Marketing Your Services

A Step-by-Step Guide for Small Businesses and Professionals

Anthony O. Putman

John Wiley & Sons
New York • Chichester • Brisbane • Toronto • Singapore

Yellow Pages is a trademark of Reuben H. Donnelley Company.

Library of Congress Cataloging-in-Publication Data
Putman, Anthony O., 1945–
    Marketing your services : a step-by-step guide for small
businesses and professionals / Anthony O. Putman
        p.   cm.
    Includes bibliographical references.
    ISBN 0-471-50948-5
    1. Service industries—United States—Marketing.   2. Small
business—United States—Marketing.   3. Professions—United States
—Marketing.   I. Title.
HD9981.5.P88   1990
658.8—dc20   89-21537
                                                              CIP

Printed in the United States of America

90 91 10 9 8 7 6 5 4 3 2 1

To
Carl Edwin Putman,
who showed me the importance of
working hard and giving good value,
and
Baba Muktananda,
who showed me the importance of service.

Please Read Before Buying This Book

Before you invest your time in reading this book, let's take five minutes to make sure this book is really for you. *Marketing Your Services* was written for a specific audience, about whom I have made three assumptions:

1. You make the marketing decisions for a small-to-medium sized company. Your firm—as small as one person or as large as fifty or so—provides services which are of real value to your clients.

2. You want to have more business in the future, which you can bring in more reliably and for less effort.

3. When you are honest with yourself, you recognize that you could do a better job of marketing your services if you just knew how.

If I have missed you on any of these points, this book was not written for you. If you are an executive of a large firm, for example, you may do a lot of selective reading here because your specific concerns are not addressed; for example, nowhere in these pages will you find the term "globalization of markets." But if you recognize yourself in my three assumptions, go ahead and buy the book. It could be the best investment you make all year.

My name is Anthony Putman—my friends and clients call me Tony—and I wrote this book for only one purpose: to help you, the reader, to become an effective marketer. It is not about *marketing*; it is about *your business* as seen with marketers' eyes. If you read this book and take it seriously, it will transform the way you see your business. The mystery of marketing will be stripped away. You will see what to do, and how to do it, to market *your* services effectively. You will leave this book seeing *your* business in the way a sophisticated marketer would see it, and your business results will improve. In short, you will leave this book with the conviction that, as one of my clients put it, "Marketing is now doable!"

To do all that, we have some work to do together. I wrote this book to be easy to read—even fun in places, I hope—but don't be misled by that. There is a lot here for you to think about and act on. If you want to read through and get the "key points," go right ahead: you will certainly get your money's worth. But this book has more to offer than key points. Its purpose is to help *you* become an effective marketer. I want you to know exactly what to do to succeed. I also want you to understand what you are doing, and why.

So if you really want to work at improving your marketing, work through the book step by step. Each chapter is designed to be a single step and is designed to give you firm footing for the chapters that follow. Within each chapter, I have provided mental exercises and worksheets which focus the content of the chapter on you and your specific business. These are not "homework"; they are "Workwork," and they progressively build your ability to market effectively. If you are like most people you will find the Workwork challenging, thought-provoking, a lot of fun, and very rewarding.

There's a lot to do. Let's get started!

TONY PUTMAN

Ann Arbor, Michigan
April 1990

Acknowledgments

Business owners pay their debts; authors acknowledge theirs. This page is in lieu of payment.

Many of the ideas in this book came to me through the teaching and example of Bruce Fritch. Bruce is an outstanding consultant whose dedication to the success of his clients is an inspiration to all who know him; he is also a loyal and thoughtful friend. His careful reading of the book proposal and the manuscript was invaluable. Had I not known Bruce, marketing would still be a mystery to me.

Ray Bard guided me with patience, calm, and enthusiasm through the arcane process of getting a book into print. His mission is to "support authors in creating good books, and getting them published." As a satisfied customer, I can highly recommend him.

Chip Bell contributed in many important ways. He introduced me to Ray Bard, read the proposal and manuscript with his usual positiveness and insight, and was steadfast in encouraging me to write the book we both believed was needed.

The original book proposal was greatly improved by the thoughtful and candid responses of Harry Cohen, Joia Jitahidi, Douglas McClennen, John T. O'Neill, David Polis, Sherry Sprague, and Phyllis Timmons. A small but dedicated group of friends read the entire manuscript in draft form and gave me invaluable feedback and support. Heartfelt thanks to Clay Carr, Sheila Feigelson, Geri Markel, Ann Perkins, Bob and Joan Rose.

Peter G. Ossorio, the founder of Descriptive Psychology, provided the foundation on which all of my work is built. A great teacher and mentor is rare; those of us who have had one are indeed fortunate. Thanks, Pete.

My wife Lisa has been unwavering in her enthusiasm and support for this book and my writing of it. She was always the first reader on every draft; once it got by her loving but pitiless critical eye, I was confident in sending it to anyone. Thanks, love.

It has been my good fortune to be influenced by hundreds of people: teachers, colleagues, friends, clients. In particular, my life has been incredibly enriched by those who have granted me the privilege of being involved with their businesses: my customers. Many of you appear in thin disguise in this book; without you, I would have had nothing interesting to say. Any list would have inevitably omitted someone important. You know who you are and you, and I, know what you've done. Thanks.

A. O. P.

Contents

1

Honk If You Hate Marketing

You Don't Have to Become a Huckster

Would you like to be really *good* at marketing your own services? If you would, I've got good news: that's what this book is for.

This book has only one purpose: to help you, the reader, to become an effective marketer. The book is not about *marketing*; it is about *your business* as seen with marketers' eyes. If you read this book and take it seriously, it will transform the way you see your business. The mystery of marketing will be stripped away. You will see what to do, and how to do it, to market your services effectively. You will leave this book seeing your business the way a sophisticated marketer would see it, and your business results will improve. In short, you will leave this book with the conviction that, as one of my clients put it, "Marketing is now doable!"

You *can* become an effective marketer. But before you get there, you have some learning and work to do.

Let's face it—if you're like most people, you're not a "natural" marketer. You're good at what you do; your services truly provide good value to the people who receive them. But you know your business could be doing better if you could just figure out how. All the business books and consultants seem to be telling you: "The solution to your problem is clear. Become a marketer." But that advice may seem about as useful as the advice an owl once gave to a grasshopper:

> A weary grasshopper had come to the owl for counsel. "Oh wise one, I despair of this constant struggle. I work all day, from Spring through Fall, just to lay in enough food to barely survive the Winter. How can I get ahead?"
>
> The owl blinked and nodded. "I see your problem, and the solution is clear. You must become a cricket."
>
> "But why, oh wise one?"

1

"The cricket does not waste his time as you do. He eats what he needs, makes music when he likes, and when the cold weather comes, he crawls into a snug hole and hibernates. Become a cricket, my son, and your days will be light and joyful."

The grasshopper was ecstatic, contemplating his coming good fortune. He thanked the owl and began to hop happily away. A small doubt struck him, however, and he turned back.

"Oh wise one, just one last small thing. Exactly how does one become a cricket when one starts as a grasshopper?"

The owl blinked in dismissal. "I have given you the strategy. The details are up to you."

Don't worry. This book is not going to tell you to become a cricket. You will not have to stop being what you are and become something else. Instead the book is going to help you become successful at marketing your services by being the best "you" that you can be.

Skeptical? That's understandable. Most people would be at this point, because the kind of marketing we see most of the time—on television, in magazines, or in the mail—too often involves simplification, mere image-making, or outright distortion. "Madison Avenue" may have a knack for it, but the rest of us would agree with a building contractor-client: "I just can't see myself doing that kind of stuff."

You don't have to do "that kind of stuff" because marketing does not have to be "that kind of stuff." Marketing can be a positive, exciting, *ethical* part of your business; you do not have to become a huckster to be a good marketer. The purpose of this chapter is to help you see exactly what marketing is and is not. Be prepared for some happy surprises.

Attitude Matters

Marketing. The very word calls up powerful images, not all of them positive. Many businesspeople regard marketing as a necessary evil. Some professionals have told me they see marketing as basically unethical. (One accountant who lives in my neighborhood calls it "the M-word.") They feel about marketing the way most eighth-graders feel about algebra: They don't like it because they are not very good at it, and they really don't understand it.

It's not hard to see why they have trouble marketing successfully.

If your attitude toward marketing is already quite positive, congratulations—you have one less hurdle to clear. But if, like many other people in business, your attitude is negative or mixed, consider some bad news: You will find it very difficult to market your services effectively unless you see marketing as an attractive, exciting, and ethical part of your business.

That's the bad news. The good news is that you don't have to change your attitude about *marketing as you know it.* You only have to change what you know about marketing so that you will come to see marketing your business as the exciting, attractive and very ethical activity it really can be.

What is *your* attitude toward marketing? Let's find out. Spend a few minutes going through the following exercise. This is the first of the *Workwork* sections I described in the Preface. It helps you to focus the content of the chapter on you and your specific situation. Whenever you see *Workwork,* I encourage you to stop and really *think* about your own business.

———— **WORKWORK: WHAT'S YOUR ATTITUDE?** ————————

Take a moment and look at that word "marketing"; just let it be there in your mind.

Now jot down the words that pop into your mind. Keep going until you have a dozen or so associations.

Consider what you have written down: How many of the words seem positive? How many negative?

Now imagine that someone is using those words to describe what goes on in your business. How do you feel about that? Does this help you to understand why you don't market as well as you would like?

What Marketing Is Not

Let's start by clearing up some very common misunderstandings.

1. *Marketing is not advertising.*
Marion is one of those people whose success story eventually gets written up in the business magazines. In the ten years I have known her, she has gone from working on a university staff to owning a hugely successful and influential consulting business that employs about a dozen professionals. She personally brings in more money each month than most people make in a year.

Marion has never spent one cent on advertising.

One of her very junior associates once suggested to her that the firm should advertise in an upcoming directory. "After all," he said, "if we've been this successful with just word-of-mouth, imagine how we would do with a little marketing."

Marion looked at him as if he had just spoken in Urdu. "What are you talking about? I have been marketing nonstop all my career! I just don't advertise."

Marion was right. She is one of those rare "natural" marketers who understands a critical truth:

> **Advertising is only one of many marketing functions. It is the most visible and perhaps the most notorious, but there is a great deal more to marketing than advertising.**

Advertising can be very useful and important; we devote an entire chapter of this book to it. But it is not always necessary. You can be successful without advertising. You have very little chance of being successful without marketing. (By the way, like everyone else mentioned in this book, Marion is an actual person. I have changed names and some identifying details to protect privacy, but the people and their situations are very real.)

2. Marketing is not promotion.

Roger may never be written up in magazines, but in his own way and on his own terms he is as successful as Marion. He has a one-man consulting firm and has all the work he wants. His biggest problem currently is making sure he gets enough time off for the travel he enjoys so much.

It wasn't always that way. When I started working with Roger he was an excellent consultant who was worried about where his next client was coming from. The problem became clear immediately.

"Tony, I have to tell you I have mixed feelings about this. I'm not sure I really *want* to market my services. I just don't feel comfortable tooting my own horn. I see these slick brochures coming across my desk every day, telling me how great this guy is or how everybody raves about this woman's work, and it turns me off. It seems unprofessional. I'm as good at what I do as any of them—better than most, to tell the truth—but if that's what I have to do to market my services, thanks but no thanks."

Roger was making the common mistake of confusing marketing with another of its rather notorious functions—promotion. You see it every day in your mail and in the newspapers: "25% Off on Oil Change This Week Only!" "Wall Street Insider's Secret Weapon Revealed!" "I lost 37 lbs. in only three weeks without dieting!"—simple, quick, tantalizing, and designed to give you that extra push you need, to decide to buy. Promotion is an important part of marketing, but it is only one part. And as Roger was aware, it's not always easy to see how to use it appropriately.

Roger never changed his mind about "tooting his own horn." He still thinks it's unprofessional and won't do it. He learned how to be a successful marketer without it.

3. *Marketing is not sales.*

Let's look at you for this one. You already know how you feel about selling: you either enjoy it or you don't. That here-and-now interpersonal back-and-forth that winds up with a signature on the dotted line is high-octane pleasure for some people and pure agony for others. Whichever way you are is fine; you can market successfully without ever having to "sell." (You can also be an excellent salesperson and a lousy marketer. I was that for many years!) Better yet, those of you who are allergic to "selling" can learn how to get that signature on the dotted line without having to become a salesperson. You'll be using a more effective way to sell.

What Is Marketing, Anyway?

OK, now we know that marketing is *not* advertising, *not* promotion, and *not* sales. So what *is* marketing? We will define it soon, but first let's identify it with an image we can return to in our discussions throughout the book.

> **Marketing is a set of lenses you use to look at your business—your *entire* business.**

In other words, marketing is not just one part or function of your business; it's not even the primary or most important part. Marketing is a *perspective*, a distinctive and essential way of looking at the whole enterprise. The purpose of this book is to enable you to see your business with marketers' lenses. Then you can use what you see to build an effective, high-performance marketing organization.

——— **WORKWORK: THE POWER OF PERSPECTIVE** ———

Let's illustrate the power of perspective. Take a moment right now and focus your attention on the room you are sitting in. Try to clear your mind; picture a blank screen before a slide show. Now look around you; spend about thirty seconds noticing everything in your surroundings. Clear your mind (the blank screen again) and look around you again, but this time notice everything made of paper. Clear a third time, then look around again, this time noticing everything that uses electricity.

What did you notice about the three looks around you? Isn't it true that you saw some things the second time that you missed the first time, even though the first time you were to notice "everything?" And the third time, didn't some things almost seem to leap out at you that you had not noticed the first two times? This is the power of perspective. What you see and what you are therefore able to do depend fundamentally on what lenses you are looking through. When your perspective makes such a difference in something as simple as looking at your surroundings, imagine how much difference it makes in something as complex as a business—*your* business.

We will be using these marketing lenses to look at your business in detail throughout the book. Let's first look at the big picture. When you look at your business with marketing lenses three things stand out:

1. The character of your business enterprise

2. The market for your services

3. The relationship between your business and its market

Let's look at each of these three with our marketer's lenses.

The Character of Your Business Enterprise

Businesses are like children: the more you get to know them, the more you realize that they are distinct individuals. Their "parents" influence them, of course, as do their circumstances. Some are started by laid-off visionaries who work part-time out of their basements, others start life as full-blown franchises owned by no-nonsense money managers, and the rest are everything in between. Each business evolves its own distinctiveness over time; one of the genuine pleasures of being a marketing consultant is seeing different businesses grow and change from the inside.

This distinctiveness is at the heart of effective marketing. Looking at your business through marketer's lenses, you will see one fact standing out from everything else:

Your business exists *solely* for the purpose of making a specific beneficial difference in the lives of your customers.

Don't misunderstand—this is not to deny that your firm exists for other, extremely important reasons (like making money for the owners, providing livelihood and satisfaction for the employees, and making a contribution to the community, to name a few very legitimate ones). From the *marketing* perspective, however, these happen as the result of success at your fundamental purpose, your reason for existence—the positive benefit of your services to your customers.

Throughout the book we will refer to this fundamental purpose of your business as your *mission*. Your mission energizes your business and is one of two cornerstones of successful marketing. The importance of knowing and communicating your firm's distinctive mission cannot be overstated.

Every business also faces predictable challenges, opportunities, and confrontations. A key challenge is making the most of limited resources.

No matter how well you have done or how positive your mental attitude, you nonetheless have only so much time, money, prestige, creativity, energy, and opportunity (to mention only a few of your resources). As a businessperson, you learn to respect resources and the need to use them wisely and productively. You come to appreciate the absolute necessity of getting an appropriate return on your investment of resources. Without it, you will quickly go out of business.

And this leads directly into a dilemma:

> **Your firm is capable of delivering far more different services than you can market effectively.**

_____ **WORKWORK: SERVICES AND RESOURCES** _____

Look at your business honestly for a moment. Think about the services you currently provide to your customers. Think about all the services you actually could provide to anyone who asked for them.

Now imagine you have the Midas touch—suddenly all of those services are in demand. Do you have enough capable people to provide them? Enough money? Time? Organized systems?

Do you have the time, money, and other resources to _market_ them all? How about half? Be brutally honest: give your best estimate. How many different services do you have the resources to market effectively? (If you said more than three, you may be kidding yourself. Most people say one or two, and they are realistic.)

If you hope to market effectively, you must make hard choices. We will work on them in the next chapter.

The Market for Your Services

I assume you are good at what you do. (Let's face it, if you are not good at what you do, you probably won't find many buyers for your services.) But just being good at it isn't enough. You have to find people who are willing to _pay_ you to be good at it. These people are your market, and finding them is not always easy.

Richard Drake found that out the hard way. Richard is a skilled career consultant who specializes in helping people move from jobs that bore them to careers that match their skills and interests. He moved to a large university town and began advertising his Career Transition Service (which involves extensive testing, evaluation, strategizing, and coaching) in the Yellow Pages.

Great service. Wrong market.

It turned out that almost everyone who called was a recent graduate of the university, looking for some inexpensive help in putting together a résumé. New graduates can't afford and seldom see the point of paying several thousand dollars for help in "finding a job"; but people who are bored in their current jobs and would see the value in Richard's service rarely look in the Yellow Pages for help because they seldom recognize what their problem is. Richard switched his strategy to reach the people who really needed his services and, with time and determination, he succeeded. (You will read more about Richard and how he did it in later chapters.)

Your services have a number of different markets:

- *Actual Market*—the people who have bought and are buying your services already.

- *Potential Market*—the vastly greater group who might, given the right circumstances, buy your services.

- *Target Market*—the group on which you will concentrate your marketing efforts. This group represents your best opportunity to get a good return on your marketing resources.

Your mission is one cornerstone of effective marketing; your market is the other. We will spend all of Chapter 4 helping you identify your target market.

The Relationship Between Your Business and Its Market

Now we get to the first great insight into effective marketing:

> Effective marketing does not focus on your firm's mission or services, nor on your market or its needs. Effective marketing concentrates on one thing only: the *relationship* between your firm and its market.

In other words, marketing is fundamentally a matter of building relationships between your firm and its market—the people willing to pay for its services.

I remember very well when I first encountered this basic insight. I learned marketing the old-fashioned way—by making every mistake in the book. I have been a professional consultant to organizations for over twenty years. For quite a while, as I mentioned earlier, I was a very good salesman and a lousy marketer. But all that began to change when I met Bruce Fritch, a brilliant young marketing expert who helped me to see what marketing really is all about.

The year was 1975. I was consulting to the largest bank holding company in the southeastern United States. The bank was about to launch an exciting new retail marketing strategy, and I was asked to consult with the marketing department on how to turn internal resistance to the strategy into enthusiastic support. One afternoon about a dozen of us were sitting around in the bank's plush conference room on the twenty-seventh floor, brainstorming and inhaling coffee. We were talking about what made a business into a really effective marketing organization when the group's resident marketing whiz, Bruce, tossed in an image that drew "Aha's!" from everyone in the room. Bruce said:

"The really effective marketing organization creates a laser-like alignment between its mission and its market."

He went on to explain, "Consider the lightbulb and the laser. Both are systems for converting energy into light, but a lightbulb illuminates only a small area around it, while a laser can cut through metal or bounce a signal off the moon and back. Now here's the part most people don't realize—you can run a laser on the same amount of energy you use to burn a lightbulb! The difference lies in alignment. A lightbulb sheds its light in all directions over a wide range of frequencies; its power is dissipated rapidly. But the energy that goes into a laser emerges tightly aligned; you can focus it sharply to accomplish tremendous things. The effective marketing organization is a laser, not a lightbulb."

The new retail marketing strategy turned out to be a tremendous success—the bank remained one of the largest for over ten years, in the face of ferocious competition—and we were able to turn most of the resistance into support. Over the years, I have become increasingly impressed with the power that comes from that laser-like alignment of the relationship between mission and market.

That relationship is so important that it is at the heart of our definition of marketing:

> **Marketing is the intentional process of creating and maintaining the relationship of "customer."**

Look at that definition carefully. Memorize it. Think about it. We will take that definition apart, phrase by phrase, as we go through the chapters of this book. As we do, your view of what marketing is and how to do it will change dramatically. When you have thoroughly grasped this definition and its implications for your business, you will have mastered the marketing perspective.

And exactly how do you "create and maintain the relationship of 'customer'"? The short answer is "The same way you create and maintain any relationship: by what you say and what you do!" (Marketers like to talk about "communications" and "transactions" with the market: they just mean "what you say" and "what you do.")

A somewhat longer answer will help to orient you for the chapters ahead. To create and maintain the relationship of "customer" you have to:

- Commit yourself to being in business—instead of, for example, doing whatever happens to come up or look interesting. To start every day not knowing what the day will bring may be fun or exciting, but it's not good business, and you can't market it. Chapter 2 will help you with your commitment.

- Define your business mission so that everyone knows *exactly* what you do, starting with yourself. That's in Chapter 3.

- Identify the best target market for your services. (First you have to decide exactly what you mean by "best"; it's different for different people.) Chapter 4 will help you.

- Cause your firm and its services to stand out from the crowd. An almost magically effective strategy for doing that is in Chapter 5.

- Create that laser-like alignment between your firm and its target market, so that your energies are aligned and your marketing efforts are very powerful. You'll learn how to do that in Chapter 6.

A few other things: you have to get your pricing right (Chapter 7), set up a "marketing machine" that will support you in turning prospects into customers (Chapters 8 and 9), package and present your services (Chapters 10 and 11), and so on. (I never said it would be easy; I said it would be doable!) In short, you have to look at every aspect of your business with your marketer's lenses and do what you see needs doing. This book was written to help you do that, step by step.

There's a lot of work to do (but you already knew that, didn't you?). Don't worry; it's doable and, believe it or not, it's mostly a lot of fun!

Shall we begin?

2 | Meaning Business

How to Get and Stay Focused

It had been one of those mornings: telephone tag, missed connections, unavoidable delays. By the time noon came I seemed to have nothing at all to show for my efforts. I glanced at my calendar and noticed that I had a lunch date with Sharon. I smiled despite the morning.

I always look forward to seeing Sharon. Maybe you know someone like her—curious, enthusiastic, always getting into new and interesting things. You never know what she's going to show up with, but you know it will be fun. I headed for the restaurant anticipating a light and refreshing lunchtime chat.

By dessert it was clear that something was not quite right. As I ordered coffee, I remembered that she had called me this time and suggested lunch. I leaned back in my chair. "Something you want to talk about, Sharon?"

Her smile was a little stiff. "Yes. Well. I guess . . . it's just . . . my business isn't doing so well, Tony. Actually, I'm really frustrated; I'm good at what I do, I know that, but . . . well, I think I could use some help with marketing."

"Most people could use some help with marketing, Sharon. Let me play dumb for a while and ask you a few basic questions. Like, what work do you do?"

She looked surprised. "Why, you know. I'm a planned change consultant."

"And what does a planned change consultant do?"

"Well, whatever it takes to facilitate planned change. I do futuring sessions and workshops on running meetings; sometimes I consult one-on-one with key leaders; sometimes I interview people in the system and feed back their ideas in group sessions; whatever. You know, one of the things I like most about my profession is that I'm always learning something new."

"Somehow that doesn't surprise me. But tell me: Whom do you do this planned change work for?"

"Oh, all kinds of people—school systems, health care organizations, community groups, business . . . anybody who is facing change, and wants to be proactive rather than reactive."

"Sounds like you shouldn't lack for prospects."

"You wouldn't think so, would you? That's what's so frustrating. I can't seem to figure out how to reach those prospects. I do networking and I've made up a brochure." She took one out of her briefcase and handed it over; nice paper, good clean graphics and type face. "But it's like pulling teeth to get a client. Almost all of my business comes from people who call me, who were referred to me by my previous clients, and frankly my phone hasn't been ringing off the hook lately."

The coffee arrived. I took a sip and looked over her brochure. It confirmed what I had observed from our conversation. "Sharon, I appreciate your willingness to be open with me about your business. I will be equally frank with you. I think I have spotted what's wrong, and I know how to help you solve it. Problem is, I'm not sure you will really *want* to solve it. You see, Sharon, you are a classic example of what I call 'Zorba the Professional.'"

Sharon looked amused. "And what, do I dare ask, is 'Zorba the Professional'?"

"It's what you wind up being when you haven't yet made a business out of practicing your profession.

"In the film the Boss asked Zorba the Greek: 'What work do you do?' And Zorba replied: 'Listen to him! I've got head, hands, feet—they do their job! Who the hell am I to choose?' You're Zorba the Professional, Sharon: 'I do futuring, workshops, one-on-one consulting: Who the hell am I to choose?'"

Sharon laughed. "OK, I see the point. So what do I do about it? How do I get focused?"

Making a Business Out of Your Profession

"How do I get focused?" This is probably the second most frequently asked question a marketing consultant hears. (The most frequently asked question, of course, is "How can I get more business?") It comes up when, like Sharon, you realize that you can't be successful just doing whatever happens to come along. You have to focus your energies instead of scattering them; you have to move toward that laser-like alignment we talked about in the first chapter.

But how? The short answer is: by making a business of your profession. You have to learn to see your enterprise as a business. You have to be a businessperson—*not instead of* being a professional *but in addition to* being a professional. And that means you must make sure that you get a good return on your resources; you must choose how you use your time and money and creativity and reputation and opportunities, instead of letting circumstances determine how they are used.

_____ **WORKWORK: FOCUSING YOUR ENERGIES** _____

Take a moment and think honestly about how you use your time at work. What determines what you do and when? Do you mostly just show up and do what seems most urgent? Do you tend to simply respond to whatever comes up? Or do you usually have an agenda, a list of things to accomplish? Do you really give these "to do" items priority, or do you set priorities in theory only? Suppose you do have an agenda and mostly follow it, where does the agenda come from? Is it just a list of what's due or what has to be handled? Or do you choose the items on some basis? What basis?

In short: What determines the way you use your time and energy at work?

_____

In a business there are only two ways to get focused: you either focus on your mission or you focus on your market. Ask yourself: To what extent do I pay attention to my mission or my market in making day-to-day decisions about how to use my resources? Depending on your answer, your business stance is one of the four shown in Figure 1: Zorba the Professional, the Missionary, the Mercenary, or the Marketer. Each of the four stances has implications for your business.

Stance 1. Low Mission, Low Market: Zorba the Professional
Like Sharon, most professionals and most owners of small businesses are Zorbas. Like a lightbulb that radiates its energy over many frequencies and in all directions, a Zorba's energy is spread over a wide variety of services and many different markets. Priorities are dictated by circumstances and other people. Zorba's days get used up just "taking care of business."

How can you tell whether you are a Zorba? I suspect you already know, but just in case, here are some tell-tale clues:

- Quickly now: What is your firm's mission? You should be able to state it quickly, clearly, and accurately. Any hesitation or fuzziness is a good clue that you're in the Zorba camp. What? You don't have a mission? Zorba, without a doubt!

	Low	High
High	*Stance 2* The Missionary	*Stance 4* The Marketer
Low	*Stance 1* Zorba the Professional	*Stance 3* The Mercenary

Mission Orientation

Low   High

Market Orientation

Figure 1

- One of my clients was so proud of his mission statement that he had it printed on the back of his business card. When I pointed out that it read like a definition of his profession, he smiled and admitted that he had copied it from his favorite textbook. This is another good clue: when you are so identified with your field that your mission and the definition of your field are essentially the same, call yourself Zorba. One accountant worked for hours on his mission statement, and the best he could come up with was: "We provide the full range of accounting services to business." Zorba the Accountant: "I do taxes, audits, management consulting—who the hell am I to choose?"

- Forget the mission. What are your services? Write them out—*all* of them—and take a hard look at the list. Can you see what they have in common? Yes? Good, so far. Could any half way intelligent person off the street see what they have in common? No? (Sharon could see a common thread running through futuring sessions, workshops on running meetings, one-on-one consultations, and group feedback sessions; but I can't see it. Can you?) You say that your services look like a list of "this and that and these" to someone else? Sorry, Zorba.

At this point in my marketing workshops, someone usually speaks up: "OK, OK; so I'm Zorba the Professional—so what? What's so wrong with that? I *like* variety. I don't want to specialize. Why can't I just do what I was trained to do and make a living at it? Good questions. Good because they deserve thoughtful answers; but also good because they show clearly why people stay stuck as Zorbas even though their business suffers. Let's look at your situation once more, carefully.

Service business used to be a lot simpler. You worked hard to finish your apprenticeship or your schooling, you were certified as a professional, and then you hung out your shingle. You prided yourself on being able to handle whatever came through the door, and as a practical matter you had to; nobody starting out could afford to turn down work. Over time word would get around that you knew how to do this or that; people would come to you for what their friends came to you for, and you might become known as a "specialist." But you would always try to keep as broad a scope as possible, so you could provide whatever service was needed. Many service providers even today have this implicit model in their heads of how to do business.

What's wrong with that? In one sense, nothing; this is a fine model for how to practice a profession. The problem is, successfully doing *business* that way is awfully hard. If you sit back and wait for clients to show up, you can get very hungry waiting. To succeed in your service business, you have to actively create new customer relationships (that's marketing, remember?). You have to choose and then act on your choices.

But you don't have to become a narrow specialist or stop taking whatever business interests you. You can stay flexible and take on any new challenge that comes your way, if you like. We are not talking about how you *respond to* new opportunities; we are talking about how to *create* them. Over time, the scope of your work will narrow, so it is very important that you choose well. (Still not convinced? Don't worry; you've gotten this far without marketing, haven't you? With luck you can keep it up. And don't forget: even though Zorba was a poor man, he was the happiest character in the film. Good luck to you.)

The rest of us need to get on with the next step: choosing where we intend to focus our energies.

Stance 2. High Mission, Low Market: The Missionary

Keith goes to work every morning with a spring in his step and a spark in his eye. When he talks about his work, he speaks with such passionate conviction that his face almost seems to glow. He works long hours and gets tremendous satisfaction from his work.

Keith is a Missionary.

No, not *that* kind of Missionary. Keith is not in the business of saving souls. But in his own way he is out to make the world a better place. He has seen the Promised Land, and to anyone who will listen Keith is ready to preach the gospel of the Computer Operating System according to Pick.

Go ahead, laugh; Keith is used to that. He takes it with good humor, but in truth he is puzzled. Can't you see what is so obvious? The Pick

Operating System really *is* a better way! It really *does* save you time and money and it's *so* much easier to program in it! What does it take to get people to *see* . . . ?

Keith exhibits the two tell-tale signs of the Missionary: he truly, deeply believes in the value of what he has to offer, and he finds it bafflingly difficult to convince other people. In his darker moments, he suspects there is a conspiracy in the industry ("All that money tied up in those primitive IBM operating systems") or something perversely wrong ("resistance to change" or "Not Invented Here syndrome"); after all, something this good shouldn't be this hard to get across.

Recognize anyone you know? It shouldn't surprise you; the world is full of Missionaries, people who through experience or training or blinding revelation have become convinced that what the world *really* needs is quality circles, chiropractic adjustment, graphical user interfaces, interactive laser disks, reliable childcare, and so forth. You see their ads and brochures every day.

Missionaries are Zorbas who have seen the light. No longer do they just do whatever comes up; they have a mission and they pursue it with zeal. Their emphasis in on getting the word out: "If we can just get people's attention, they will see for themselves the value of what we have." They pursue "marketing" (which they see as half-page ads and glossy brochures: a bigger and better pulpit from which to preach the gospel) with excitement and conviction, but with disappointing results. They respond to failure by "upping the wattage"; instead of lightbulbs, their organizations become like searchlights. They increase their advertising budgets and worry about cash flow, all the while asking themselves: "Can't they *see* . . . ?

Well, no. They can't see. And you can't make them see either. Missionaries are so focused on the mission that they fail to see what is obvious: the market. We will be looking at this in detail later, but for now, Missionaries, think about an important principle:

> You will not succeed in getting the market to see things from your point of view. You will only succeed when you see things from your market's point of view.

Want to know the "funny" part? By and large, *the Missionaries are right!* There are always some impractical crackpots, but most Missionaries are solid folk who in fact have seen something of value; what they have, people really *do* need! Actually, that's not funny at all; it's tragic. We have people in this world who have valuable services to offer, and other people who genuinely need those services—and these two groups are not getting together! I believe that's a tragic waste. My personal mission is to help those two groups get together. To do that, I help you move beyond being a Missionary and become a Marketer.

Please be clear, however, that I am not advising you to become a Mercenary.

Stance 3. Low Mission, High Market: The Mercenary

By now you know how important the market is; why don't business-people pay attention to it? Why do so many of us, so much of the time, resist the idea of marketing? Of course there are many reasons, but I think the biggest reason we resist becoming marketers is that we're afraid we'll start thinking like Harve.

Harve calls himself an "unabashed self-promoter." (Like almost everything else Harve says, he stole that phrase from someone else and makes no apologies for it.) He talks and dresses like an aging Vegas lounge hustler. Ask him what the mission of his business is and he snorts in contempt. "Mission! I'll tell you my mission, Tony, and it's the same as yours and everybody else's: my mission is to make as much money as possible for as little work as I can get away with. All this mission stuff is just so much crapola. I'll tell you the only three words you need to know to succeed in business, baby: marketing, marketing, and marketing. You find out what the customer wants, and you give it to him. He wants it in purple with bells on, you give it to him in purple with bells on. And when he gets tired of that, you give him something else. You gotta stay close to the customer, baby; you gotta know what's hot, what's the latest buzz."

"So you give them what they want, Harve. What if that's not what they need?"

"So what? I suppose you think smoking Marlboros really makes you look like a cowboy, right? You think people really need fifty-dollar designer jeans? What's-it-called really gives your mouth sex appeal? Image, baby, image; that's what makes money."

Is this what you are afraid of? Are you worried that "pay attention to your market" means "give the customers what they want, whether they need it or not?"

Relax. Remember what I told you at the start of Chapter 1: you *don't* have to become a huckster. With all due respect for Harve, he is not a good marketer—in fact, he's not a marketer at all. Harve is a Mercenary. (He's still looking to make his first "big killing"; he's not there yet but he tells me, "I'm keeping my ear to the ground, baby.")

The difference is simple. You are a provider of services that make a positive and beneficial difference in the lives of your customers. Your customers know a positive difference in their lives when they see one; but they don't always know in advance how to get it. Your job is to help them see how to get it, and then to help them get it. Yes, you have to market your services, and you also have to provide services that make a genuine difference. It's *not* just image; it's image and reality, combined and aligned. You can't only be "in it for the money" and expect to succeed.

So how *do* you succeed?

Stance 4. High Mission, High Market: The Marketer

Marion is a natural Marketer. I doubt if she has learned a thing from me; I've learned a lot from her. Let her tell it: "There's really no secret, Tony. I've just been in the right place at the right time with the right solution. The only thing I really know how to do well is to get groups of people working together toward common goals. Of course, a lot of American industry really needs that right now. That's why I got into this business in the first place: I was on a personal mission to help save the auto industry. They *really* needed more effective ways of working together and I could help them with that."

"So how do you market your services, Marion?"

She laughed. "I talk to people and I listen, Tony! That's all I do in my professional work, and that's all I do in marketing! I tell someone that I help groups work together toward common goals, and they say, 'Sounds like something we could use!' So I ask them what their main frustrations are, and what it would look like if things were working as they want them to, and pretty soon we are working out the first steps of a program for their organization. It helps that I speak their language, of course; they can see that I understand their concerns. But they expect that; I'm a consultant, so what I do is, I consult."

Sounds easy, doesn't it? It is, if you are a natural Marketer like Marion. The rest of us have to work at it some. But you *can* work at it and you can get to be as successful at marketing as Marion is, if you are willing to practice. That's what this book is for.

The Two Key Steps

Notice something about Marion: she started out as a Missionary. That's important, because marketing services is not like marketing toothpaste or soap or designer dental floss; you have to *believe* deeply in the value of what you have to offer, in order to convince other people of its value. (You also have to deliver the services once you get the business, so it had better be something you can put your heart into!) Being a Missionary is not enough. To be a Marketer you must pay attention to *both* your mission and your market—both the light you have seen, and the life they see.

What if there is conflict between the two? What if your mission says one thing and your market another?

That's when the all-important ingredient is added: alignment. You must create such laser-like alignment between your mission and your market that there *cannot be* conflict between them. You and your market must become like two tuning forks that are so well-aligned that when one vibrates, the other vibrates in response. Then, and only then, will your energies have laser-like focus and power.

So how do you become a Marketer? Simple:

> To become a Marketer, *first* become a Missionary. Then find the best possible market for your mission, and align yourself thoroughly with that market.

Chapter 3 will help make you into a skilled Missionary. In later chapters you will find the best possible market for your mission and will see exactly how to bring about a laser-like alignment.

Before we get to all that, you have some choosing to do, remember? All you Missionaries are now excused to get on with Chapter 3 (I assume the Mercenaries skipped this chapter). But all you Zorbas, listen up. We need to work on focus and choice.

___ **WORKWORK: CHOOSING THE BEST SERVICE** _____

Step 1: At a family reunion, you run into your Aunt Mary, an intelligent older lady who lives in the Midwest. She is not big-city sophisticated but she understands almost anything so long as it's in plain English. With genuine interest she asks you about your work. You tell her about all the work you have done the past year—what you did, for whom, and what your clients and customers thought of your work.

What would you say to Aunt Mary? Think it through and write it down.

Aunt Mary then asks about your plans, and you tell her about the exciting work you will be doing in the coming year, assuming all goes well. Again, think it through and write it down before you go on.

You now have a fairly complete list of your services. Look it over. Have you left anything off? Add it.

Step 2: Look over your list of services to find "packages" of services that tend to go together. For example, my dental hygienist cleans teeth, takes Xrays, teaches people to floss, checks for cavities, and checks for gum problems. These are five different services, but they usually go together into a single service package called "Prophylactic checkup." (I kid you not! That's what it says on my bill!) Identify each typical package of services on your list as a separate item. You can make up names, or call them "Package 1," and so on. "Service" from now on means either service or package of services.

Step 3. Put an asterisk beside the services on your list that you especially enjoy. Maybe you find them fun, or challenging, or rewarding—whatever the reason, these are the services that you genuinely get excited about.

(No asterisks? Friend, we need to talk. Why are you spending the greater part of your waking hours doing something you don't enjoy? And why are you trying to market these services so you can get to do *more* of this thing that leaves you cold? You need the money? I can understand that; but you don't have to do this to yourself to get it. Trust me on this one, please: *You can do work you find satisfying and still make money!* Read the two books listed under "Finding Your Work" in the Resources section at the end of the book. You can come back to this later.)

Step 4. Now look at each service on your list and put a circle around the services that your market has found to be especially valuable—the ones that make the biggest or most important beneficial difference in people's lives.

Step 5. You now have a smaller list of services to consider: the ones that both have an asterisk and are circled. (You say none of the circled ones has an asterisk. Are you *sure* you are in the right field?) If only one service is both circled and asterisked, you are done—that's your best service! Focus on it.

If more than one service is both exciting to you and especially beneficial to your customers (you lucky dog, you!), here's one last task.

For some unimaginable offense, a marketing tribunal has sentenced you to providing for the next two years or so, one—and only one—of the services remaining on your circled-and-asterisked list. You get to choose which one.

Pick the one your heart says "Yes!" to the loudest.

3 | Your Most Important Task

Defining Your Mission So That Everyone Knows Exactly What You Do

Sometimes life confronts you with a "moment of truth."

These are the times in life when all the preparation and preliminaries are over, when the test comes and you find out where you really stand. In bullfighting, it comes when the matador actually kills the bull—or, on occasion, is killed himself. In personal relationships, it comes when the talking stops and we are called upon to act on the commitments we have made. ("Ms. Jones, we need one more coach for your son's soccer league.")

In marketing, the moment of truth comes when a person you have just met finally finishes the amusing anecdote about getting a taxi to LaGuardia, looks you in the eye, and says: "So tell me—what do *you* do?"

_____ WORKWORK: "WHAT DO YOU DO?" _____

Go ahead, try it out. Run the tape in your mind. Here comes your cue now: "So tell me—what do *you* do?"

_____

What did you say? How confident did you fee while you were saying it? Overall, how did you do?

I call this the marketing moment of truth because it is the clearest test of how well you have done the hard work of clarifying your mission and your market, and then aligning them. From time to time I give talks to professional and industry groups. (I enjoy this because it's a speaker's dream: a few dozen to a few hundred people, all with an intense need and burning desire to know what I have to tell them!) Invariably, someone asks: "What is the single most important task in marketing my services?

What will make the biggest difference in my success?" And just as invariably I answer with this description of the single most important task in marketing:

> You must be able to say in one clear sentence *exactly* what you do, so that anyone hearing you will say to themselves: Wow! "Sounds like I could use some of that! I want to know more!" or else "Interesting, but I don't need it right now."—and that response will be accurate.

Now do you understand why I call it the moment of truth?

How close are you to being able to do that? Can you already do it? If so, congratulations; you may not need the rest of this chapter. (But make sure you aren't kidding yourself! Try out your single sentence on some strangers as a test.) Are you saying to yourself, "Come on, get real; nobody could do that with *my* business"? Then settle down for some hard but tremendously important work, friend; you *can* do it, and if you expect to succeed at your business you *must*. This chapter will prepare you to face and conquer the moment of truth in marketing.

Let's start with where you are. A useful slogan of Descriptive Psychology reminds us: "When people are called upon to do something they can't do, they do something they can." When people are called upon to say what they do, they respond in different ways. Which fits you?

Dazzle Them with Your Importance

Linda dresses for success. She looks you right in the eye when she talks to you, and her tone is confident. Networking is her middle name. Ask her what she does, and she almost glows: "I own my own research firm. We do work for several Fortune 500 firms, and I'm leaving for Washington tomorrow morning to negotiate a contract with DARPA. Here's my card."

Be honest: don't you feel a little intimidated by people like Linda? And isn't there a part of you that wishes you could be like her: confident, important, *impressive*? Do you respond to "What do you do?" by trying to sound as important as possible?

Don't. You are making a big mistake. You may be winning the status contest, but you are almost certainly losing something more important to your business: the marketing contest. You are playing the wrong game.

You have to ask yourself one key question: "What do I want to accomplish in this interaction?" People like Linda want to impress you with their importance. They see the interaction as a social transaction in which the basic purpose is to establish a certain standing, to be taken seriously, perhaps even to be admired or envied—and that's what they accomplish. In that light, notice the reactions Linda is after: "I own my own research firm. [Wow! An owner!] We do work for several Fortune 500 firms [And a big-league player!] and I'm leaving for Washington tomorrow morning to negotiate a contract with DARPA. [Got any stock for sale?] Here's my card. [Can I have your autograph, too?]"

There's nothing wrong with wanting to be seen as Somebody Important. We all have status needs. But from the marketing point of view, Linda is winning the wrong contest. When you set out to impress people with your importance, you are throwing away a crucial marketing opportunity. From the marketing point of view:

> **Every "What do you do?" transaction is an opportunity to help listeners discover that you have something they really need.**

In other words, they can end the transaction feeling "Wow! This person is impressive!" or "Wow! This person has something I really need." The choice is yours. I would recommend that you do as Omar Khayyam suggested in a somewhat different context: "Take the cash and let the credit go."

Sign Them Up on the Spot

Then there are people like George Haney.

I met George in a comic strip. The entire strip showed a man talking on the telephone. In the first panel he says, with a look of amazement, "George? George Haney? Is it really you?" Then, with increasing delight, "I can't believe it! How long has it been—since high school? Great to hear from you! What are you up to?" And in the last panel, with an expression of immense disappointment:"Oh—selling life insurance."

You know the type: ask them what they do, and they give you a sales pitch for a water filter. Or they offer to "tell you about my business" and try to sign you up as a distributor of vitamins or soap or prepaid legal consultation. You wish you could rewind the tape and try again with something like: "So . . . do you think the Cubs have a chance this year?"

I am not knocking insurance agents or salespeople in general. Sales is hard work and salespeople need every break they can get. The point is: Social interaction has certain implicit ground rules, and using a social inquiry as an opportunity to make a sales pitch strikes many people as a violation of the rules. Trying to sign people up on the spot may be a good sales tactic but it is poor marketing. (Remember, marketing is not the same as sales.) Your task is to get your listeners to recognize that they (or someone they know) need what you have to offer. Getting their signature on the dotted line happens after a serious professional discussion, and that usually does not take place in a social setting. In sales terms, you are creating a "qualified prospect," not a customer. (More on this in Chapter 8.)

Give It the Old College Try

"I *know* what I do! So why do I always feel like a tongue-tied idiot when I try to explain it to someone?" Some version of this complaint has popped up in every marketing workshop I have done. Many of us are a lot better at *doing* what we do than we are at *saying* what we do. But we keep on trying . . . and trying . . . and trying . . . like Dr. John.

"Tony, I've been a chiropractor for over ten years now, so you would think I would be used to it, but it still bugs me. I tell somebody I'm chiropractor, and they get this funny look on their face, so I start talking about spinal alignment and low-force technique and they *still* don't get it, and I wind up feeling like some kind of snake-oil salesman. What can I do?"

Dr. John is neatly illustrating just about every mistake you can make. We will come back to Dr. John and his question a little later in this chapter. For now just ask yourself: Is this me? Do I try and try and still never feel I do justice to what I have to offer?

Get It Over with and Change the Subject

Remember Roger, the consultant who hates self-promotion, whom you met in Chapter 1? As you might guess, Roger always hated being asked "What do you do?" because he could never figure out what to say. Our first conversation on the subject went something like this: "One sentence! Tony, I went to graduate school for five years to learn how to do OD! [organization development] I would have trouble doing justice to it in a ten-page paper, and you expect me to do it in one sentence?"

"Actually I would love to see the ten-page paper, Roger, but that's just me. How many people have that level of interest?"

He shrugged. "That's why I usually don't bother. I just tell them I am an organization development consultant, wait for them to say something like 'Oh—you mean like quality circles?' to which I say 'Not exactly, but that sort of thing,' and change the subject."

"Pretty slick footwork, Ace. Got any new clients recently?"

Roger winced. "No, dammit! But you can't sit there and tell me that I could get a new client from a social interaction. In my experience, it just doesn't happen that way."

"I can easily believe that has been *your* experience, Roger. What would you say if I told you that over half of Marion's new business comes just that way—from follow-up on her telling someone what she does in a social setting?"

"You're making that up, right?"

"Not at all, Roger; ask her yourself. And in *my* experience that's dead average for a good marketer. The main reason you're not getting new clients, Roger, is that you are running away from your best marketing opportunities. Not even someone as good as you can afford to do that."

Are you like Roger? If so, don't worry; with a little work he learned to conquer marketing's moment of truth, and so can you. Let's get started.

_____ **WORKWORK: WHAT'S YOUR MISSION?** _____

OK. Time to get down to it. First, go close the door. Switch on the answering machine and unplug your phone. Get comfortable and ready to concentrate. What you are about to do is *the single most important task in marketing*. It's not hard, necessarily, but it's *important*.

We're going to do this in three simple steps. First, you will decide for yourself what your mission is. Next, we will look at that mission through the eyes of a prospective customer and discover what difference your mission makes in the customer's life. Finally, we will figure out exactly how to *say* what your mission is so that you will conquer marketing's moment of truth. Remember how we phrased the three steps in Chapter 2: First become a Missionary; then align yourself with your market; then become a Marketer.

"OK, John, Let's try it out. What do you do?"

"Uh—I'm a chiropractor."

"No, John, that's what you *are*. What do you *do*?"

"Huh?"

"John, you are falling right into the social expectations trap. People ask what you do, and they expect you to hand them a label they can apply to you—banker, mechanic, social worker, whatever. Problem is, in handing them that label you are now completely at the mercy of their prejudices, ignorance, and projections. You are in effect saying to them: 'Go ahead. Drag out whatever image you have of chiropractors and slap it on me.' Do you really want them to do that?"

John almost shuddered. "Definitely not."

"OK then. Just because they expect a label doesn't mean you have to give it to them. They ask, 'What do you do?' So tell them that. Try it again, now. What do you do?"

We will come back to Dr. John soon. It's your turn now. Remember that giving people a standard label to apply to you is bad marketing.

Do not tell people what you are; tell them what you do.

In Chapter 1 we said that from the marketing point of view your business exists for one purpose only: to make a specific beneficial difference in the lives of your customers. Let's work backward from there. Use this fill-in-the-blanks formula to get you started on your mission statement:

I support _____

in their desire to _____

by means of _____

The first blank identifies your market. If you start to get bogged down there, just write "my customers" in that blank and move on.

The second blank is the real heart and soul of the statement; it will contain what marketers call "the benefit," which is marketer shorthand for "what they want that you help them get." Take a shot at filling in that second blank; we will work on it, progressively, until it clicks.

The third blank is where you specify the actual services you perform which result in that benefit. For now just write down the results of your Workwork: Choosing the Best Service, in Chapter 2. (What! You skipped Chapter 2? Look, there's some Workwork at the end of Chapter 2 that you really need for this. We'll wait for you.)

Choose the Right Words

How does your mission statement look to you so far? Basically on the right track? If you have gotten bogged down, here are two tips. First, you may get confused about who your customers are. I once did an in-house marketing workshop for the personnel department in a huge organization. They were very confused about which of their many "clients" were the customers. "We can't just please the people who sign the checks. After all, we have all these people in training classes; we have to satisfy them too." I pointed out a simple distinction: as a service professional, you may have many clients or consumers of your services. You of course must produce value and satisfaction for them. But your customers are a little different: they are the people who authorize the use of your services in the first place. They have to see the value in what you propose before you will be authorized to do it. (In that light, the personnel people decided that their mission was "to support the executive group in their desire to have and manage a productive work force.")

Second, don't worry if the benefit part seems weak or fuzzy at this point. It usually does. That's the part we will work on most.

"OK, John, try it again. What do you do?"

"I do chiropractic adjustments to people who have chronic or acute back pain, or who have headaches that have failed to respond to standard medical treatment, or . . ."

"Whoa! Down, boy! You remember that old joke, John, about the kid who did a report on a book about penguins? His report was, 'This book told me more about penguins than I ever wanted to know.' You've just told me more about your business than I ever wanted to know. But at least you are telling me what you *do* instead of what you are. Now let's clean it up a bit.

"First big problem: You lead off with something the average person doesn't understand: 'chiropractic adjustments.' Do people generally know what that means?"

"Not really. Sometimes they think they do—'Oh, you crack backs, right?'—but that's wrong, and mostly they don't even know that."

"So you have lost them from the first words. John, this moment of truth goes by in a flash. You can't afford to fool around. I know you're not going to like this, but here it is anyway:

> **When you tell somebody what you do, you must do it in words they *already understand accurately*. If you have to educate them even a bit to get them to understand what you have said, you have lost."**

John looked unhappy. "I don't know how to do that."

"We'll work on it. Second big problem: your laundry list of potential patients. It begins to sound like you can cure just about anybody of anything, like an old-time patent medicine."

John looked very unhappy. "That's a problem chiropractors face all the time. But, Tony, that's just a list of the kind of people I really do help! What am I supposed to do—specialize in one or two types of patients?"

"No. Let's work it out step by step. First, let's look at the 'chiropractic adjustment' part. Remember the principle: What you are going to say must be in words that people already understand accurately. So what can you say instead of 'chiropractic adjustment'?"

"I guess I could say I promote spinal alignment . . ."

"But . . . ?"

"But that's probably as bad as 'chiropractic adjustment.' Most people have only a vague idea of what spinal alignment is, and why it's important."

"Good, John. You're getting the point. Try again. Any other way to say it?"

John was beginning to look depressed. "No. That's the problem with my field, Tony—the public doesn't understand what we do."

"John, would it help any if I told you that's the problem with almost any professional service you can name? The public doesn't know how most professionals get their results; and frankly, my dear, they don't give a damn. What the public is interested in are the results, not the way you get them.

"You have discovered for yourself one of the hardest marketing principles to accept and apply:

Tell them *what* you do, not how you do it.

"I know, I know—what makes you a chiropractor is how you do it. And there's plenty of time to tell them about how after they say, 'Wow! Tell me more!' But what makes yours a desirable service they will want to buy is *what* you do—for them. We have to drop from your mission statement all the stuff that refers to how, and see what's left."

Let's leave Dr. John to digest that for awhile. Look back at the benefit part in the middle of your own mission statement. Have you done what Dr. John did: have you told how? Ask yourself: Have I used any words or phrases that mean something special in my field—words that my average prospective customer would not understand accurately, or would fail to see the importance of? If so, *get rid of them*. Replace them with plain English if you can; otherwise, drop them out. The place for how and technical words is later, when you have conquered the moment of truth and they ask for more.

Don't worry if knocking out the how essentially strips everything out of your mission. If it doesn't belong, get rid of it. As a wise old teacher of mine once said, "Sometimes it is better just to make a fresh start."

"What's left after we drop all the how stuff is that 'laundry list of potential patients' you disliked so much, Tony."

"Well, if the only thing left in sight are your customers, John, you're in pretty good shape. Tell me about that list. What do the people on it have in common?"

"They all can benefit from chiropractic services."

"And what about them makes them good candidates for your services? Big picture, now—not all the details."

John thought hard for a moment. "Well, they all suffer from some degree of spinal misalignment. . . ."

"Not that technical stuff again, John! What do *they* see that makes them good candidates for your services?"

"Well . . . they are all in pain of some sort . . . except a few aren't really in pain, they are chronically stiff or sore . . . discomfort is more like it. . . ."

"So your customers all suffer from pain or discomfort and they know it. What do you do for them?"

"I adjust their spine and musculature so that they are aligned."

"And what does *that* do for them?"

"It gets rid of what is causing their problem and frees them to lead healthful lives."

"So you help people lead lives free of pain and discomfort."

John stared at me. "Say that again!" I did. He wrote it down and looked at it with obvious excitement. "That's it, isn't it? That's exactly what I do! But . . . can this be right? I mean—it's so *obvious!*"

"That's how it's supposed to be, John. Obvious—once you see it. Congratulations; I think you've got it."

Your turn again. Look back at your mission statement and think—think hard!—about what you see. What do your prospective customers all have in common? ("They all need my services." "Good. What about them makes them good candidates for your services? No technical stuff—what do *they* see that makes them good candidates for your services?")

Now look at what you do for these customers. Don't look at the how part; drop the details and look only at the outcome of what you do from their point of view. Ask yourself: Is this something that they would immediately say "Wow! Yes!" to? If not, ask yourself: When I do this for them, what do they get that they really value? Stuck? Here are some tips:

1. Get rid of all jargon and technical terms.

If you insist on clinging to your own jargon, you will have a lot of trouble seeing what your customers see. Cindy kept insisting that her customers all shared a "desire for good graphical design" until she finally acknowledged that most of her customers barely knew what "graphical design" was. Then she was able to see what her customers really had in common: They wanted professional-looking brochures that would help them get more business.

2. Look for a valued outcome, not a valuable feature.

Keep asking "What do they get from *that?*" until your answer is an outcome that they value. May owns a bookstore specializing in "escape" reading. She felt that her mission was to provide "variety and wide selection" to her customers. That wording's almost right, but not quite. What do readers get from having variety and wide selection? They can be assured of finding exactly the kind of escape they are looking for. That's May's mission.

3. Do not assume your market values the same things you do.

It probably doesn't. Jenny does workshops on negotiation. Like most trainers, she saw "skills" as very important; giving people better negotiating skills seemed valuable in its own right. A hard-nosed salesman in her workshop pointed out that "good negotiating skills plus fifty cents will get you a cup of coffee in a cheap diner"—his way of pointing out that what was valued was not the skills but rather the results of successful exercise of those skills. In other words, we don't value the means (negotiating skills); we value the results (better deals).

4. *Be careful not to go so far that you lose plausibility.*

Naive marketers seem to think that all they have to do is invoke the latest buzz word, or the ultimate "bottom line," to get an instant benefit statement. For a while in business circles, the buzz word was "productivity"—Leadership for Productivity, Listening for Productivity; then it was "quality"; then "excellence" or "competitive advantage." And there's always that old favorite: Make More Money! Notice how your mind filters out these claims? Advertisers refer to them as "noise"; they only clutter up the communications channels.

Usually when people wind up with such outcome statements it's because they have taken the "What do they get from my services?" logic one step too far. Your service as you describe it, has to be the service that *could*, on the face of it, bring about the result you claim. We can believe that negotiation training could result in better deals; and it's true that better deals will result in making more money—assuming the market doesn't turn against us, or a scheduling glitch cause too much overtime, or we try to grow too quickly, or any one of a hundred other things that also affect how much money we make. Negotiation training and making more money are not strongly enough linked. Furthermore, making better deals is highly valued in its own right. You lose credibility when you reach too far to get your benefit.

Some more examples may help you choose the right wording:

- A trainer who did "workshops on humor, communication, and futuring" realized that her mission was to "help create a positive work climate," which really gets "Wow! Tell me more" reactions from people who need it.

- One diversified consultant who was offering "employee involvement, participative management and problem solving" worked out this mission: "I help organizations construct a vision for their future that will enable them to thrive." This firm, now thriving itself, is turning away business because demand is so great.

- A self-described "leadership coach" now tells people, "I help people lead their organizations out of chaos." (If your organization is in chaos, you know it—and want out.)

Put *your* answers together now: What is the beneficial outcome of your services? What problem do all your customers have in common, that you help them solve? (Or flip it around if that's easier: What opportunity do all your customers face that you help them make the most of?) These questions have the same answer, because they are really the same question! The answer defines what your customers have in common. It seems clear and obvious once you see it. It makes immediate sense to anyone hearing it, and it will enable you to conquer marketing's moment of truth.

That answer is your mission. If you've got it, congratulations! If you're still not there, show what you've got so far to a friend and ask for help. Keep working on it and keep testing your revisions until the statement clicks.

Now What?

"Great, Tony! 'I help people lead lives free of pain and discomfort.' That's right. So what now?"

"Now you practice, John. Practice saying what you do until it comes out smooth and clear. Memorize that mission statement. I know that sounds silly but you'll be amazed how often you will stumble over the words until you do. Write it down on a piece of paper and tape it next to your business phone as a reminder. Take every opportunity you get to tell people what you do, and pay attention to the response—theirs and yours. Does anything seem flat or missing? Do you lose conviction when you use this word rather than that? Keep fine-tuning until it seems to flow directly from you to them: both what you do, and your sense of how valuable this service really is."

"OK. But I can see already I will have a problem. I know you don't like labels, Tony, and I agree with you, but how can I *not* say I'm a chiropractor? It feels like I'm trying to hide something."

"No problem. *Now* you can get away with the label. Just say, 'I'm a chiropractor. I help people lead lives free of pain and discomfort.' Think you can do that?"

John grinned. "No problem."

4

Zeroing In

Finding Your Natural High-Opportunity Market

A farmer needed water for his crops. There was no river nearby, so he set out to dig a well. After surveying the land carefully, he chose the most likely site and began to dig. Ten feet, no water; 15 feet, no water; 20 feet, still no water. The farmer thought to himself, "This is a poor spot!" He filled the hole back in and went to bed.

The next day he picked a new site for his well and began to dig. Ten feet, 15 feet, 20 feet—no water. He went to bed discouraged but still determined. The next day he picked a new spot and began to dig.

In this way the Spring passed into the Summer. The farmer dug 70 wells and never found a drop of water. Finally, exhausted and out of money, he sold the farm for a few coins and moved to the city.

The new owner could find no new site to dig, so he went to the site of the very first well and began digging. Ten feet, 15 feet, 20 feet—no water; 30 feet, 40 feet, 50 feet—no water.

Finally, at 60 feet, the well suddenly began to fill, and from that day on the second farmer always had an abundance of cool, sweet water for his crops.

Recognize anyone you know in this story? Have you tried service after service, market after market, attempting to find the one that you can build your business around? If so, you're caught in probably the most common dilemma in business. Take heart: with few exceptions, every successful business I know started out like the first farmer. The key is to become like the second farmer before you exhaust yourself and your opportunities. That's what this chapter is all about.

Marketing is a lot like digging that well: you will virtually guarantee failure if you divide your energies among a number of different markets. The only way you can hope to succeed is to concentrate your marketing

32

on a very small number of well-chosen segments into which you pour all your resources. ("One" is an appropriate candidate for that "very small number.")

"But what if I'm wrong? What if I've misjudged? Shouldn't I hedge my bets by appealing to a variety of markets?" That's first-farmer talk. "Hedging bets" is for gamblers, not for business owners, and experienced gamblers know that hedging bets just speeds up the rate at which the casino takes your money. You should do what makes sense to you, of course; it's your well. I recommend you think like the second farmer. And that means we have to find you a target market segment.

What's a "Segment"?

Like every profession, marketing has some favorite words. "Segment" is up near the top of the list. It's a simple idea, really: a segment is an identifiable piece of your total market. Take the entire universe of your prospective customers—the people, organizations, businesses, or media that logically could benefit from your services—and divide it up however you like and as often and finely as you like, and then stop whenever you like. "Males" are a segment; so are "red-headed, left-handed females under 25 years of age who live in the Sunbelt and drive Hondas." However you divide up your market, you arrive at market segments: the process is called "segmentation."

As you might surmise from the examples, segmentation can be an endless exercise in accomplishing nothing much, unless you bear in mind *why* you are identifying segments. The basic idea is common sense: Some segments are better prospects for your services than others. To create and maintain the relationship of customer will take more effort in some segments and less effort in others. You want to find segments for which your efforts will get very good return, so that you can put your marketing resources where they will do you the most good. You want to dig your well where you have the best chance of finding water with the least amount of digging.

In this chapter we are looking for your "target market segment," the single segment that represents your best chance of getting a good return for your marketing efforts. That's the segment you will work with to achieve the laser-like alignment that is the real secret of successful marketing. Segmentation turns out to be one of the simplest tasks in marketing for most people; all it takes is willingness to think analytically for a while and do some digging for facts. It won't be fun or exciting, like some of the other tasks, but it will be rewarding.

How important is segmentation? No less an authority than Ted Levitt, the Harvard Business School professor who has influenced an

entire generation of marketers, states flatly: "If you're not thinking segments, you're not thinking." So let's think!

Let's get you started with a list you will add to and refine throughout this
chapter. But first, a pop quiz:

Quickly now—in one clear, crisp sentence, what is your mission?

(Can't say? You skipped Chapter 3, didn't you. Then you're headed
for a rough time: You can't identify the market for your services until you
know with great clarity what your services are, and that means knowing
your mission. I recommend you work through Chapter 3 before you
continue here.)

Let's expand your view, with a brainstorm. (If possible, do this step
with a partner or colleague or with one or two savvy friends or family
members.) Take ten minutes or so and write down, just as fast as you can
think of them, the answers to the question:

Who *could* benefit from my services?

Remember, in brainstorming you write down whatever comes to
mind, no matter how silly or farfetched it may seem; the time to weed out
the list is after you have a list. Duplication or overlap is fine; you may
discover later that what looked like overlap was actually useful segmentation. Your goal is to list as many potential segments as you can in a short
period of time. Ready? Go!

Good. This is the beginning of your potential segments list. Now
put the list aside while we look at how to refine it.

How Do You Segment the Market?

Anything that distinguishes one group of prospective customers from
another can be used for defining a segment. Many ways of segmenting
may turn out to be "no big deal" for your particular service, but hold off
on evaluating the segments until after we have defined them. For example, does it really matter in your business whether your customers are
right-handed or left-handed? (It does if you sell scissors!)

Let's look at the "segmenters," the bases on which customers can be
divided into segments.

Whom They Are Buying For

Are your customers buying for themselves, for their companies, or on
behalf of other people? The usual ways of describing these are: sales to
consumers, sales to industry, or sales to agents, respectively. Marketing

to an individual who is buying on her own behalf, as a consumer, is quite different from marketing the same service to the same person when she is buying on behalf of a large company. You may have great success with one and no success with the other.

Industry Type

The potential divisions here are almost endless. You can use the big headings: Manufacturing, Retailing, Health Care, Financial Services, Education, Government, and so on. Or you can break them down by what they manufacture (heavy-industry machinery, high-tech components, finished goods, autos, computers, consumer electronics, industrial tools and equipment); by what they retail (food, clothing, electronics, books); and so on for each category. You can segment by who your customer's customers are (for example, a manufacturing consultant who works exclusively with suppliers to auto manufacturers); by how your customers distribute their products (software services for direct-mail companies); or even by the specific technologies they use (repair and maintenance of bar-code readers).

Are your potential customers privately held companies, or public corporations? Big, medium, or small? Well-established or start-up? Emerging technology or mature technology? Bureaucratic or entrepreneurial? Conservative or aggressive? Are there many different companies of this type, or few? Most of these issues will become completely irrelevant to choosing *your* target segment, but you can't be sure which those are in advance. Look at each one carefully before you decide whether to dismiss it.

Demographics

You can segment your market on the basis of "census" type information: age, income, education, employment, sex, race, weight, family status, religion, professional and social affiliations, and so on. Direct-mail marketers and heavy media advertisers love to use demographics to create an image of the "typical" prospect for their marketing plan. Pick the demographics that seem relevant.

Geographics

Where are your potential customers located? Are they where you are? (You may succeed at opening a surfing school but you will probably have to move out of Nebraska to do it.) Are you really willing to spend most of your life flying around the country to service your customers? (Trust me, it only sounds glamorous.) Will you concentrate on your local community? The northeast side of town? The Midwestern states?

Buying History

Your best segments may be people who have a certain kind of buying history. If you are opening a video-rental service, for example, you will find it useful to market to people who have purchased VCRs. Or perhaps the linkage is not quite that direct: if you are a day-care provider, you might market to people who have purchased diapers. Or, you may find it worthwhile to market accounting services to individuals who have recently purchased a fax machine (getting serious about that basement business!). You might market to people who have been customers of one of your competitors. Or the linkage may just be statistical: all things considered, you will sell more financial planning services to Mercedes owners than to Corvette drivers. What buying history will increase the likelihood that someone will be receptive to *your* services? (Don't overlook the best buying history of all: people who have already bought from you—your own customers.)

Personal Characteristics

These come in two varieties: plain and fancy. The plain variety looks for traits, attitudes, abilities, and so on, that increase the likelihood that people will need or want your services. Impatient people may be good prospects for services that save them time; people who are self-conscious about their use of language may see the value in a home-study course; people with restricted physical abilities are in greater need of many services such as lawn care and snow removal. These are mostly common-sense matches of services to types of people.

The fancy variety is called "psychographics." This science divides a potential market into psychological types (such as the VALS system's Survivors, Sustainers, Emulators, Achievers, and so on) and attempts to market differently to different types. In the hands of a marketing pro, psychographics can be dynamite; however, it's much harder to use effectively than you might think, and can quickly get complicated and costly. I suggest you stick to the plain variety.

Identifiable Situations

Segmenting by situation can be very powerful. Let's spend extra time on this, because it's not completely obvious and you may just strike gold.

The trick is to identify a state of affairs that greatly increases the likelihood that a prospect will need your services. The old stereotype of the ambulance-chasing lawyer is a crude but direct image of how this works. Some examples:

- One firm routinely markets to every publicly traded company that has merged with another company, acquired a company, or been acquired. The firm's service? "Outplacement" counseling for employees who have become "surplus" in the reshuffling.

- A consultant specializing in "downsizing organizations" focuses on public agencies that have received a significant budget cut.

- Welcome Wagon has made a long-standing business of helping merchants and professionals reach prospects who have just moved into a new home. This is an excellent situation for many service businesses to build a relationship.

As we shall see in later chapters, identifying situations that activate need for your services is a key move in many of your marketing communications. For now, ask yourself: "Does some identifiable situation define an important segment of my market?"

OK, OK; calm down. You don't have to consider all these factors at once, or even at all. The whole point is that your market can be divided into a tremendous number of segments, most of which will be useless to you. But some will be solid gold for your marketing, so look over the possibilities and pick out the ones that work for you.

___ **WORKWORK: PANNING THE STREAM** _____

Let's clean up and refine your potential segments list. Start by crossing off the segments that are obviously ridiculous. (Dermatologists do not *want* your high-intensity tanning lamps!)

Now look for connections: Do certain of the segments go together into an identifiable larger segment? Write it down as a separate segment.

Next look for refinements. Scan the list of "segmenters" above. Do you see any that suggest a further division of some segment already on your list? Or perhaps an entirely new segment? Write them down. Keep going until you are fairly sure your list is complete.

Look over your list quickly once more (you may want to copy it over on a clean sheet of paper if you are having trouble reading it). Every segment on your list now should seem at least a potentially viable market for your services. If you look at any segments and get the feeling that there is no way you could reach them, put a big question mark beside them.

Lots of possibilities here, right? Now we start narrowing them down to one. Look back over your list of potential segments. Without trying to be too analytical yet, we want to narrow the field down to about 10. Pick 10 or so segments that seem to you to be candidates for your target segment.

(Only one candidate? Are you *really* sure it's as clear-cut as all that? Do you look at that segment and drool in anticipation? Yes? Sounds like a pretty good target. Congratulations.)

On a clean sheet of paper, write down the 10 segments, one per line; allow five or six lines of space after each. We'll be using this sheet as a "scorecard" for some analytic stuff in a few minutes.

How Do You Evaluate Segments?

By now you have noticed the good news: there are far more market segments for your services than you could possibly reach! All you have to do is find the cream of the crop and get to work.

To do that, let's do a quick probe of your values (it's won't hurt, I promise). The reason is simple: We are looking for your "target market segment," the single segment that represents your best chance of getting a good return for your marketing efforts. Those words "best" and "good" don't mean the same thing to different people, so we need to find what *you* will consider the "best" segment.

("The best segment is the one that will make me the most money. End of values exploration." Do you honestly think that's all there is to it? And are you *really sure* you can spot the segment that will make you the most money? If so, skip the analysis that follows. But if that segment doesn't work out, come back to this page and try thinking a little harder—if you're still in business.)

What makes a segment a good one? I once asked a workshop group to write down their personal criteria for saying that a segment was a good opportunity; when we pooled the answers, we wound up with over 35 distinct criteria! Experience with that list led me to boil it down to 10 statements about the people in the segment:

1. *They have the money.*

If they can't afford to pay for your services, you can hardly get a good return on your marketing efforts. Specialized versions of this criterion are: "It's in their budget," when dealing with units within large organizations; "They are authorized to contract for it," when dealing with government; and "They pay their bills," when dealing with any private organization.

2. *They will pay a premium for better service.*

Some industries, and types of consumers, are notorious for buying at the lowest possible cost. Others are known for their willingness to pay extra for better service. All else being equal, you'll do better marketing to people who know quality and will pay accordingly.

3. *There are a lot of them.*

Two apple trees stand side by side: one is loaded with hundreds of apples, the other has a dozen or so on its branches. Which tree would *you* shake?

(10) *They will make excellent references.*

In the long view, the quality of your references and word-of-mouth is one of your most valuable assets. You may choose a segment specifically with that in mind. There are three major versions of this criterion:

- "You worked with *Them*? I'm impressed!"

✓ ■ "If *They* say you're good, that's good enough for me."

- "If you helped *Them*, you can help anybody!" (I occasionally get this reaction when I tell people that I have helped certain federal government groups improve their marketing.)

Understand now why I said that different people have different ideas of what the "best" opportunity is?

_____ WORKWORK: YOUR TARGET SEGMENT _____

Time for a little analysis.

Review those 10 criteria for saying a segment is a good opportunity. Pick five or so that really count for you. Write them on a clean sheet of paper. (Make up criteria of your own if something important to you is not on the list. We're looking for *your* values.)

Now pick the criterion that is most important to you. Write the number 10 beside it. Now assign a number between 1 (lowest) and 10 (highest) to the other criteria on your list, to show how important each one is, compared to the most important one. You can give them all 10 if they are equally important in your estimation.

You now have something like this:

Have the $$$	10
Lots of them	9
Credibility	9
Greatest need	7
Easy to get message to them	10

Now pull out your "scorecard" sheet of paper, where you wrote your 10 or so segments. Your task is to rate each of your 10 potential segments using your five criteria. In the space below the first segment, write numbers that say how well it meets each of the criteria. In my example above, if my first segment has absolutely no problem with finding the money, I

4. *Competition in this segment is weak.*

How hard will you have to compete for customers? You get better returns with weak competition (but look twice to make sure potential competitors are not staying out for a good reason).

5. *We can easily get our message to them.*

This criterion probably trips up more beginning marketers than any other single oversight. To create the relationship of customer you have to be able to communicate to your prospects. How will you do that? To reach accountants you can put ads in their professional journals, or mail something to all the accountants listed in the Yellow Pages. But how do you reach "people who want to be proactive in managing change?" What do they read, or listen to? How could you get their address?

6. *We already have credibility with them.*

A pivotal task in marketing is getting your prospective customers to take what you have to say seriously. You must cut through the semiautomatic "Oh, yeah? Sez who?" response most people have to most marketing communications. Credibility is the major factor in getting them interested, and you are way ahead of the game if you already have it with some segment. (A variation is: "We can easily get credibility with them.")

7. *They have the greatest need.*

Perhaps it's important to you to be making a contribution through your work. You need to make your living, of course, but in addition you want to help where help is most needed. If this is a strong value of yours, it's self-defeating to ignore it. Another version is: "They fascinate me." If your life-long dream is to work with authors and other creative types, go for it. (But remember criterion #1!)

8. *They already know they need what I have to offer.*

This is the pragmatist's version of "greatest need." It's hard work to get people to see a need they didn't know they had (but not impossible: consumer products advertising does it all the time, at great cost). Your return is much greater if their reaction is, "I was just thinking about that yesterday!"

9. *They are in the right geographic area.*

Want to consult to the auto industry? Better move to Michigan. (Or Tennessee. Or Ohio. Or Ontario. Or, come to think of it, certain parts of California. Oh well—get a frequent-flyers card and live near a major airport.)

will give it a 10. If there are only a few and not "lots of them," I might give them a 3 score on my second criterion, and so on.

Two important points before you write down your five numbers for each segment. Even if some segment has the greatest imaginable need, I should score it only 7, since that's the most I said this criterion was worth. And *very* important: If you don't know, don't make it up! Put down a question mark if you're not sure how some segment rates on one of your criteria. The fact that you don't know something that makes an important difference in your decision should concern you a bit.

When you have rated all 10 segments (that wasn't so bad, was it?) you will have five numbers (or question marks) for each. Add the five numbers up, so that you have one total score for each segment. (If you have any question marks for a segment, the total score is question mark.) As you look over your total scores, does one stand out as clearly the best opportunity (highest total score)? Look at it carefully—that's your target market segment. Aligning you with that segment is our task for the rest of this book.

Are two or more segments essentially tied at the top? Which of them looks best to you? Choose one of the criteria as a tie-breaker; or go back over them again, to see if you've been overly optimistic; or go with your gut feeling as to which one you want to align yourself with. You've got more than one good site for your well; about the only way you can go wrong is not to pick one of them and start digging.

Do you think one of your question-mark segments might actually be the best? Then find out what you need to know, before you make your commitment. But do it quickly; the sooner you start digging your well, the sooner you will find water.

Filling in the Blanks

Now that you have chosen it, you need to find out as much as you can about your target market segment. This is not "market research" in any high-falutin sense; it's just plain digging out the facts you need, to market successfully. The more you know, the more likely you are to be on target. (And you may find out something that makes you reconsider the wisdom of targeting this segment. A software engineer was ready to go after federal government business, only to find that it takes over 18 months on average to award a federal contract! That would have been about a year after the software engineer's business had gone under. Better to find these things out *before* you invest your life's savings.)

Again, you do not need any magic insight here—just common sense, some sweat equity, and knowledge of some of the characteristics of your target market. If you are not sure about even *one* of these characteristics, you are taking a bigger risk than I personally would feel comfortable with. Find out! That's what libraries and the telephone are for!

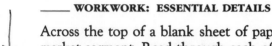

—— **WORKWORK: ESSENTIAL DETAILS** ————————————

Across the top of a blank sheet of paper write the name of your target market segment. Read through each of the questions below and answer them to the best of your ability. Write both the answers you have and any answers you don't have but need. Put big stars beside the ones you don't have. Those starred items should occupy your attention until you have answers.

1. How large is this segment, measured by number of potential customers?

   What do you know about them demographically—age, income, education, employment, sex, race, weight, family status, religion, professional and social affiliations, and so on. (Don't forget: even if you are marketing to companies or organizations, you are actually marketing to specific *people* in these organizations. What kind of people they are *matters*.)

   If you don't know, how can you find out?

2. What personal experience do you have with this segment?

   How well do you know the people you have had contact with?

   Have you ever sold anything to them, or talked to anyone who has?

   What key insights or cautions have you developed about them through experience?

   Do you know anyone who knows this segment well?

   How can you get that person to share this expertise?

3. What important need of this segment does your service fill?

   In what terms does this segment think of this need? Of this service? (Industry thinks in terms of "developing skills" and "workshops"; school districts think in terms of "continuing education" and "in-services.")

   How important is this need relative to others, in the minds of the segment? ("Nice-to-have" is a lot harder to sell than "need-to-have.")

4. What services already exist to fill this need?

   Are they well known to the segment?

   How do the people in the segment view the service you offer?

   How do they feel about it?

   What are its most desirable features in the minds of the segment?

   What aspects of the service and/or its delivery do they find most off-putting? ("Having to wait so long for my glasses. I need them now!" said prospects for eyeglasses. Lenscrafters built their business around eliminating this off-putting factor; they make glasses while their customers look around the mall.)

   How can you find these things out?

5. Who actually makes the decision to purchase your services?

   Who recommends or influences the purchase?

   Who could block it?

6. What phrase or term identifies members of this segment?

   How would I know if I were part of that segment?

   Do I actually think of myself as "one of those?"

   Would I merely recognize the segment when you point it out?

   Would I resist thinking of myself as "one of those?" (Nobody sees himself or herself as a "Yuppie." They see other people as "Yuppies.")

   What term or label might I prefer?

7. What kind of information impresses people in this segment? (If you want to influence an engineer, put it on a graph. Seasoned business managers want accounts of your experience with "people like us.")

   What magazines, newspapers, and journals do they read?

   Whose endorsement of this kind of service would count with them?

   What kind of endorsement would count most?

   What kind of image of myself do I like to have? (No-nonsense bottom liner; risk taker; trail blazer; "with-it"; workaholic; shrewd judge of value, "nothing but the best will do.")

Does my service support this image?

Does it conflict with this image?

Seem overwhelming? It's not; if you take it one item at a time. You could go ahead and market your services without answering any of these questions. It is *your business* and nobody's holding a gun to your head. But think of it this way: you are about to go for a walk through a minefield. Just because there are mines out doesn't mean *you* will step on one. Think of the answers to these questions as telling you where the mines are.

Now it's your choice. Want a map?

5 | Standing Out from the Crowd

The Relationship Strategy for Differentiating Your Services

Did you ever try to find a good dentist? It's not easy.

Several years ago I needed a good dentist fast. I had just moved to a new city and brought a vicious toothache with me. As I sat staring at the Yellow Pages listings for "Dentists" I had one of those sinking insights: I had no idea how to tell them apart! From past experience I knew some dentists were great and some were not;—but which was which? I didn't know and I didn't know how to find out. In desperation I started calling orthodontists and asking who cleaned *their* teeth. When I heard the same name twice, I went to him. I didn't much like him, but he did take care of the toothache.

Like anyone who has ever faced the problem of finding a good dentist (or mechanic, lawyer, psychotherapist, accountant, day-care provider, employment counselor, and so on), I was seeing from the consumer's side the most difficult task facing the provider of professional services: standing out from the crowd.

How can *you* stand out from the crowd? How can you get prospective customers to choose you instead of all those other people who seem to be providing the "same service?" We will look at that "same service" notion in some detail in Chapter 7; for now let's just recognize that, until you know better, all dentists look pretty much the same.

So do all accountants, which is what brought this issue home to me professionally. I was sitting in an office in New York a few years ago, talking with a senior partner of one of the major national accounting firms. We were discussing what his firm needed in order to thrive through the next decade. (It was one of those beautiful Spring days that make you understand why senior partners jockey for the corner offices; between the buildings I could see a long swatch of Central Park.) Emerson had just finished telling me that accountants typically don't know the first thing about marketing.

"Tony, what we really need help with is differentiating the audit." ("Differentiating" is marketers' jargon for "standing out from the crowd.")

"OK, Emerson. Why the audit, in particular?"

"Two reasons: the audit is still our firm's bread and butter. And to an increasing number of our prospective clients, the audit is a commodity." (In marketing jargon, a "commodity" is what you definitely do *not* want to be—like pork bellies on an Exchange, bought and sold solely on the basis of price.)

"Why's that?"

Emerson sighed. "Tony, the way accountants tend to treat it, an audit *is* a commodity. An audit is an audit is an audit. It doesn't much matter to the client *how* you do it, as long as you don't get in their way too much. They are interested in getting that signature from the Firm that certifies their financial statements. And, of course, they are interested in what it costs them. And frankly, that's about it."

"But you know the audit is not a commodity."

"Yes—at least, I believe it isn't." Emerson went to his bookshelf. "And if you believe Levitt, there's no such thing as a commodity. There are only unsuccessfully differentiated services."

"Far as I'm concerned, nobody understands the marketing perspective better than Ted Levitt."

Emerson nodded. "I agree. Look, Tony, let's do this. Put together for us a program that will put into practical form the concepts in Levitt's chapter on differentiation." He handed me his copy of *The Marketing Imagination*. "Accountants are in kindergarten when it comes to marketing. Let's put together a program that will at least get our partners through the first few years of college."

The first thing I did after leaving Emerson's office was to hire Bruce Fritch, the young marketing whiz who invented the "laser-like alignment" image (you met him in Chapter 1). By now he was a somewhat older, independent marketing consultant living in Charlotte, North Carolina. Together we set out to put together the differentiation program.

First we sat down with Levitt's book and re-re-*re*read his chapter called "Differentiation—Of Anything." (Bruce was as big a fan of Levitt's as Emerson and I were.) In concept, differentiation is both simple and challenging. *Anything* can be made to stand out from the crowd in a positive and valuable way, if enough marketing imagination is applied. The challenge is to figure out exactly how. And according to Levitt, almost anything can be a source of differentiation. So far, a piece of cake.

Then we started pulling together everything else we knew from practical experience about differentiating services. Suddenly the challenge didn't look so easy.

You see, almost anything about a firm or its services can help it stand out from the crowd. There are only two small qualifications: whatever is used has to be both distinctive and visible to the prospective customer. The problem is, most things flunk one or both of those tests. For example, both research and common sense say that a telephone directory listing in red will capture the customer's attention better than black type. Red is visible. And if your listing is the only red one on the page (or one of a very few) it will also be distinctive. Visible and distinctive: *Violà!* Differentiation! Unfortunately, you may not be the only advertiser who has noticed the power of red. If many other listings are also red, it is no longer distinctive: no differentiation.

So Bruce and I knew this audit differentiation project was going to be a challenging job. We got down to work.

We got Emerson and his partners to identify their target market for the audit: "medium size businesses." (Their firm's definition was businesses with annual sales of from $5 million to $100 million!) We researched that market thoroughly: we talked to some satisfied clients, some dissatisfied clients, and some clients who had recently switched from other accounting firms. We talked to experienced partners about what works in marketing the audit and what doesn't. We talked to the "troops" who actually go in and do the audits. In every case we were looking for concrete answers to the bottom-line question: Why did you choose this firm to do your audit, and not some other? What caused this firm to stand out from the crowd?

Ultimately we found the answers we were looking for, in a place we might never have thought to look. We helped Emerson's accounting firm create a practical strategy for differentiating the audit—or any other professional service—that works almost like magic. We called it the "Relationship Strategy" and you can use that same strategy to cause your services to stand out from the crowd. We will do that in this chapter. Along the way, we took note of some ways of differentiating services that look like they ought to work but don't. Let's get those out of the way first so you can see clearly what *does* work, and why.

You Can NOT Differentiate Your Services on the Basis of . . .

Features

Accountants may not know the first thing about marketing, but that doesn't stop them from having opinions on the subject—especially the young, aggressive, new accountants who are hired by big-time accounting firms. Bruce and I found plenty of accountants eager to tell us exactly why their Firm's audit is superior.

"We have the best level of automation." "We use teams made up of . . . ." "Can you believe, those guys still use . . . ." Like all good professionals, these accountants had given considerable thought to their jobs and were convinced that their methods were the best. For all I know, they were right. Our talks with their clients, however, made it quite clear that the clients knew little about how an audit was done and cared less. As Emerson had told us, what clients care about is the result. How you get there is your concern, not theirs.

This is true of virtually all service professionals. Some aspect of what they do and how they do it ("features" in marketing lingo) helps make their service distinctively superior. ("We certainly don't use those cheap synthetic polishes.") Unfortunately, they rarely can get their customers excited about these features.

Dr. John, the chiropractor you met earlier, phrased it best. I asked him, "John, what distinguishes you from other chiropractors?"

"Well, I take a very holistic approach, and I use low-force technique."

"What happens when you tell people that?"

"They either look at me blankly or else they say, 'Oh, Dr. So-and-so uses low-force technique.' Now I know what Dr. So-and-so does, and I wouldn't call it low-force at all, but they don't know the difference."

They don't know the difference. That one sentence explains why you can't differentiate using features. Technical and professional distinctions that are important to you are not visible in a motivating way to the customer.

Like most rules, this one has exceptions, but they don't last long. If everybody really wants it "in purple with bells on," as our Mercenary friend Harve put it, and you are the only one who has it in purple, you will stand out from the crowd nicely. Just be prepared to watch your competitors quickly paint theirs purple.

There are good uses for features in marketing—in packaging, for example—but the simple fact is: You can't differentiate your services on the basis of features.

Brand Names and Slogans

We all grew up watching television. It has a funny effect on how we see the world. In particular, it has had a strong effect on how we think about marketing. For most of us marketing is the same as advertising, and its essence is found in The Quest for the Perfect Slogan—preferably set to music.

This is not the time or place to talk about the value of advertising; we'll get to that later. And please don't get the wrong idea: I like slogans and brand names as much as anyone, in their proper place (packaging and presentation, for example). But you have about as much chance of successfully differentiating your services by using a slogan as you do of winning the big prize in the state lottery. Slogans have the same problems as features: if they are distinctive, they don't say anything valuable; if they say something valuable, everybody else is saying the same thing.

But people do keep trying. I recently saw a flyer with the bold slogan: "Chiropractic: It's Not Just Back Pain." (No, it wasn't Dr. John; he *knows* better.) I overheard the fellow walking next to me mutter to himself: "Gee, you mean they also do windows?" Almost every week I receive a mailing from some medical facility, telling about its great services. Medical programs all have brand names now. I can't remember any of them.

If you are trying to stand out from the crowd using slogans or brand names, save your money. A scalpel is a wonderful tool for surgery; it's not so great for cutting birthday cake. Brand names and slogans are great for what they are intended to do, but you can't differentiate your services using them.

Slick Presentations

The "proposal" is to an auditing firm's business what Saturday night is to a teenager's social life: everything. An incredible amount of time is spent preparing for it, worrying about it, and debriefing it. Gleeful reminiscences ("Did you see their faces when Jack said . . .") and pained second-guessing ("Why didn't we think to . . .") follow the announcement of the winner. Most accountants are convinced that auditing engagements are won or lost during the presentation.

Unfortunately this turns out to be another case of: "When you are called upon to do what you can't do, you do what you can." Accountants may not know how to differentiate the audit but they sure can do slick proposals. They use desktop publishing and laser printers, skillfully mixing personalized pitches with tons of boiler-plate; their overheads are clean and in color. Sometimes it seems like an arms race: *they* bring in their senior partner who has a big reputation in the industry, so *we* fly in the heavy hitters from the Washington office to show that we have a direct pipeline to the law and current regulations.

According to the clients, the net result of all this effort is *not much.* By the time the presentation comes, any differentiation that works has already been done; seldom does a Firm stand out on the basis of the slickness of its presentation. The overheads and so forth serve the same function as a man's tie during a job interview: wearing a good tie will not cause him to stand out from the crowd, whereas wearing a bad tie or no tie at all *will* cause him to stand out, usually in a negative way.

You may need slick presentations just to stay in the game. But they won't be enough to cause you to stand out; you can't differentiate your services with slick presentations.

Price

The next chapter deals with pricing your services. For now, take my word for it: You can't differentiate your services on the basis of price, either.

Well, actually, you *can* differentiate your services on the basis of price, but in a service business you shouldn't want to. Becoming the "low-cost provider" in a product business like steel or soap is a viable competitive strategy; becoming the low-cost provider in a service business is an almost certain strategy for bankruptcy. Try it if you want to; but pay for this book first, please.

How to Differentiate Successfully

If you can't differentiate a service on the basis of features, brand names or slogans, slick presentations, or price, *how do you differentiate a service?* Here's the awful truth: You don't. You can't. When you try to stand out from the crowd by trying to differentiate your service, you almost certainly will not succeed. You are looking in the wrong place.

The situation reminds me of the old joke about the drunk who was standing under a streetlamp looking at the ground. A passerby asked him what he was doing. The drunk replied, "Looking for my car keys." The passerby offered to help, and asked, "Where were you when you lost them?" The drunk gestured toward a dark alley: "Over there." The passerby asked, "If you lost your keys in the alley, why are you looking for them under the streetlamp?" The drunk replied, "The light's better here."

We look to our services for sources of differentiation because that's where the light is; that's where we know how to look. But that's not where the sources of differentiation are.

The problem (and therefore, fortunately, the solution) lies in how we think of differentiation. Common sense tells us that a service will stand out from the crowd only if it is actually different. In this case, common sense agrees with the current "expert" opinion; books on marketing and competitive strategy emphasize creating a service that is in some important way unique (this is supposed to give you that all-important competitive advantage). Unfortunately, in this case both common sense and expert opinion fall a bit short.

This "objective" approach to differentiation fails to do justice to two simple facts: many unique services fail to stand out in the marketplace; many successfully differentiated products are in no discernible way unique. (One of Levitt's favorite examples of differentiation is Frank Perdue and his chickens. Perdue's chickens stand out from the crowd: he sells them for a premium price. Could you pick out a Perdue chicken in a taste test? If so, you have better taste buds than I do.) We need to dig a little deeper to see where sources of differentiation actually lie.

Let's revisit the task of standing out from the crowd. When can you say that differentiation has been successful? Think about it. You have succeeded in standing out from the crowd only if, when the moment comes for the prospective customers to buy, you and your services stand out positively and distinctively in the prospects' mind. In other words:

> **Differentiation is the task of creating, in the minds of prospective customers, a *perception* of you and your services that is both distinctive and valuable.**

This seemingly small shift from an "objective" to a "subjective" view opens the door to a powerful strategy for standing out from the crowd. It helps us realize that we should be paying attention to the prospective customers' *perception,* not to some aspect of our service.

What do we know about perception that can help us here? Actually we know a great deal, and not just from academic theory; a lot of folk wisdom points in the same direction. "Seeing is believing." "A taste is worth a thousand testimonies." "Try it, you'll like it!" These and hundreds of other commonplace observations point to a simple reality: perception is grounded in experience. I can tell you about it and describe it and cite a dozen witnesses; I can show you pictures and sing you songs; all of these will have an effect on your perception. But only one thing will make the perception sharp and clear and lasting in your mind—your own experience. To stand out positively and distinctively in the prospective customers' mind, you must manage their experience of you and your services.

Here's how that works. For years I have been hearing about how wonderful compact disks are. Almost everybody I know has switched over to CDs. I know a bit about the technology, and I have seen the technical specs that prove how superior the sound is. It all made good sense, but my basic reaction for years was: "Who cares? I've got all the sound equipment I need; why spend all that money?"

Then one day a friend sat me down with two copies of one of my favorite recordings. He popped the cassette into the tape player and hit "Play"; from the speakers came that beautiful, familiar sound of the first cut. I smiled as I listened. Then he put the CD into the player—same recording, remember—started it up, and moved the amplifier switch from "Tape" to "CD."

I was stunned. It sounded like suddenly the piano and saxophone were in the room with me.

I listened to the CD for a minute or so; then my friend moved the amplifier switch back to "Tape." Instantly it sounded like I was hearing the music through a thick layer of mud. Back to the CD—beautiful clarity. Back to the tape—terrible! After a few switches back and forth I couldn't bear hearing what that tape was doing to my favorite music. The next day I bought a CD player.

Perception is grounded in experience. To stand out clearly in the prospect's mind, you must manage their experience, just as my friend managed my experience of CDs.

There's a small, obvious problem. Maybe you can see how to do something in your business that exactly parallels my CD experience. If so, go do it! But most businesses are like the auditing firm: there's really no way to manage a company's experience of your auditing services before they hire you as their auditor. You need a different strategy.

The strategy virtually falls into our lap as soon as we recognize one simple additional truth:

> **Whenever customers hire you to provide a service, they are simultaneously purchasing *two* things: the service itself and a relationship with you as the provider of the service.**

And while it may be difficult to manage their experience of the service itself before they buy it, it is comparatively easy to manage their experience of the relationship!

This leads us to the Relationship Strategy for differentiating your services in the marketplace:

> **Stand out from the crowd by deliberately creating a positive and distinctive professional relationship with your prospective customers.**

In other words, when it comes time to buy, what will stand out distinctively and positively in the prospect's mind will be their perception of the relationship you have created with them. The services may all look the same, but you and your firm will stand out in their mind, and that will often be enough to make the difference.

And here's the best news of all: you already are very skilled at creating professional relationships! You may not know that you have these skills, and you usually use them unconsciously and without giving them much thought, but let me assure you: *Nobody* gets to be a functioning adult in our culture, let alone a professional service provider, without being very skillful at creating and maintaining relationships. We just need to make you more consciously and deliberately aware of what you are doing so you can focus your efforts.

To do that, we need to answer some pointed questions: What relationship do you create? How are relationships "created," anyway? What do you need to do to bring this off, and how exactly do you do it? Let's take them, as usual, one at a time.

What Relationship Do You Create?

About this time you may be asking, "What's all this relationship stuff?" Bruce and I ran into that with quite a few younger accountants, who said in effect, "I'm an auditor, not a social worker. I'm not in business to make friends." That's a common reaction, and we need to clear it up, because it's based on a fatal misunderstanding of what relationships are and how they work.

Roger, whom you met earlier and who views marketing of professional services as nearly unethical, looked glum the first time we talked about the Relationship Strategy. "I know I need to work on this, Tony, but I don't look forward to it. Relationships are not my strong point."

"Really?"

"Yeah, really. I know I should have joined the local Chamber of Commerce years ago, but I just feel so awkward standing around making small talk, building relationships. . . ."

"Oh. You mean *that* kind of relationship. Roger, those are social relationships. They may lead to professional relationships, and frankly people who are comfortable standing around at the Chamber have a definite advantage over you, but it's not that big an advantage. What I'm talking about is building professional relationships. You're good at that, aren't you?"

"Well, it depends. Once I have a contract with somebody and we get down to work, of course I'm good at it; part of my job is building and managing the consulting relationship. There I'm a pro. But it's before I become their consultant that I have problems—then it's mostly like the Chamber."

"I see. So before you get the contract you have one relationship with the person, and after you get the contract you have another, very different relationship that you are much better at. Right?"

"Right."

"Here's what you have to do. Remember how you are when you are at your very best as a consultant. Notice how you feel and act, what you say and do, and how you treat your client. Got it clearly in mind?"

Roger nodded.

"Good. Now *that* is the only professional relationship you can afford to have with any client, prospective or otherwise. Create that relationship consistently from the first word out of your mouth *before* they officially hire you as their consultant."

What gives you the decisive advantage when customers decide to buy is this: When they ask themselves, "What will it be like to have this person as my [whatever you are]," they will have to guess or imagine in the case of your competitors. In your case, they will *know* because they will have had experience with you *as the professional you are.* The difference is like choosing among three pictures, two of which have been described to you and one of which you have seen. All else being roughly equal, you will almost always choose the one you have seen.

Roger, after a bit of thought, was almost ecstatic. This was better news than he could have imagined:

> **To stand out from the crowd, positively and distinctively, requires nothing more than the ability to act as the top-quality professional you are—consistently and visibly, from the first words to the last.**

Let's work on that news for a few minutes.

_____ **WORKWORK: WHY FOCUS ON RELATIONSHIPS?** _____

You are sitting at your desk early one Monday morning. The phone rings. After the usual initial greetings the voice on the other end of the line says: "I need that report on my desk by close of business Friday." You acknowledge that, and the conversation ends. You hang up the phone.

How do you feel about that narrative? Obviously you need more information. Put yourself in three different contexts for what happened:

- You have been working hard to get a consulting business going. You have been pursuing business with one particular company, and have submitted a detailed proposal to do a certain analysis for them. The voice on the other end of the line was your contact at that company; "I need that report on my desk by close of business Friday" was your contact's way of saying, "You've got the job." How do you feel? What is your motivation level? How do you feel about doing that report?

- The voice on the other end of the line is your boss, asking you for a routine report in a reasonable time frame. How do you feel as you hang up the phone? What is your motivation level?

- Last scenario: same Monday morning, same phone conversation— but this time the voice on the other end of the line is an IRS agent. The report asked for is documentation of your expenses for the last three tax years. How do you feel as you hang up the phone? What is your motivation level? How do you feel about doing that report?

Same interaction; three different relationships; three very different meanings and responses. Now do you see "why all this relationship stuff?"

We need to get very specific now about that professional relationship you want to create. It's not as simple as saying, "Just be your professional best"; that's the professional or Missionary point of view. We have to add an extra element: alignment.

That's exactly how Bruce Fritch and I approached the audit differentiation project. Again and again we asked clients, "What do you want your auditor to be to you?" It usually took some probing before they got the point of the question, but once they saw what we were asking, their response was strong and consistent: "I want my accountant to act as my business adviser."

This was not exactly a revolutionary insight. Major accounting firms had known for years that these medium size businesses wanted business advisers; in fact, one firm used "Your business adviser" as a slogan. But calling yourself a "business adviser" is different from actually being one; according to the clients we talked to, the overwhelming majority of accountants were simply accountants. They would happily keep your books, set up management systems for you, audit your books, and help with your taxes— but that's just accounting. That's a long way from being a business adviser.

The rare exceptions were instructive. Some accountants had established a very satisfactory business adviser relationship. We asked their clients: "What is it about them that makes them such good business advisers?" and we listened carefully. From their comments we extracted a list of simple declarative statements; with the help of Emerson and his partners we boiled these down into nine statements which together formed a "role description" for the "business adviser" relationship. A good business adviser:

1. Knows the client's business.

2. Is responsive to the client's needs.

3. Anticipates the client's needs.

4. Has the knowledge, skill, and capability to meet the client's needs.

5. Wants the client's business.

6. Is not afraid to speak up and doesn't pull punches, but never forgets that the client makes the decision.

7. Respects the value and limits of the client's resources.

8. Is trustworthy and can maintain confidentiality.

9. Accepts and deals appropriately with different statuses and cultures.

Now we were getting somewhere! This list was something the accountants could sink their teeth into. The nine statements served as a specific target. During the proposal stage, before the decision on the auditor was made, the objective was to deliberately and consistently create the business adviser relationship by establishing each of these nine perceptions sharply in the mind of the prospective client. The next obvious question was: how?

✓——— WORKWORK: ROLE DESCRIPTION ————————

Before we see how the accounting firm did it, let's work on your target. To create a "role description" for your professional relationship, let's take a quick trip into the future, *your* future. Since this trip will involve some creative, imaginative work, you may find it more fruitful to have a partner or two as traveling companions.

In this future, you have already done the hard work of aligning your mission with your market, and are having great success both marketing and delivering your services. You are, to your customers, exactly what they want you to be.

You are eavesdropping while I talk to some of your satisfied customers. They have said that they are delighted with your work and with the way you go about doing your job. I ask them: "What is it that makes _____ [fill in your name each time] so good? What do you especially value about the way _____ does the job? About the way _____ treats you? What is _____ always careful to do? To not do?"

Write down the answers as your satisfied customers would give them. Don't be too concerned with wording just now; write down everything that comes to mind. Feel free to steal or modify any statement from the "business adviser" list. Keep going until you feel the ground has been covered.

Now prune and polish the list. First eliminate any statement that says nothing more than "Does a good job" or "A real professional." These are essentially content-free judgments—nice to hear, but no help when it comes to "how to."

Next, try very hard to see the remaining statements as your market would see them. Have you included something that is professionally important but essentially invisible to the customers? ("Always uses the best statistical method.") Get rid of it. Have you used your own jargon to describe the relationship? Change it to English. Work on the list until every remaining answer is the sort of thing your satisfied customer might actually say.

How many statements are left on the list? If you have fewer than four, you are being much too global; there are more aspects to your professional relationship than you are taking into account. If you have more than about 10 statements you are probably including too many details or some "nice to have" elements that are irrelevant to this relationship. ("Easy to talk to" is probably not a major requirement for a gardener.) Expand or tighten up your list until you get a sense of "Yeah, that's it. If they say those things about me, I have succeeded in establishing exactly the right professional relationship."

We've been looking at the trees; now back up and look at the forest. Take a mental step back from the list and see what it adds up to. Can you see a single phrase that describes the desired relationship well, as "business adviser" does for accountants? Often, no single label is adequate; that's OK. The important thing is the list, not the label. But if you can spot a label, write it down; it can serve as an easy reminder to you in marketing.

An important last step: Check your list with some real customers! You have been relying on your own ability to see things from your customers' point of view; it would be wise to have them check your work. Do they see anything on the list that seems irrelevant, or off the mark? Have you left off anything important? Refine your role description until it seems right to both you and your customers.

You now have a detailed, exact target to use for standing out from the crowd!

How Do You Create Relationships?

Mostly relationships just happen—or so it seems. Like the weather, we usually take relationships for granted and don't give them much thought unless they get particularly stormy.

But relationships *don't* just happen. We make them what they are, and we can create them consciously and intentionally. Psychologists who study relationships have formulated two useful insights about them:

1. Relationships are created, maintained, and changed through exactly the same process: action and reaction.

2. It is easier to establish a relationship from scratch than to change an existing one.

An acquaintance smiles and says "Hello!" whenever he sees you. He asks about your work and seems interested as you talk; you find what he says about his work interesting too. You discover you are both long-suffering Cubs fans; and so on. Without giving it much thought, through the largely unconscious process of action and reaction, your relationship moves from "acquaintance" to "friend." Every relationship, no matter what kind, is created in this same, ordinary, action-reaction way.

The Relationship Strategy depends on realizing that creating relationships can be done deliberately and consciously. You do not need to rely on chance or circumstance in creating relationships; you can deliberately choose what you say and what you do so that the resulting relationship is what you need it to be. And you can do that beginning with the first words you say: better to create the right relationship to begin with than to have to change it later.

You have already defined the relationship you need with your prospective customers, and it is exactly the relationship they most want with you. To create that relationship, you have to notice what actions are congruent with each perception. Emerson and his partners, in that wonderfully systematic way accountants approach things, took each of the nine statements in the "business adviser" role description and asked themselves: "What can we do or say that will create this perception?" They listed every reasonable action they could think of that would contribute to building each perception during the proposal phase.

For example, consider their sixth perception: "A good business adviser is not afraid to speak up and doesn't pull punches, but never forgets that the client makes the decision." This led to a planned responsive tactic: Be sure to watch for an opportunity to advise prospects on some business matter, preferably one where they seem to be leaning in a direction they can be warned against. Speak up and outline the reasons for not taking that course, suggest an alternative, and conclude with a recommendation phrased something like: " . . . so we would recommend that you consider this alternative carefully before you make your decision."

This is an excellent example of intentional relationship building because it combines a planned tactic—be sure to do this—with a responsive approach—watch for a good chance to do it. Relationship-creating activities may be purely planned (always conclude by saying, "We would like to do this for you."), strictly responsive (if they reveal confidential material, say, "I realize that this does not go out of this room."), or a combination.

Notice that if this tactic is done skillfully (we recommended that the accountants rehearse it) it leaves the prospect with exactly the experience you wanted: they have seen you speak up and offer good advice, but not in an arrogant or presumptuous way. This part of the relationship is well on its way to being established. One or two more deliberate, congruent actions on your part will nail it down.

Notice also that a well-chosen responsive tactic can help create more than one perception. If the accountants' "no punches pulled" advice shows particular skill in applying business principles, a perception of "skill and capability" is created; if the advice hinges on unnecessary cost involved in the ill-advised course, a perception of "respects the value and limits of our resources" can be established as well.

In this way, the accountants came up with a repertoire of planned and/or responsive moves to establish each of the needed perceptions.

_____ **WORKWORK: PLANNING THE MOVES** _____

Your turn again. Look back at the statements on your role description Workwork. Write each statement at the top of its own clean sheet of paper. We are going to create your own repertoire of relationship-creating moves. You may find it useful to do this with a partner or two, to help stimulate ideas.

Look at the first statement. Ask yourself: "What specifically could I do or say that would establish this perception in my prospective customers' mind?" Think about it. Identify one specific thing clearly and write it down. (Having trouble? Try this: You have had that perception about other people. What have you seen them do or heard them say that gave you that impression of them? What would you expect that kind of person to do? Write that down.)

Got something? Good. Now, what else might you say or do that would create this perception? Write down that statement or action, then another, and another. Keep going until you have a good list for this statement.

There, that wasn't so hard was it? You _do_ know how to create relationships after all.

Repeat this same process for each of the statements on your role description (that's why you have a clean sheet of paper for each one). Feel free to steal from yourself—the same move can appear on more than one sheet—but don't get lazy and just copy! Don't forget that moves can be planned, or responsive, or a combination of both.

Keep going until you have a solid repertoire of possible relationship-creating moves.

How Exactly Do You Stand Out from the Crowd?

The Relationship Strategy was almost complete. All we needed was something to pull it together for the individual accountants, so they could put it into action. After a few false starts, we finally hit on an idea that did the job: the Relationship Agenda.

Ever been to a meeting that had no agenda? If you have, you know the difference a good agenda makes: without one, the meeting has virtually no chance of accomplishing much. A marketing transaction will accomplish a great deal more when it is guided by a specific Relationship Agenda.

It works like this. Before any transaction with a potential client, the accountants ask themselves, "What is my Relationship Agenda for this meeting?" The role description and relationship-creating repertoire serve as the overall orientation; within that orientation, certain perceptions are chosen for attention in the meeting, and certain moves are selected to create these perceptions.

For example, in the first meeting it is critical to establish that the Firm knows the clients' business and has the skill and capability needed to meet their needs. The accountants might choose a responsive tactic such as: "Wait until they have revealed enough about their situation for you to make some intelligent extrapolations. Respond with: 'If that's the case, then I imagine you are also finding that such-and-such is also a problem, and it wouldn't surprise me if your salespeople were saying that. . . .' Be sure to use some of their technical vocabulary correctly while you are doing this." This becomes the accountants' Relationship Agenda for the meeting; they will make sure that it is accomplished before the meeting is finished.

Using the role description, the relationship-creation repertoire, and the discipline of Relationship Agendas gave that Firm what was needed: a way to stand out positively and distinctively in the prospects' mind when it came time to choose an auditor. The audit itself still was not differentiated, but the relationship with the auditing Firm *was* differentiated—and that, it turned out, was enough.

—— **WORKWORK: RELATIONSHIP AGENDA** ————————————————

Let's put this into practice for you by creating a Relationship Agenda for your critical first transaction with a prospective customer. Once you have practiced this and become comfortable with it, you will find it fairly easy to create a Relationship Agenda, for any other marketing transaction.

Look over your role description Workwork again, to determine a sense of priority. Ask yourself: "Which of these do I need to nail down in the first interaction?" Put a 1 beside each perception that *must* be in place by the time your first interaction with the prospective customer is finished.

Everything has a 1 beside it? Could be—but is that really possible? Can you really establish that whole relationship, in its full complexity, in the first transaction? If you must and you can, then go for it. Otherwise, look those perceptions over again. Which can you *really* not leave without?

Now go back to your Workwork pages from planning your relationship-creating moves. For each perception with a 1 beside it, pick the move that will be most effective in the first transaction. Imagine you have completed that move successfully. Now ask yourself, "Will that be enough?" If not, then look for a second move for this perception; will that do it? Stop when you have the sense: "If I bring these off successfully, that should nail down the perception."

As you select the moves, write them on a clean sheet of paper. This is your Relationship Agenda for your first transaction with a prospective customer. Practice it. Rehearse it; get feedback; rehearse it again until it feels natural and comfortable. Then use it in every first transaction with a prospective customer. If you have read your market right, and you discipline yourself to use your Relationship Agenda, you will succeed almost magically at the most difficult marketing task of all: standing out from the crowd.

The Genuine, Final, True Secret of Successful Differentiation

Roger spotted the paradox, of course; Roger is that kind of guy.

"Tony, this relationship stuff is great! I can't believe the difference it has made in my marketing. But what happens if everybody is doing it? Won't it stop working then?"

"Good point, Roger—but, no, I suspect it won't. In the final analysis, when all is said and done, what stands out in the customer's mind is *you*. The relationship is with *you*; you as a professional, certainly; you embodied in the practices of your firm, even; but, nonetheless, you.

"And although an audit is an audit is an audit—there is, and thank goodness always will be, only one you. If you and your services are the right match for this customer, the customer will be able to see it. And that's not only all you can ask for from marketing—when you think about it, that's really all you want."

Now What?

OK, where are we? You have focused your business and your mission is clear. You have identified your high-opportunity market. You have defined in detail the relationship between you and your market, and know how to use it to stand out positively from the crowd. You've done a lot of good work for yourself!

Next we need to work on alignment with your market. If you have done the work in this chapter carefully, you are already well on your way to that "laser-like alignment" that characterizes the truly effective marketer. We will see how to complete that alignment process in the next chapter.

6 | Laser-Like Alignment

The Secret Ingredient in Effective Marketing

"The really effective marketing organization creates a laser-like alignment between its mission and its market."

I first heard that statement over fifteen years ago, from a brilliant young marketer named Bruce Fritch. It was the first statement I had ever heard that made sense of this mysterious thing called "marketing." It took some time and experience for me to appreciate just how profound his insight was, but I can tell you without hesitation or reservation:

> **Alignment is the secret ingredient in effective marketing.** *Every* successful marketing effort succeeds as the result of alignment. There are no exceptions.

This chapter focuses on helping you create laser-like alignment with your market.

What Is Alignment?

Alignment is a concept that shows up in important ways in a remarkable number of places. My favorite image for it is the laser. Consider the laser and the lightbulb. Both convert energy into light, but because the energy that goes into a laser emerges tightly aligned, it can accomplish tremendous tasks. Yet a laser runs on the same amount of energy used to burn a lightbulb; the difference lies in alignment.

The effective marketing organization is a laser, not a lightbulb.

Alignment comes when the energies in a system are all working congruently, in harmony, toward the same ends and without conflict. Hard-won experience shows that the only way to have a powerful manufacturing company is to create alignment among the different individuals, functions, and divisions of the organization. According to people who work intensively inside the auto industry, this was the most important difference between the two largest American auto makers in the 1980s: people in Ford Motor Company, from the chairman on down, worked conscientiously to create internal and external alignment. People in General Motors did not. GM's Chevrolet lost its position as the best-selling car to Ford, and GM lost tremendous chunks of its market. Ford grew and became profitable.

Alignment shows up in other places as well. People who do "body work" (chiropractors, Rolfers, acupuncturists, and the like) tell me that their whole aim is to create alignment of the various parts of the body: alignment of the parts of the spine, alignment of the skeletal and muscular systems, even alignment of the skeletomuscular system with the forces of gravity. Family therapists tell me they work to achieve alignment among the needs and aspirations of the various family members. I have even heard a great teacher say that the true secret of spiritual mastery is achieving alignment between the individual will and the Supreme will.

In marketing, alignment between your mission and your market shows up in a simple rule:

> Everything you say to your market, and everything you do in interaction with your market, must be *congruent*. It must be congruent with the way your market sees things; it must be congruent with the way your market thinks and talks; it must be congruent with everything else you say and do.

In other words, all your actions and communications must send one single, powerful message to your market—and it must be exactly the message your market most wants and needs to hear. That is alignment.

At this point in my workshops I can count on some attendees to figuratively throw up their hands in despair and blurt out: "That's impossible! I can't see how I can possibly be that on-target and that consistent!" That's perfectly true, of course; *they* can't see it. Fortunately, the problem contains its own solution. To be that consistent and that on-target requires you to figuratively get up out of your chair and move to where your customer is standing. Then you will see it.

Imagine that your customers are looking down into a valley that has rocks, streams, trees, fields, farms, and all manner of interesting things. You have heard reports of what that valley is like, and of course you've seen a valley or two in your time, but from where you are standing you cannot see into this one. Your task is to talk to your customers about that valley in such detail and with such conviction that what they hear from you matches exactly what they see before them—you can even point out landmarks they have overlooked. Impossible? Of course, until you make a simple and obvious move—you look at the valley from where your customers are standing. Then you need only to keep your eyes open.

That valley is your customers' life, or at least that portion of it in which your services make a beneficial difference. To achieve alignment you must first move to where you can see things from your customers' point of view. And one of the very interesting things you will see from that point of view is—*yourself.* Your services, your actions and communications, what you do and how you do it: all of these must be seen as your customers see them. Throughout this chapter (and the rest of the book) you will be asked to see things "through your customers' eyes." (I will give you as much help with that as I can.) What you see will enable you to align yourself with your market.

What Does Alignment Look Like?

I have a confession to make. What you are about to read is the result of my breaking a firm resolution. Before I started writing this book, I promised myself that I would illustrate it only with examples drawn from businesses like yours: small-to-medium size service businesses. Too many books about marketing and advertising assume that all they have to do is tell how Procter and Gamble or Marlboro did something and the point is made. I have not found most such books particularly useful. (Be honest: Did *you* learn anything useful for your business from the "Old Coke to New Coke to Classic Coke" fandango?)

I am breaking my resolution because there is a huge company, known worldwide, that is a superb example of the power and process of alignment. This company has had unprecedented success in one of the most rapidly changing and competitive technological fields of this century, yet it has never been seen as having the best technology, and it is notorious for its high prices and incredible margins. In an industry that lives and dies on the innovations of its technical people, you could fill a large book with the names of those who have left this company for a work environment more supportive of their creativity. In fact, it would not be stretching things too far to claim that the *only* thing this company has going for it is alignment, both internally and with its market—but that alignment is really all it needs.

The company, of course, is IBM.

Surprised? You wouldn't be if you were in the computer industry. Some friends of mine, who have been in computing since before the first microchip, once made a year-by-year chart of "who had the best" hardware, software, and peripherals (printers, disk drives, and so on) since the dawn of the computing era. Their conclusions were interesting. Since at least the mid-1960s, the best hardware has been made by companies other than IBM: if you want the fastest, most powerful computer, you don't buy IBM. The best software has been made by companies other than IBM: great fortunes and respectably sized companies have been founded on non-IBM software written to run on IBM's computers. The best printers, the best disk drives, and so on—all by companies other than IBM. And price? If you can't beat IBM on price, you're just not trying. Looking at this chart, anyone might wonder (as many computer people do; IBM-bashing is a time-honored tradition among hard-core computer types): How has IBM succeeded in the computer business?

What my technically minded friends failed to recognize was that IBM is not in the computer business. IBM is in the business of helping its customers' enterprises succeed by using computers. *That* is what I call alignment.

Since IBM has been a thundering success by almost anyone's standards, it is very instructive to look at what alignment IBM-style means. You should be able to pick up some useful insights for your own business.

Live with the Customer

In the mid-1960s I was walking through the programming section of a large aerospace manufacturing company, when I spotted a fellow wearing a white shirt and a tie. Programmers in those days were more likely to work in tie-dyed T-shirts than white dress shirts, so I stopped and said hello. His ID tag said "IBM."

"Visiting?"

"No, I work here."

"But your tag says IBM."

"That's right. I work for IBM, on permanent assignment to this company. This is my desk. I'm here to make sure the operating system keeps running, and to get it back up when it goes down."

Computer pros tend to snort when they hear this story: "Who else but IBM makes operating systems that need a full-time customer-rep to keep it running?" And from their point of view, of course, that's right. But move over to where the customers are standing and take a look: "I've got so much money invested in these computers, and everything grinds to a halt when the system crashes. IBM sends me somebody who's right there when I need him; with those other guys, who knows how long before they get out here?"

Looks a little different from where the customers stand, doesn't it? That fellow in the white shirt was not there to take care of the operating system; he was there to take care of the customer.

We heard a lot of good advice in the last decade about "getting close to the customer." IBM *lives* with the customer. The on-site fellow in the white shirt was there day after day to spot problems as they arose, but he also watched as little improvements were made, and heard the complaints that only show up when you're using a system hard. He was there to see what the customers used and what they didn't use, what they really needed and what they only said they needed, what worked well and what worked poorly or not at all. And every complaint, every compliment, every request or problem or opportunity, was relayed back to the people who designed and built and marketed these IBM systems.

IBM takes every opportunity to hang out with customers while they talk shop. IBM people join the professional and industry groups in every market they serve. They do more than just join; they attend the meetings, and listen, and take notes. They take ideas from anywhere, but most of their new ideas come from listening to customers. And they are not passive note-takers; they actively stimulate discussion of where the industry is going and how computing can help get there, by sponsoring innumerable meetings and conferences and special-interest groups. (As I was writing this chapter, a few months short of the 1990s, I received in the mail an invitation to speak at a conference for business school faculty, co-sponsored by Penn State University and IBM! The white shirt is still on the job!)

So why doesn't IBM do a better job of building computers (and software and components)? Let's clear up one thing right now: IBM builds excellent computers and computer systems. It's not surprising that computer professionals are not impressed, because IBM *does not build computer systems to impress computer professionals. IBM builds computer systems to impress its customers.*

Who are IBM's customers? That population has changed somewhat over time, but throughout its history IBM has consistently addressed itself to the needs and perspective of the people who make the decisions: owners and presidents, executive directors and administrators, CEOs and CFOs and their designated proxies for technical matters, MIS directors. These are people whose primary concern is: Does it help our enterprise succeed and thrive? Who cares whether it's the fastest or most modern or even the cheapest; what matters is: Does it do the best job of helping us do what we need to do? And by these standards (which for an aligned firm are the only standards that count) IBM makes outstanding computing systems.

—— **WORKWORK: IMPRESSING THE GHOSTS** ————————————

Whom are *you* trying to impress? (Sorry, I know that's a rude question, and it may make you very uncomfortable to answer it, but try. You may discover why your marketing has been so hard and unproductive.)

It's a very natural human tendency. We tend to value the opinion of our heroes, or teachers, or peers; we want our services and marketing messages to look good in their eyes. We unconsciously play to a ghost audience of critics, whose approval or disapproval of how we do our job matters sometimes more than the market's. We write novels that are critically acclaimed but unread; we build computer systems that are technological marvels but are terrible to use; we write ads that win awards but don't sell more soap.

Are you doing "textbook perfect" consulting but having trouble getting clients? Are your peers blown away by your skill or creativity while less-acclaimed people get the business? Are you "fighting the good fight" while other people quietly walk off with the customers?

Look at your own work. What *really* counts for you? Do you find that what gives you the most satisfaction about a job well-done is essentially invisible (or unimportant) to your customers? Do you find that your customers seem to want, or even ask for, things that seem irrelevant or even wrong-headed to you? You may in fact be upholding standards of excellence or craft that are important, that the "lay" person can't see; but are you *sure*? How is it that your customers wind up being so wrong so often? Is it possible that you are missing something here; that your customers see important things that you do not because you haven't really stood where they are standing?

Whom are you trying to impress? If you are a true professional you will want to impress two people: yourself and your customer. And if you are an aligned professional (in other words, a marketer) what impresses you *will* impress your customer, and vice versa. But this can only happen when you stop trying so hard to impress those ghosts.

IBM understands about alignment. You decide who your customers are, and then you learn to think, see, speak, act and even *dress* like your customers. If IBM were building computer systems for computer professionals, that customer-rep back in the '60s would have worn jeans and a beard. Instead he wore a white shirt and a tie, the flaming stereotype of business dress. Without saying a word, the IBM rep's shirt told you: "IBM means business."

In the light of alignment, IBM's business practices make a different kind of sense. IBM is notorious for letting someone else pioneer a technology and only stepping in when the market is proved (and then taking it over). Occasionally an important segment is lost that way, as when Digital Equipment Corporation walked off with the minicomputer market, but typically the strategy has stood IBM in good stead. Many theories have been put forth to account for this strategy, ranging from the tiny competitors' view that "They're never the first because they never invent anything worthwhile" (demonstrably false, but comforting) to "They are too large to move quickly" (some truth to this; but have you ever seen a 747 take off?) to "They have an intentional competitive strategy of crushing potential competitors by waiting until the market is proved and then moving in with pre-emptive pricing and distribution." (This latter is the favorite of certain business school professors who read too many Scrooge McDuck comics as children.)

Why not acknowledge the obvious: It's not IBM that dictates this strategy, it's IBM's customers. This is a risk-reducing strategy. IBM is aligned with customers whose entire life is devoted to taking risks only if they can estimate their exposure and return (in other words, business people). And there are few risks more difficult to assess in advance than those involving new technology. As a venture-capitalist once told me: "I can rationalize a marketing risk. I cannot rationalize a technological risk." IBM's customers want to invest in technology that has a predictable pay-off and predictable risk. "Let it get a track record, then we'll look at it." So IBM does what its customers want, while simultaneously investing phenomenal sums in inventing and developing and testing new technology. (Nobody in the world comes within light-years of IBM's chip manufacturing technology, for example. That's an area where the technological risks are invisible to the customer, and are happily assumed by IBM itself.)

What are the lessons here? We will take this notion of alignment apart piece by piece and apply it to your business next, but first look at the obvious: Like IBM, you must live with your customers. You can't just do some reading and research and then launch your campaign; you can't just learn the buzz words and hot buttons and then do your thing; you can't just spy on the enemy camp and then direct the battle from behind the lines. That's how too many companies think of their customers! A software engineer who works for one of IBM's competitors summed the attitude up memorably when he asked me: "I wonder what they really want out there in Userland?" You have to pick your customers and then move in with them. Only then will you have a chance of seeing what they see.

Laser-Like Alignment Between Your Services and Your Market

I introduced Richard Drake to you earlier—and his unsuccessful job-finding service in a university town. He was summing up his present condition. "I'm tired of working with college students, Tony. They don't really have the work experience to appreciate what I have to offer, so it's impossible to get them to sign up for my full job-finding program. What they want is a résumé, and they can't understand why I won't give them one for fifty dollars, like the word-processing shops will."

"Sounds like your services are not congruent with the student market, Rich. Who would you rather work with?"

"Managers and professionals—people with some real job experience who want help making a major career shift. They have the background to understand what a big move they are making, and how much help they need in making it."

We will look in on Richard Drake again a little later, as he moves into alignment with his market. But first let's dig into the fundamental place in which you must create alignment: your services. It is fundamental for a simple reason:

> Your services are the specific form through which your mission is accomplished.

If there is to be laser-like alignment between your mission and your market, it must begin with alignment between your services and your market. Everything about your services must be made to be congruent with your target market.

"Everything?"

Everything. If it looks like a duck, walks like a duck, and quacks like a duck, prospects assume it's a duck. But if it looks like a duck, walks like a duck, and barks like a dog, *then* what do they assume it is? They don't know, so they probably won't buy one for the pond. If even one thing is incongruent, the picture can blur badly enough to keep prospects from becoming customers.

We already know that your mission and your target market are a good match (you *did* work through Chapters 3 and 4, didn't you?). But are the specific services you want to market congruent with your target market? Here are some common ways in which your services and your market may be missing each other:

Wrong Size Package

Richard supports people in finding jobs that match their skills and interests. Sounds perfect for recent college graduates, right? The problem is, what Richard really does best and believes in fervently is working with people over the long haul, strategizing and coaching from start to finish. This requires more commitment—and money—than makes sense to most college students. They want support in much smaller, cheaper doses. Basic rule: Anyone hoping to sell milk to preschoolers had better not count on selling it a gallon at a time.

Wrong Type of Package

Lucinda supports business owners in controlling their finances and operations with computer software. Every owner of a small business could benefit from such a service. But Lucinda wanted to sell her software "off the shelf" for owners to install on their own computers. Most of her prospects wanted a "turn-key" system installed for them, ready to run as soon as they turned it on, and they wanted training, technical support, and general "hand-holding" while they got used to it. Her way was a lot "cheaper," but is it really cheaper to pay less for something you can't use rather than to pay more for something you can? Lucinda decided to offer her software in a "turn-key" installation.

Wrong Service

Joe provides management support to health professionals and their staffs. He designed a fine program for dentists to "build your high-performance office team." Nobody bought. Dentists were more interested in programs designed to market their services or to get their billing and record keeping in order. As Joe put it ruefully, "This was the best nice-to-have program they had ever seen. Unfortunately, they were up to their ears in need-to-haves." Joe took his team-building program to the insurance industry, where they loved it.

——— WORKWORK: YOUR SERVICES, THEIR EYES ———

Let's look at *your* services with the eyes of your target market.

Put yourself in the place of one of your prospects. Imagine a real setting: where would your prospect be when thinking about your services? In an office, sitting at a desk? On the factory floor? At home? Imagine yourself being there, doing what your prospect does, seeing and hearing what your prospect sees and hears.

Now take a hard look at your services through the prospect's eyes. What do you notice? Is the service delivered in a form or format that suits you well? Are all the "pieces" you want included? Are there pieces included that you can't use or don't want? Is it "complete dinner" or "cafeteria style"—and which do you prefer?

When and where does the service occur? Is this how you prefer it? Does the scheduling meet your needs? Does the service require training for your people, or documentation? Is it provided in a way that pleases you?

Is the price about what you would expect to pay? Too much? Too little? How about the terms of payment? Are they selling a package deal but the billing by the hour or by the service? Is help with financing included? Do you want or expect help?

Overall, what do you think of the service? Do you see items that seem out of sync with your needs? With the other aspects of the service itself? What would you like to see changed?

Now that you've seen yourself through others' eyes, ask yourself seriously: What do I need to change to bring my services into complete alignment with my market?

Don't be too alarmed at some misalignment between your services and your market; I have never seen a service business that couldn't benefit from periodic review of this sort. Just go ahead and make the revisions you see are needed. But if you have spotted a major mismatch between your services and your target market, take decisive action, soon. You might do as Rich and Joe did—find a target market that is better aligned with your services—or you might change your services to align with your market, imitating Lucinda and IBM. Either way works, but it makes a whopping difference which you choose. If you have chosen your target market carefully (as we did in Chapter 4), chances are you will be better off to redesign and repackage your services to bring them into alignment with your market. Chapter 10, "Packaging for Maximum Benefit" will show you how.

Laser-Like Alignment Between Your Firm and Your Market

"Are you sure you want to work with professionals and executives, Rich?"

"Absolutely."

"You realize you will need to make a few changes if you intend to work with that market, don't you?"

"Like what?"

"Oh . . . let's start with your office."

"What's wrong with my office?"

You have to understand about Richard and his old office. When Richard started out in business, he was just a few years out of social-work school and he had a bit of "store-front agency" mentality. (He also didn't have much money.) He was delighted to find an inexpensive space in an older downtown building, which he proceeded to fix up and furnish in a comfortable, welcoming style. Richard's office was really very nice, once you got inside the door.

"Nothing's wrong with your office, Rich. I feel very comfortable here. But let's look at the surroundings as a prospective customer might see them. Pretend you are a young executive looking to make his career move. You park your car in the structure down the street and start walking toward Richard Drake's office. What's the first thing you pass on the street?"

"The adult book store."

"And next to it?"

"The Red Cross blood donors office."

"A little off-putting, no? Now you get to Richard Drake's building. Up one flight of stairs and down the hall—past how many empty offices?"

"Three."

"Past three empty offices. By the time you get to Richard Drake's office what's your dominant impression?"

"Seedy, I guess. Second-rate private eye."

"Rich, how much confidence has this inspired in your young executive's mind so far? Isn't it reasonable to assume that he is having serious second thoughts about whether he's in the right place?"

"I suppose so."

"And you expect him to open the door, walk in, and sign up for a program costing $2500 or more?"

"I see your point. But have you looked at rents in the better buildings? It scares me to think of paying that much for an office."

"I sympathize, Rich. You are talking to one of the world's biggest fans of keeping your overhead down. Never spend a cent on frills. And this office has been fine up to now. Students love the ambience. But if you start marketing to professionals and executives this office won't save you money. It will cost you money, in customers you will lose because your setting is so very much out of alignment with your service."

We'll get back to Richard Drake. But let's pause to state an explicit rule:

> **Your setting must be congruent with your service—and, of course, with your market.**

Nothing should be out of sync. If you are a "helping professional" your setting should be warm and welcoming. If you offer "creative" services your setting should reflect creativity. High-tech services fit most naturally in a modern, up-to-date setting. Your setting should promote an immediate sense of "I've come to the right place." Anything that creates a sense of discomfort or uncertainty in your customers should be eliminated.

This does not mean you have to spend a lot of money on ostentatious display. The key notion here is appropriateness. A banker said he knew Delorean Motors was headed for trouble when he saw their office in New York: impressive, but does a start-up manufacturer really need Italian marble floors? Your setting should feel right to your market. I consult to quite a few small firms, as their "free-lance marketing director." I either go to their offices or, more often, meet them for a working breakfast or lunch. I picked up this custom from an outstanding consultant who lives in San Francisco. He explained to me: "I don't want these business owners sitting in my fancy office, wondering if their little business can really afford somebody with an overhead like this. The fancy office I use to meet the big companies, who want the reassurance that you are successful enough to handle this kind of overhead."

Let's look at your firm for a moment. Again, imagine you are one of your prospective customers. You are approaching the place of business; what do you see as you approach? There's the door. What's your first impression? Open the door and look in. What strikes your eye? Overall, what is the message you get from the physical plant and setting? Is it congruent with the service? With you, the customer?

What do you see that needs to change?

Laser-Like Alignment Between Your People and Your Market

"So I need a new office. What other changes do I need to make?"

This was not going to be easy. How do you tell someone he dresses like an over-age graduate student? "Well, Rich, once you're past the setting, you meet the people providing the service. If you are a professional looking to change careers, what kind of person do you want helping you? You want somebody who seems very congruent with your own self-image: Competent. Experienced. Successful. Professional."

"Sounds about right."

"You've got most of the bases covered already, Rich. You know what you're doing and it shows. You have good credentials, and a good track record. But . . . Rich, you counsel people on how to prepare for job interviews, right? Pretend you are about to apply for a job counseling professionals on career changes. Look into a mirror and give yourself some advice."

"Hmmm . . . nice mustache, Rich, but it needs a trim. And get a better haircut."

"How would you say you're dressed?"

"Comfortable. Like a college counselor. Maybe a therapist."

"Think that will inspire confidence in executives?"

"Hardly!"

"Rich, you are putting yourself forth to these professionals and executives as someone who knows how the business-and-career world works. But you are dressing like they do on their days off. This raises doubts in their minds that you just don't need. Get yourself some clothes that make you look like the successful people you work with."

This whole issue of appearance is a little tricky. It's not quite as simple as "look successful and you will be successful." The rule is slightly more complex:

Your image must be congruent with the relationship you have with your customers.

If the relationship hinges on your professionalism and business savvy, as does Rich's, then you must look successful and professional. But a graphic designer who dressed like Rich would be incongruent; more taste and visual flair would be expected (that's what you're paying them for!) Therapists tend to dress more comfortably and informally because that's the nature of the therapeutic relationship. "Creative types" make a point of not looking like bankers. To be called a "suit" in Hollywood is not a compliment (as in "We wanted to shoot on location, but the suits said no.") The relationship is the reality. It is an expression of the alignment between who you are and who your customers are. The image follows that reality; the image must be congruent with the relationship.

Two examples show this nicely. A large bank decided to emphasize its "private banking" services. These are aimed at wealthy customers whose banking needs create the opportunity for juicy margins, but who require substantial individualized service.

The setting was brilliantly planned and executed to create alignment with this wealthy, privileged segment. The bank set up a private section with its own entrance separate from the public lobby. The section was furnished and decorated in luxurious style—leather, fine woods, thick carpets, art work, fresh flowers, coffee poured from silver pots into fine china. The place looked like a fine private club with impressive bankers' desks. Emphasis was on personalized service even down to details. "Just call and we'll handle the transfer for you. Of course we'll pay those routine bills for you. Deposit slip? Oh no, just endorse the check; we'll handle the paperwork."

After six months the private banking section was doing less than half the business the bank had projected.

As soon as you stepped into the private bank you could see the problem. The bank thought of its private banking services as part of its "fast track"; assignment to it was a plum, given to its brightest young MBAs. But the private banking clients were mostly people in their 50s and 60s, and their idea of a private banker was someone with some distinguished grey in the hair. They did not feel terribly confident letting someone who looked like one of their children handle their money.

Great setting, great services. Wrong image for the relationship.

By contrast, consider my neighbor Billy. He looks like a teenager until you look closely and notice he's old enough to have teenage children. He has longish hair and '60s-style glasses, dresses like a Harvard undergrad, and drives a Porsche. He always has a smile and a wave. In recent years, in deference to his advancing age, some people have taken to calling him Bill.

The diploma on his office wall reads William Robbins Levinson, MD. Billy is without a doubt the most successful family practitioner in our area.

How can this be? Billy is a classic example of alignment. He believes strongly in "holistic medicine" and has made professional alliances with the best of the "nontraditional" medical practitioners in the area, while continuing to use traditional medicine for what it does best. He has come to be known as "the doctor for people who don't trust the medical establishment but still want a *real* doctor." He is perfectly congruent with that relationship: he doesn't look like a Doctor, he doesn't dress like a Doctor, he doesn't act like a Doctor or relate to people like a Doctor. He's just a very good doctor. People who are uncomfortable with Doctors are comfortable with Billy. He is aligned with his market.

——— **WORKWORK: MIRROR, MIRROR** ———————————————

Your turn now. Review the Workwork you did in Chapter 5. What is the relationship you are working to create with your market?

Now look at yourself through the eyes of someone in your target market. Start with the obvious physical things: height, weight, physical condition, gender, race, age, general appearance. Is anything incongruent with that relationship? Is it something you can change? Is it something you should compensate for? Is it really important, or are you just self-conscious?

Look at your grooming and how you dress. What message do you convey? Is it exactly the same as the relationship you are creating? If not, what do you need to change to bring it into line?

Think about your manner and style of relating to people. Are they congruent with the relationship with your market? (If you're not completely sure, ask somebody whose opinion you respect and trust.) What do you need to modify or develop in your personal manner to become congruent with your market?

If you see major incongruity but do not see how to eliminate it, ask yourself: Is this really the best target market for me? Can I find a segment with which I can create better alignment?

Alignment Through Tangibles and Materials

Everything your customer sees and hears from you—*everything*—should communicate your single, clear message. We have looked at your services, your setting, and your people in the light of alignment; now let's look at what's left: all the tangibles and deliverables that represent your company to your market. These include business cards, letterhead, envelopes, brochures, flyers, ads, posters, and handouts through which you communicate with your market. Ask yourself the two following questions.

1. *What tangible pieces do I need?*

You should have every single tangible piece you need—and not one thing more. Most businesses need business cards, letterhead, and envelopes. All businesses need some sort of promotional or advertising pieces; these may be a brochure or two, flyers, posters, presentation books, catalogs, mailers, and so on. We will look at these in depth later; for now, ask yourself: "Which of these tangibles will my market expect me to have? Which will make them feel uncomfortable or odd if I don't have them?" ("No business card? But how do I get in touch with you?") "Which will make them feel uncomfortable if I *do* have them?" ("Why is my therapist putting up posters on telephone poles?") If your market expects it, you must have an extraordinarily good reason for not giving it to them. If your market does not expect it, you can still give it to them, but be sure their reaction is, "I never would have thought of that myself, but it was useful." An example of this is a commercial plumber whose "business card" is two Rolodex cards. One is filled out with his firm's name, address, phone numbers (one for after-hours emergencies), and business hours; the second is filled out for "Plumber" with the same information.

2. *Are my materials congruent with my mission, my market, our relationship, and each other?*

Along with your work setting and your people, the appearance of your tangible materials communicates a powerful message about you and your services. Often your tangibles form prospective customers' first impression of your firm; even more often, they send subtle signals that either reinforce or blur the message you are trying to send. Well-designed and well-executed tangible materials are crucial in marketing.

People *looking* at your materials should get the same sense of you and your firm that they get from reading your materials or hearing you tell them about your business. A natural-foods co-op will use a color scheme and logo that seem earthy, friendly, and somewhat egalitarian; these are poor choices for a high-fashion boutique. A concrete paving business uses strong typeface, simple photos, and darker colors in its brochure; it would not use calligraphy on slick eggshell paper. The appearance must be congruent with the content.

If you are going to be serious about marketing your business, you will need professional help in creating your tangible materials. (Again, we will discuss this at length in later chapters.) For now, recognize the importance of having a professional graphic designer create a "look and feel" for your tangible materials. This involves, at a minimum, a set of conventions regarding color of paper and ink, typeface and type size, logo (if any), and general layout for your cards, letterhead, and brochures. (Graphic designers often call this a "corporate identity package." Don't be intimidated by the label; that's what you want.) Your materials should be like your personal style and appearance—completely appropriate to your mission, market, and relationship. Tell the designer what your mission and market are, and then insist on a "look and feel" that seems congruent with them. (That's one good reason why we do all this mission–market alignment work first, before you run the printing presses.)

> Your tangible materials need to not only look *good;* they need to look right.

This is not the place to cut corners. Good graphic design is hard to do and easy to recognize. You wouldn't dream of making your own business suits or wearing one whipped up on the weekend by your next-door neighbor (unless one of you is a professional tailor). Neither should you assume you or your talented tenth-grader can design your tangible materials. (You are amateurs in a job calling for a professional, and it would show.) You don't have to spend a ton of money, but you really have no choice about getting this right. What you spend now will be returned many times over, in the effectiveness and efficiency of your marketing efforts.

_____ **WORKWORK: A SINGLE IMAGE** _____

Line up one copy of every tangible item your customer sees: a business card, letterhead, envelope; one of every brochure and catalog you use; any leaflets, posters, flyers, ads; any standard letters or proposals, presentation books, overheads or slides; report forms; applications, or customer information forms, invoices or bills. Spread them on the table in front of you and look at them hard.

First, what's missing? What have you been "making do" without, but really need? Make a note to yourself to fill in that gap.

Next, what's unnecessary or irrelevant? Did you make up a brochure because you thought you needed it, but then found it doesn't work? Get rid of it.

As you look at each piece in turn, ask yourself, "Is this piece completely congruent with my mission and my market?" Do you get the right sense of your business and your relationship to the customer from its appearance? Put the pieces that are congruent in one pile; put the pieces that are not congruent in another. (If you're not good at judging this sort of thing, get some help from someone who is, preferably a customer or competent designer.)

Now look at the "congruent" pieces. Are they congruent with each other? Do they present a clear, consistent image, or do they present several different images? You can afford only one image if you expect laser-like power from your marketing. Do you need a professional designer to help you create that single image? If so, be sure to show the designer the pieces in your "congruent" pile, as a starting place.

Make notes to yourself about which pieces need to be worked on to make them powerful, congruent marketing pieces. Pick the most important one and get to work! You'll be busy with this for a while, but don't worry— it's worth it. Once these materials are powerfully aligned they will keep you busy for a long time, serving paying customers.

Now What?

I have good news and bad news. The good news is: You are now ready to market your services with power and efficiency. You have defined your mission clearly and selected a market segment in which your services are needed and valued. You have defined exactly the relationship between you and your customer, by means of which you can stand out clearly and positively from the crowd. You have examined your services, your setting, yourself, and your materials and seen how to bring them into laser-like alignment. You are ready to become a high-performance marketing organization.

The bad news is: You will have to keep working at it for the rest of your life.

A natural force works against order and alignment. Physicists call it "entropy"; they tell us that all systems have a built-in tendency to decay into disorder. You can't tune up your fiddle once and expect it to stay in tune. Even a Mercedes needs the occasional oil change. A retired merchant seaman aptly summed up my bad news. When asked for a slogan to live by, without hesitation he replied: "Rust never sleeps."

Alignment is never finished. What works perfectly today may work well next year but be only so-so three years from now. Today's approach should be seen as a working prototype: good for what we knew when we built it, but not nearly as good as it will be as we refine what we know. The market changes; what we know changes; what we know how to do changes. The relationship between us and our market must change to reflect how things are *today*.

There is no substitute for living with your market.

For the rest of this book we will assume the laser-like alignment you have worked so hard to achieve. As we look at the more technical aspects of marketing—packaging, presentation, promotion, prospecting—we will build on this foundation. Make sure the foundation is sound before you start to build on it.

7 Money Matters

"We lose money on each of these, but we make it up in volume."

Sometimes a marketing consultant makes house calls. You do it when your client is a friend and runs a small publishing business out of his house. You do it especially eagerly when your client's brother—and business partner—is a talented baker who always brings fresh coffee-cake to the meetings.

I was just biting into a warm pecan roll when a memorable, great eye-opening event occurred. Anders looked up from his notepad with a wry smile and said, "Tony, I worked up those cost figures you asked for on our last book. I've got good news and bad news."

I nodded encouragement and mumbled, "What's that?"

"The bad news is that we lost $1.15 on each copy we sold last year. The good news is, we didn't sell enough to put us out of business!"

After I stopped laughing (and choking on coffee cake) I made a mental note:

Never take pricing for granted.

Pricing is a very simple matter that can be made very complex if you are not careful. The simple part is this:

Price your services too high and you won't get the business; price them too low and you will wish you hadn't gotten the business.

How should you price your services? Things can get complex quickly here if you let them. After all, you can't charge more than the market will bear—whatever that is. And you shouldn't charge more than your competitors, assuming you can find out what they charge, but then aren't you

79

really better than they are? Aren't your services worth more? And just how much are your services *really* worth, anyway? Compared to, say, a neurosurgeon's? Or a rock star? Or . . . . (That clammy feeling is thick mental fog rolling in.)

Fortunately, some simple business principles can cut through the fog. They depend on understanding the marketers' view of two basic but tricky concepts: "worth" and "profit." Accountants can probably skip this chapter; everybody else will find that this chapter alone will save you many times the price of this book. Let's look at "worth" first.

What Is a Seminar *Really* Worth?

In the early 1970s, Time Management became a hot topic on the business seminar circuit, largely due to a best-selling book by a business consultant named Scott MacDonald. After the book was published, MacDonald had a nice business giving one-day seminars based on his book, for which he charged his usual consulting fee of $300—not bad by pre-OPEC standards.

One day MacDonald was looking over his correspondence files when he noticed to his horror that his secretary had made a mistake on one invoice. Instead of billing the usual $300, she had inserted an extra zero and had sent a bill for $3000! He was just about to dictate a letter of apology to the company when the mail arrived. In the mail was a letter from that same company, thanking him for the workshop, exclaiming over how well it had been received, and enclosing a check for the full $3000.

MacDonald looked at the check for a while. He thought for a few seconds. Then he raised his standard fee for a one-day workshop to $3000. In the next month he booked more workshops than ever before, and the increase continued steadily from then on. Nobody seemed to care or even notice that he had raised his rates; in fact, the only effect seemed to be that his income suddenly increased tenfold!

Granted, this is an unusual situation. I'm not recommending that you try raising your rates tenfold! But MacDonald's experience illustrates in a dramatic way an important but seldom appreciated point about pricing of services:

> The range of prices that people willingly—even happily—pay for the same service is many times greater than the range they will pay for the same product.

There are three good reasons why this is so.

1. *Price information is scarce.*

Hungry? Want a candy bar? Walk into any typical large drugstore and you will think you have gone to Chocaholics Heaven. You'll find an entire aisle of candy bars three or four shelves high, with 50, 60, even 100 or more different types side-by-side, attractively presented with the price per bar neatly displayed under each box. Walk down that aisle a few times and buy a candy bar now and then. Without even thinking about it you will get an accurate sense of how much a candy bar ought to cost.

Want a VCR? Look in this evening's newspaper—there are full-page ads from five different discount chains, each advertising several different makes. If you even glance at the ads occasionally it's hard not to get a pretty good sense of what VCRs cost. And you can always look them up in the Sears catalog.

Products are displayed and advertised side-by-side. Many routinely available sources give information about their costs in ads and catalogs. We take it for granted that certain things are "worth" a certain amount, and we either know how much or can easily find it out.

Services, in marked contrast, are *not* displayed, side-by-side or otherwise. They are seldom found in catalogs, and ads for services rarely give more than perfunctory price information. As a result, most of us have only the foggiest notion of what services cost (unless we have used them recently) and accordingly—here's the important part—are prepared to accept as normal an almost startling range of prices for services.

One of my clients is a nationally known singing duo who specialize in family concerts—mostly original compositions that the whole family can enjoy. Suppose they are available to come to your town and put on a concert in the local high-school auditorium; you might use it as a fund-raiser for the local PTO. How much would you expect to pay them for the concert? Unless you sit down and carefully work out the figures, you probably have no realistic idea; intelligent people have guessed as low as $75 and as high as $5000.

2. There is no such thing as "the same service."

You have finally decided on that new color TV. You narrowed it down to a few models, looked at the features, and decided on exactly the one you want. Now the only thing left is to shop, for price. A few phone calls if you are in a hurry, a little gas and shoe leather if you want to play hardball, and you quickly buy from the store with the lowest price because, after all, *they are all selling the same TV.*

Now try that logic on arranging for a face-lift—your face or your spouse's—or rewiring your den. Or a haircut; but have a wig ready, because unless you are very lucky you will quickly find out a simple truth: *they are NOT all selling the same haircut.*

Services vary with the service provider. Some are good, some are *very* good, and some are unspeakably awful. They may call themselves by the same name; they are *not* the same service.

3. *The value of a service to the customer is always substantially greater than the price.*

Have you ever had a cracked filling? I do not recommend the experience. You can imagine my surprise. Like you, I assumed that once they were stuck into your teeth those silvery metal things were permanent. My dentist, as he was efficiently buzzing the old filling out and putting a new one in, assured me that mine was not an uncommon occurrence. This news was not much comfort.

As his office manager handed me a bill for $45, the consumer in me was wondering, "How much is this procedure really worth?" The marketing consultant in me replied, "What's it worth to you to avoid going through life with a cracked filling?" The sensible coward in me responded instantly, "One helluva lot more than $45!"

We are so accustomed to this implicit value equation that we seldom give it much thought: the value to us of a service we buy must be many times greater than what we pay for it, or else there is no sale. You make a Xerox copy of a letter, instead of typing another copy for your files; is the time you saved worth only the five cents you paid for the copy? Your back goes out and you can't sleep because of the pain; is being pain-free worth only the few hundred dollars you pay the therapist who puts it back in place? MacDonald's clients gladly paid him $3000 to teach their executives to use time more efficiently because even if the seminar saves each of them only ten minutes a day, it will pay for itself ten times over in the first year. We always pay many times less than the service is "worth" to us, or else we won't buy at all.

_____ **WORKWORK: THE VALUE OF YOUR BENEFIT** _____

Think about the services you provide to your customers. Remind yourself of the benefit to the customers: the beneficial difference your service makes in their lives. Get that benefit very clear in your mind.

Now assume this benefit has already been provided. Imagine that an evil magician comes to your customers and says, "I am going to take away this benefit permanently unless you pay me not to."

- How much would your customers pay to *keep* that benefit?

- How much do you charge to *produce* that benefit?

- Is it clear that the *worth* is many times greater than the price?

From the marketing viewpoint, *price* and *worth* are completely different concepts that have very little to do with one another. What you charge is only remotely related to the value of your service. Let's make that statement an explicit slogan:

Price is NOT based on worth.

What *is* price based on? How *do* you know how much to charge? Fortunately a simple business principle comes to our rescue here. I call it the KWIC *principle,* and I recommend that you memorize it and cling to it whenever issues of pricing and worth arise.

I learned the KWIC principle from Grant Gregor more than 15 years ago. Grant owns a very successful job placement firm that finds jobs for professionals like accountants and computer programmers. (Grant had once been a cost accountant himself.) He only takes jobs for which the company pays the placement fee, which assures him of first crack at the best talent, and he has an excellent track record. But since the companies pay the fees, they often try to negotiate a reduction, and they always use what they are sure is a crushing argument: "Grant, your fees are double what your competitors charge. What makes you think your services are worth twice as much?"

Grant always replies calmly, "What my competitors charge is their business, not mine. My fees are what they are because I *know what it costs me* to make that placement."

Grant has held the line on his fees. And year by year, Gregor Associates has grown and prospered while one by one his competitors have gone out of business.

The KWIC Principle

Know What It Costs to provide your services.

———— **WORKWORK: WHAT *DOES* IT COST?** ————

Think about the service you most commonly provide. Consider your costs of doing business. Take into account *all* your costs, not just the obvious ones. Now—how much does it cost you to provide that service, to the nearest *cent?*

How do you know? How sure are you? Suppose an accountant looked at your books and told you that you had underestimated your costs by 25 percent—how surprised would you be?

Pricing is based on cost, so all you have to do is figure your costs, and that determines your prices, right? Not quite. First we need to look at that other basic concept: profit.

You *Must* Make Your Margin

Brenda radiates warmth, the genuine kind, that makes you feel great just to be around her. She is sensitive and caring and appears infinitely patient; she seems exactly the sort of person who would make a wonderful psychotherapist, which she in fact is.

She was also rapidly going broke when I first met her.

Brenda has a healthy orderly streak. She had kept careful records of income and expenses, so she met the KWIC test: she already Knew What It Cost her to provide the service. She had set her prices to pay her an adequate salary and meet her costs of doing business. When I suggested that we reexamine her pricing decisions, Brenda frowned.

"I feel *very* uncomfortable with that, Tony. I am a helping professional. I feel OK with making a reasonable living practicing my profession. But I believe it is wrong to *profit* from the suffering of others, and I refuse to see only people whose insurance can pay for it. I'm sorry."

I could hear that she was *not* sorry; in fact, she was principled and determined. To her, profit was the "P-word." This called for some quick reframing.

"Brenda, what do you think of the idea that some children are just naturally 'bad kids?'"

She looked puzzled at the change of subject but her response was firm. "There's no such thing as a bad kid."

"Really? I was talking to a philosophy professor at the U. just last week who said that we blame parents too much these days, that some kids are just bad, and . . . ."

"That may have some relevance to philosophy, but in my experience, Tony, in therapy [and in real life, her tone implied] there is no such thing as a bad kid."

"I couldn't agree with you more, Brenda. Now I want you to understand something equally clearly: Profit may have some relevance to economics and political theory, but in marketing and pricing, *there is no such thing as profit.*"

Brenda looked mildly stunned. Before she could recover I moved on. "You are making a very common mistake, Brenda. You are using the notion of profit, with all of its value implications, where it doesn't fit. You should not try to make a profit in your business; I'm not even sure what a profit in this context would mean. But what you *must* do is something quite different: you *must* make your margin."

Brenda is a great listener, and she was listening now. "What on earth is a margin?"

"Imagine you are driving along a mountain road—no railing, and a sheer drop-off of hundreds of feet just to your right. Now you *could* drive with your right front tire exactly on the edge of the road, and if you are very lucky you will make it to the top. But if your attention wanders for a moment, or you hit a bad bump, or the steering is a little loose, over you go. So you don't drive on the edge; you leave a healthy space between you and the edge so that, when these things occur, you have time to recover. You leave yourself a margin of safety.

"Brenda, your business is that car. Pricing your services to just cover your salary and costs is like driving with the tire right on the edge. When the unanticipated occurs—and it *always* does—when you are sick and can't work for a while, or the economy slows, or you need new office equipment, or your lease goes up, or you need to add staff, you will be over the edge in no time. Out of business. You have to price your services so that some money goes into a reserve, to allow time to recover from these bumps. That is what margin is."

Brenda is also a quick learner. She estimated what her margin should be, calculated a new pricing structure, and put it into effect the next month. She has had a successful business ever since.

The (Almost) Ultimate Pricing Formula

Price to cover your costs and make your margins.

At the end of this chapter (no fair peeking!) we will add one last little piece to round out the pricing picture. But first—let's get to work on *your* pricing!

——— **WORKWORK: PRICING YOUR SERVICES** ———

This is the most tedious piece of work you will have to do in this book. To accomplish it, you will need a calculator, your records of business expenses for the past year or two, an hour or so of uninterrupted time, and the firm conviction that finding out the truth about your financial situation is best done now, before it is too late. We will be using the Pricing Worksheet on page 86. If you are like me and cannot bring yourself to write in a printed book, make a Xerox of the page or hand-copy the Worksheet line-by-line as we go through it.

Warning: Prepare yourself to discover some unsettling facts. The large majority of smaller service businesses I have encountered are pricing their services too low, sometimes dramatically too low (which helps explain why the large majority of such businesses fail). You may find yourself disbelieving your figures. I have seen mature adults go into a mild panic as they go through this section in workshops. *Take the Worksheet step by step.* Convince yourself that you have done one section right, before you go on to the next. You *must* understand and believe the figures you come up with, or else you will undercut yourself continually by cutting your prices "just this once" until you hit a tough stretch of road and . . . . Or you

A. My Annual Salary			$_____
B. My Annual Costs of Doing Business			$_____
C. My Breakeven Figure		$_____	
D. My Total Work Days	_____		
E. My Utilization Rate (%)	_____	_____	_____
	Low	Middle	High
Number of Days Billed	_____	_____	_____

F. My Margin Rate

	Margin (M)	(100 – M%)			
Low	_____%	_____			
Middle	_____%	_____			
High	_____%	_____			

Daily Rate Matrix

may discover that your prices are already fine, in which case you can breathe easy and go get more business!

A. *What Is My Salary?*

"Salary? What salary? I own the business, I'm not an employee; *l'enterprise, c'est moi.*" Whoa! For the purposes of business and pricing, you need to consider yourself as your own employee. Even if you do not actually pay yourself a salary (a bad business practice, but that's your decision) you need to price as if you do. We are not talking about your salary as it is, and certainly not as you would like it to be; this is not one of those "dare to dream" exercises. This is a very practical measure. Assume one of your competitors was hiring you to deliver the services you deliver now in your business. They are not offering to pay you for your entrepreneurial spirit or to assume any business risks. They are willing to pay you only to do whatever it is you actually do, to deliver the services. (This may include designing or managing a project, of course, if that is what you do.) How much—whether annual salary, monthly retainer, or hourly fee—how much would they pay you?

Do not include in your calculations the costs of benefits, bonuses, overhead, or anything else; calculate only the salary. If you do not know, find out! Call your state's employment services, or some employment agencies, and ask. Find out from the national office of your professional association; look in the classified ads; go to the library and look at the Labor Department's statistics. You can get a good handle on this with a little effort.

Now enter that salary-only figure on your Pricing Worksheet on line A ("My Annual Salary"). If your salary figure is monthly, multiply it by 12 first; if hourly, multiply it by 2080 (40 hours/week × 52 weeks).

Super Shortcut: You are now in a position to use a quick-and-dirty method of going directly to your daily rate if you wish. I do not recommend it, because it may not be a good fit for your particular business and it gives you a single figure and no flexibility. Most importantly, since you have not worked it out yourself, you are very likely to disbelieve it and not stick to it in the crunch. Nonetheless, if you are in a hurry or cannot bear the thought of wading through all these figures, here's the quick-and-dirty method: Divide your annual salary by 2080 to get your hourly salary. Now multiply that by three. That is the amount you should charge *per hour* for your services. Multiply that by eight (assuming an eight-hour day) and you have your daily rate. Hard to believe? Then sharpen your pencil and finish the Pricing Worksheet.

(We are assuming here that you are the only owner of your business and anyone working for the business is being paid a salary of some sort by you; we will pick that up on line B. If this is not true—if you are part of an actual partnership, for example—then do the line A analysis for every partner's salary, and make line A the sum of these salaries. Your costs should reflect the market value of the labor. Partners often pay themselves more or less than market value, so taking what you pay yourselves as a cost figure may badly distort your pricing.)

B. What Are My Costs of Doing Business?

This is where you include everything else that you *must* spend in order to do the business you do: rent; utilities; office equipment and supplies; telephone; salaries other than yours; marketing expenses; insurance; subscriptions; services such as accountants, secretarial, cleaning, legal; professional education (not the stuff you want, the stuff you *need*); unreimbursed travel, and so on. Allow a reasonable amount for retirement (again, about as much as an employer would give you). Don't forget taxes: self-employment taxes, payroll taxes, sales taxes, and all those other hidden taxes that only a good tax accountant can tell you about. (Call and ask, if you have any doubt; the single biggest bump in the road for most smaller businesses is unforeseen taxes.)

Add all these up (annual basis, remember). *Don't panic.* Just write the figure down on your Pricing Worksheet on line B ("My Annual Costs of Doing Business").

C. What Is My Breakeven Figure?

Add line A and line B. Enter the total on line C ("My Breakeven Figure") on the Pricing Worksheet. As the name implies, this is the amount of money you need to make each year to exactly cover expenses, with no margin.

D. How Many Work Days Are Available Annually?

There are 52 weeks available to work each year. Of these, two weeks go to legal holidays—Labor Day, Thanksgiving and the like—leaving 50 weeks. Most people miss some work because of sickness and other personal reasons; in my case, I assume I will lose two weeks annually to these causes, leaving 48 weeks. Vacation takes some time; again, in my case, with an established business and a growing family I allow four weeks, leaving 44 weeks for work.

I assume a five-day workweek. Much less than that and it's hard to sustain a business; much more, and it's hard to sustain myself and my family over the long run. That's 44×5, or 220 days available to me for work every year. (Like most self-employed people I try to pretend that those evenings and weekends I spend in the office don't count.)

Adjust those figures to fit your situation—more or less sick leave or vacation; more or less than five days per week—and do the arithmetic. How many days are available to you for work each year? Enter that on your Worksheet on line D ("My Total Work Days)."

(Again, we are figuring this as if you are the only person in your company whose services are being directly paid for by a customer. If you have partners or employees whose services are paid for by customers, include their total work days in your line D sum. If there are two of you, for example, you probably have around 440 days in the space on line D.)

E. What Is My Utilization Rate?

Remember Marion, the hugely successful consultant who never advertises? Marion could (some months, does) get paid to work every single day of the month. This is the kind of fantastic success we all dream of; with this kind of success, you get rich. Here's hoping you and your company achieve it.

Meanwhile, your pricing should be based on realistic assumptions that can be attained with normal success. Good, successful businesses do not get paid for delivering services every available hour. Instead, they price their services so that they make their costs and their margins while billing less than 100% of the available hours. The percentage of available time for which you actually get paid by a customer is called your utilization rate.

What should your utilization rate be? That's hard to answer. A somewhat easier version of the same question is: What percentage of your time needs to be paid for before you are willing to say that your business is doing OK—not blowing the doors off, but not sputtering either: just OK?

The answer will be different for different businesses, but there are rules of thumb. The major accounting firms have looked at this carefully for many businesses, including their own. One firm I have worked with assumes a utilization rate of 65%. That is, they price their services to cover costs and margin, assuming they are able to bill 65% of their time—and then, of course, they work like mad to get their *actual* utilization rate as high as possible!

This is a reasonable starting point: about two-thirds of your time is paid for by customers. But you may need to adjust it up or down, depending on your actual business. A management consultant typically spends quite a bit of time in unpaid meetings, presentations to prospective clients, and travel. Even with efficient scheduling and long hours, this kind of business eats up time; the utilization assumption might be as low as 50%. On the other hand, a word-processing business in a competitive market might need to assume a utilization rate as high as 75%.

Instead of trying to guess it right the first time, let's look at a range for your business. On the Pricing Worksheet you will find three fill-in spaces on line E ("My Utilization Rate"). You will need three utilization assumptions: one that is as *low* as you think is reasonable, one that is a good *middle* assumption, and one that is as *high* as seems reasonable. One of your rates will be the standard 65%; you need to decide whether this is your low, middle, or high figure. Write it down on the Worksheet in whichever space is appropriate. Now make your best estimate of the other two rates and write them down. When you finish, you will have three percentages, going from smaller to larger as you go from left to right.

F. What Margin Do I Need?

A customer hands you $100 for your services. It cost you $90 to provide the service. The other $10 is margin; your margin rate is 10%.

Appropriate margin rates vary tremendously from business to business. Here are some examples:

- Like most people, you probably buy your groceries from supermarkets. What would you guess is their margin rate? Unless you already know the answer, it will amaze you: A successful supermarket chain typically has less than 1% margin. That's right: for every dollar you spend there, less than a penny goes to margin. That's cutting things mighty close. How do they stay in business? They make it up on volume. A big supermarket chain like Safeway takes in billions of dollars each year. A penny here, a penny there; make that a billion times and you are talking about some real money.

- IBM takes in over $50 *billion* every year. Care to guess what their margin rate is? For years on end it was more than 35%. That translates into over $17 billion margin annually. Outrageous? Excessive? Depends on how you look at it; don't forget that margin is not the same as profit. The computer business is a notoriously bumpy road; look at all the wrecks in Silicon Valley. To stay in business, IBM spends billions of dollars annually on research and development—more than the R&D budgets of most countries— and more billions each year on new plants and manufacturing technology. Those are not costs of providing this year's services; they are costs of providing next year's and next decade's, and they come from margin.

Both these examples, of course, are *product*-based businesses. Margin rates for service businesses like yours typically must be closer to IBM's than to Safeway's. Big accounting firms, for example, aim for a margin of around one-third: 33%. A margin of 40% is outstanding success in most businesses; much less than 20% is driving pretty close to the edge. If you have many customers each of whom pays you relatively small amounts (like a packaging service, a barber, or a chiropractor), your margin can be lower. If you have relatively few customers each of whom pays you relatively large amounts (like a graphic designer, a management consultant, or a software engineer), your margin needs to be higher. Why? Because it takes more time and money to replace a customer who pays a lot for your services. Bigger bumps on the road mean bigger margin for error.

Once again you may need some expert advice here; ask your accountant, or your professional association, or look it up in government statistics (research librarians at public libraries tend to be really helpful in finding such things). But please do not make the typical mistake of underestimating the margin your business needs.

On the Pricing Worksheet, line F is "My Margin Rate." Again, we are going for a range of low, middle, and high. Write them down on your Worksheet, and then pat yourself on the back. The hard thinking is done; only some number-crunching remains.

G. Calculate My Pricing Matrix

We are not going to try to legislate the exact, right price for your services. Instead we will calculate a matrix of prices to reflect your range of assumptions about utilization and margin, which will guide you in making actual pricing decisions. Get your calculator ready.

Immediately below line E ("My Utilization Rate") on the Pricing Worksheet, there is a line labeled "Number of Days Billed" with three fill-in lines. These correspond to your three assumptions about utilization. Fill in each by multiplying line D (total work days) by the utilization rate. Do this for each of the three utilization rates, and fill in the result immediately below the rate. For example, I have 220 days available to me to work. A utilization rate of 65% means that I will be paid by customers for $220 \times .65 = 143$ days per year. I would write 143 on the blank line immediately below the 65% rate.

Now look at your three margin rates under line F. Subtract each margin rate from 100 and enter the result in the column immediately to the right. For example, if my low margin rate is 20%, I subtract 20 from 100 and put down 80 in the blank space next to the 20%. (Incidentally, accountants call this your *expense ratio*; it is the percentage of every dollar that goes toward covering expenses.) Now, *very important*, put a decimal point in front of each number in the (100 – M%) column, to make it a decimal fraction; in my example, the figure now reads .80.

Now we use a formula to calculate your pricing matrix. (For those of you who hate to take anything on faith I have included the simple algebraic derivation of the formula at the end of this chapter.) For each of the nine squares of the matrix, calculate your daily rate:

$$\text{Daily rate} = \frac{\text{My breakeven figure}}{\text{Days billed} \times (100 - \text{M\%})}$$

That is, for each pair of margin and days billed numbers, first divide line C ("My Breakeven Figure") by the number of days billed. Now divide *that* by the (100 – M%) figure; since you have divided by a fraction, your final figure will be larger than your intermediate one. You now have the daily rate required to cover your costs and generate the level of margin under that utilization assumption. Write the figure down in the matrix square that aligns with that pair of numbers (don't panic!) and go on to the next pair, until you have completed the matrix. If you have not made an error, you will have nine daily rates; the lowest will be in the upper right square, and the highest will be in the lower left.

Congratulations! You now have more and better information about where to price your services than do 90% of your competitors. Take a break. You will think better about the implications of all this when you are less befuddled by the calculations.

What Do I *Really* Charge?

Let's get above the trees and take a look at the forest. Your daily rate is the *minimum* rate you can charge and still have a successful business. Most industries are competitive enough to make the daily rate a pretty good figure to use for your actual prices; really "knock-'em-dead" success then comes from getting your actual utilization figures up past your assumption.

But not always. Sometimes you have to charge more—maybe even much more. Sylvia is a case in point. We first met many years ago when she ran the training department of a company to which I was a consultant. Ten years ago, strongly encouraged by all of her friends, she went out on her own and immediately began making an excellent living (everyone who knew her knew she would be a great success; typical of most professionals going out on their own, she was sure she would starve). Sylvia for a number of years has had an enviable problem: the competition keeps forcing her to raise her prices!

She looked a little sheepish as she explained it. "What else can I do, Tony? I do workshops with executives who make six-figure salaries. If I quote them a price lower than $2500 per day, they think, 'Maybe we need someone a bit heavier-weight for this group.' I have to charge this much or they don't think they are getting their money's worth!"

Oh, well. Some people get *all* the hard problems.

_____ **WORKWORK: THE ABSOLUTELY FINAL LOOK AT PRICING** _____

Take one last look at your daily rate and what it implies for the current price of your services. Think about your target market: Are they accustomed to paying more for these services? Would they perhaps be concerned about the quality of your services when you charge so *little*?

If so, then do them a favor: Sell them some peace of mind along with your other services. Raise your prices to a level that makes them feel they are getting good value for their money.

Here's the derivation of that daily rate formula:

$$\text{Breakeven} + \text{Margin} = \text{Income}$$

$$\text{Breakeven} = \text{Income} - \text{Margin}$$

$$\text{Breakeven} = \text{Income} - (\text{Income} \times \text{M\%})$$

$$\text{Breakeven} = \text{Income} \,(100 - \text{M\%})$$

$$\frac{\text{Breakeven}}{(100 - \text{M\%})} = \text{Income}$$

but also: $\text{Income} = \text{Daily rate} \times \text{Days billed}$

so: $\dfrac{\text{Breakeven}}{(100 - \text{M\%})} = \text{Daily rate} \times \text{Days billed}$

$$\frac{\text{Breakeven}}{\text{Days billed} \times (100 - \text{M\%})} = \text{Daily rate}$$

8 Building Your Marketing Machine—I

Turning Prospects into Customers

I punched in the last numbers and hit the "equals" key. Little red digits lit up the calculator screen. I dropped the decimal and rounded up to the nearest whole customer.

"OK, Bob. Based on those figures, you're going to need to create at least 50 new customers this year."

Bob was speechless. (You would have to know Bob to know how rare that is.) He picked up the calculator and ran the numbers himself. Same answer.

Bob looked at me with something like panic in his eyes. "Tony, I couldn't go out and create *five* new customers if my life depended on it. How on earth can I create 50?"

"Could you go out and create *one* customer?"

"Sure."

"Fine. Then just do that—and then do it again 49 more times, and you're there."

"No good, Tony. I know how hard it is to get that one. No way I could do that 50 times a year. There wouldn't be any time left to do the work once I had it."

"Guess we'll just have to build you a marketing machine, Bob."

"Sounds great! I'd love one! But seriously, Tony, what am I going to do?"

"I *am* serious. We need to build you a marketing machine, and we don't have much time to waste if you're to get your 50 new customers this year."

Marketing Machine?

Marketing takes hard work. You knew that before you started this book; if you didn't, you do by now! But most professionals and service businesses make it much harder than it needs to be because they are not organized for marketing. Look at your own business for a moment. Suppose you were to realize that you need to generate 50 new, good, solid prospects for your services in the next three months. What would you do? Would you even know where to begin? Or would you be like the cook using the famous Scottish recipe for rabbit stew that starts, "First, catch the rabbit." (For many people like Bob it's actually worse than that; it's more like, "Buy an axe to cut down the tree to make into the trap to set in the woods to catch the rabbit.") No wonder marketing is so tough!

It needn't be that way.

In the previous chapters you have created the basic elements for powerful, aligned marketing. In this chapter we concentrate on creating a system that uses those elements to do routinely, systematically, efficiently, and in large numbers, what you probably have been doing on an ad-hoc, one-at-a-time basis: convert a prospect into a customer. In other words, we're going to build you a marketing machine, one that will make your marketing like the modern recipe for rabbit stew: "Pop the frozen rabbit stew into the microwave and heat for ten minutes. Eat and enjoy."

Could you use a good marketing machine?

After all our talk about relationships and alignment it may seem a bit odd to talk about a "machine." Please don't get me wrong—I'm not suggesting you begin to treat your customers like cogs in your machine! That's not good marketing.

I simply mean that there is an orderly progression in your relationship with your market—from prospect to customer and beyond—that you will need to monitor and control. In the "intentional process of creating and maintaining the relationship of customer" (that's marketing, remember) you will need to keep track of who is where in the process, and take specific, efficient action designed to move people along.

Your marketing machine has two main parts: the activity part (which we will call your Customer Creation System), and the information part (which we will call your Marketing Information System). The Customer Creation system moves people in a predictable, routine way through the process. The Marketing Information System keeps track of who is where in the process, and helps you decide what to do to move them along.

Think of your marketing machine as being shaped like a funnel (see Figure 2). At top are your Prospects. Prospects are anybody who could potentially benefit from your services.

You have already narrowed the field considerably by segmentation, choosing a high-opportunity market with which to align your firm. These

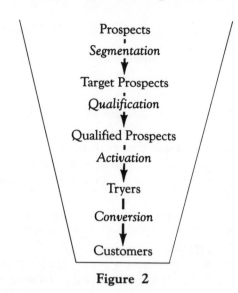

Figure 2

are your Target Prospects. Prospects become Target Prospects when you establish that they are in fact part of your high-opportunity market.

Next come Qualified Prospects, people who have said or done something to let you know that they have some interest in your services. A great deal of your marketing efforts will be directed toward qualification, that is, creating Qualified Prospects.

After Qualified Prospects come Tryers. Your efforts at this stage are oriented toward activation of their expressed interest. Tryers have actually sampled your services (perhaps through a free sample or a no-risk first session).

Finally comes conversion from Tryers into Customers. As any frozen yogurt server knows, it's a fairly short step from Tryer to Customer. (It's an even shorter step from Customer to Customer, which is where "maintaining the relationship of customer" comes in.)

The whole purpose of your marketing machine is to make sure that enough people move through the funnel to give you the number of customers you need. It's a "machine" because you create specific, efficient methods for moving people from one stage to the next, and then see to it that these methods are applied routinely. If you set up your marketing machine carefully, all you have to do is continue to crank it. These are the directions that come with the machine:

- Put Target Prospects into the top.

- Use your qualification methods for turning them into Qualified Prospects.

- Use activation methods to make them into Tryers.

- Apply your conversion methods.

- Customers are created.

To get enough Customers, just put in enough Target Prospects and crank the machine.

This is not meant to imply that everybody *must* go through each of these stages. Sometimes people call you up out of the blue and buy; sometimes people go directly from Target Prospect to Customer; very frequently Qualified Prospects become Customers without first becoming Tryers. These categories are just ways of keeping track of your safest assumptions about the specific people you are telling your story to, and what you need to make happen next.

The machine is based on one simple statistical fact: the further down the funnel you go, the better the response will be to your offers. Your odds progressively increase and your "hit-rate" improves as you move down through the funnel. If you make an offer to Prospects in general, perhaps one in 10,000 will take you up on it. Make the same offer to Target Prospects and you may get one hit per 1000; make the offer to Qualified Prospects and you may get four or five per 100. (I'm just making these statistics up for now; in your actual case the odds may be considerably better or worse. An important job of your marketing machine is to help you find out over time exactly what your specific response rates are.) By the time you get to Tryers your hit rate is usually terrific—better than one in 10, maybe much higher. (If a frozen yogurt stand can't get over 90 percent of Tryers to buy, the stand needs better flavors!)

It's like refining gold. You start by loading lots of ore-bearing rock into the top of a processor that progressively treats it until pure metal emerges. It takes tons of rock to produce a pound of gold; the exact amount depends on how ore-rich the rock is and how sophisticated the refining process. In the same way it may take hundreds of Target Prospects to produce one customer; exactly how many depends on how well you have chosen your segment and how aligned your marketing materials are. But think how much a customer—your pound of gold—is worth!

So your overall strategy is simple: Find lots of Target Prospects. Set up inexpensive, efficient ways of getting your message to these Target Prospects and persuading them to qualify themselves. Make these Qualified Prospects attractive, beautifully aligned offers that make it very easy to become Customers, including along the way, as needed, a quick stint as Tryers. And make sure that nothing gets in the way of Tryers becoming Customers. The further people move down the funnel, the more resources you put into moving them along, and the more likely it is that you will get a good return on your efforts.

Let's build your marketing machine!

Loading the Top of the Funnel

The critical first task in refining gold is to find an ore-body large enough and rich enough to be worth bothering with. You already did that work in Chapter 4, when you selected your target market segment.

Your next step is similar to digging up truckloads of ore and shipping it to the refinery, where it's dumped into the hopper. You need Target Prospects, specific individuals (or organizations, if that's how you have segmented) who are in your target market. These are people to whom you can tell your story and make your offer; people whose names and important information you can capture for your Marketing Information System; most importantly, people you can move to the next stage of Qualified Prospects. Where do you find these people and how do you reach them?

You're going to hate this answer but it happens to be both true and useful.

> **You find Target Prospects where they ordinarily are. You reach them when they are doing what they ordinarily do.**

If that sounds like one of those smirky "I rob banks because that's where the money is" quips, think for a minute. You know what target segment you are going after (you identified it in Chapter 4). You know what kind of people you need to turn into Qualified Prospects. Where do you ordinarily find people like these?

- At home
- At work
- Meeting in their clubs or professional organizations
- Moving around the community

And what are they ordinarily doing when they are at these places?

- Reading their mail
- Reading their favorite magazine or newspaper
- Listening to someone talk

- Talking on the telephone

- Just looking around

- Looking for someone who does exactly what you do

Plus a whole lot of other things that are none of your business or mine and would not make them receptive listeners.

I'm bothering you with the obvious so that you can see for yourself that there is no big mystery in finding Target Prospects! It's the simplest kind of common sense combined with a little roll-up-your-sleeves get-out-and-do-it. Start with one or more of the following:

- Get their address, at home and/or at work.

- Get their phone number.

- Find out what they read.

- Find out what they listen to or watch.

- Find out what clubs or professional organizations they belong to.

- Figure out where their eyes tend to fall when they are just looking around.

- Figure out where they would ordinarily look to find someone who does exactly what you do. (The Yellow Pages? Probably. Anywhere else?)

What information do you need right now?

_____ **WORKWORK: THE FIRST CONTACT** _____

What information you need depends on how you intend to communicate with your prospects, so let's work out communication first.

Remember, this is the first time the prospects have heard your story. You are just trying to get them to say, "Tell me more!" How can you tell prospects your story?

- Send them a personal letter.

- Send them a mailing.

- Put a flyer under their windshield wipers or on their doors.

- Put a flyer on bulletin boards—the old-fashioned kind, the new-fangled electronic kind, or both.

- Call them up.
- Place an ad in their magazine or paper.
- Place an ad on radio or TV.
- Place an ad in the Yellow Pages.
- Write an article for their professional group's journal or newsletter.
- Join their clubs or organizations and go to meetings.
- Give a talk to their clubs or organizations.

You will probably use more than one of these methods; you probably will not use them all. Which ones make most sense to you? Are you a good speaker or writer? Then by all means include talks and/or articles. Are you better one-on-one? Then show up at some meetings. Does advertising make sense for you? (If you're not sure, Chapter 13 will help you figure it out.) Is your business the type that could benefit from putting flyers under windshield wipers or a "free-standing insert" in the Sunday newspaper (you know, those "giblets" that fall all over the floor while you're looking for the comics)? You almost certainly want to include some sort of mailing. Does a letter or brochure make sense?

You *have to* get your initial message out somehow. Jot down the ways you intend to use. Review your list carefully. Will it get your message in front of enough people? If not, what other ways do you need to add? Jot them down.

Now that you know how you intend to communicate, it's easy to match up the information you need.

- *Giving talks or writing articles*: What professional organizations, associations, or clubs do your Target Prospects belong to? What journals or newsletters or magazines do they read?

- *Advertising*: Which periodicals or newspapers are read by your Target Prospects? Which are most influential? Where do prospects look when they are actively seeking services like yours? (Yellow Pages? Specialized directories? Classified ads? Bulletin boards?)

- *Circulars*: Where do your Target Prospects park their cars? What neighborhoods do they live in?

- *Direct-mail letters or brochures*: What are your Target Prospects' mailing addresses at work or at home?

- *Calling on the phone*: What's the Target Prospects' business, home, and fax numbers?

Jot down what information *you* need to get your initial message in front of your prospects.

You have loaded up the top of the funnel. You know where your Target Prospects are, and you know how you intend to communicate with them. Now you begin creating specific, powerful marketing communications to accomplish a critical task: refining your Target Prospects into Qualified Prospects.

Qualified Prospects, remember, are people who have done or said something to let you know they are interested in your services. Qualified Prospects are the mother lode of marketing: once you have them, success is a downhill ride. (I know of one company that sells the names of Qualified Prospects to its sales force for $10 each. The sales force is happy to pay the fee; their alternative is knocking on 100 doors in hopes of getting inside one.) Let's look at how to create Qualified Prospects.

The First Critical Step: Self-Qualification

Once you realize the mistakes they are making, it can make you ill to look at some people's marketing materials.

Not because they're sloppy or tasteless or cheap; quite the contrary. What can make you ill is that someone put so much time, effort, and *money* into materials that won't get a good response. Materials are almost *guaranteed* not to get a response, because they have violated one of three inviolable rules.

The first, most frequently violated rule has the highest potential for harm. If you violate this rule, you have lost: nothing else you do will matter. The first rule is:

> The first thing you must do in a marketing communication is to get the Prospect to recognize: "Hey! They are talking about *me.*"

Sales people call this "self-qualification." It's the critical first step toward a Qualified Prospect; before I can tell *you* that I'm interested in what you have to say, I have to first recognize it myself. Ad copywriters talk about it as the first two steps in their AIDA process (get their Attention; create Interest; create Demand; ask for Action).

Whatever you call it, it's crucial. Until I recognize that you are talking specifically about me, none of your carefully crafted points will register. They will bounce off that stainless-steel wall of indifference and inattention we have all learned to erect to filter out the irrelevant noise in our environment.

This rule is actually based on a profound insight into human psychology. You've probably experienced it yourself many times. Here's a typical scenario. You are at a party, making the usual party-time small talk. Crowded room. Choppy murmur of many simultaneous conversations blending into background noise. Suddenly in the midst of the babble you hear—Your Name!—and your mind and attention lock onto that voice. The voice says something about your business or your personal style and suddenly it's as if you tuned into a powerful radio station—that's all you can hear! They're talking about you!

Now notice something interesting: That same voice was talking before and you didn't even register it. But as soon as your mind decided the talking had to do with you, your attention became automatically focused, like a compass needle pointing North. You couldn't *not* pay attention if you tried.

That's the kind of attention you need for your marketing communications, and you can get it only if you follow the rule.

How, specifically, can you get your Prospects to recognize that you are talking about them? There are two classic methods, which have been refined to a high art by direct-response copywriters.

1. Ask me a pointed question to which I say "Yes."

2. Describe my situation in a scenario that is so accurate I say "Hey! That's *me* they're talking about!"

The most powerful communications use a combination of both: usually a question for the headline and scenarios for the first paragraph or two. By the time your Prospects finish the first 30 seconds of reading, they will be paying careful attention. (Or, they will have realized your message is *not* addressed to them and will stop reading. As long as their response is *accurate*, you win either way.) Let's look at some examples of both methods so you can see how they work.

The Power of the First Yes

My all-time favorite story about using a pointed question to qualify a prospect appears in Frederic Pohl's memoir, *The Way The Future Was*. Pohl is one of the most talented and honored science-fiction writers of his generation; he was also, at the time, earning his living writing copy for mail-order advertising. He tells it far better than I could:

> Almost the first problem George laid on me was a big coffee-table picture book called *Outdoor Life's Gallery of North American Game*. Mostly it was full-color reproductions of the cover paintings from *Outdoor Life* itself, and it was really quite handsome, if you like that sort of thing. But in the market it was no wily white-tailed deer or battling steelhead salmon. What it was in the marketplace was a dog. The company had printed fifty

thousand copies of it, and forty-nine thousand-plus were still in the warehouse. They had tried everything: buckeye four-color circulars the size of a bedsheet and personalized we're-all-art-connoisseurs-together letters on embossed stationery. And nothing worked.

I decided to test some new copy appeals. At the time, penny postcards still cost only a penny, so I wrote up a dozen or so sample appeals for postcard testing and we sent out thousand-piece mailings to test them out. I tried all the angles I could think of—

> The book is beautiful and will impress your friends . . .

> With this book you will be better able to kill, crush, mutilate and destroy these beloved game beasts . . .

> This book will teach your children the secrets of wildcraft and keep them from turning into perverts and drug addicts . . .

And then I tried one more card, which said:

HAVE YOU GOT A BIG BOOKCASE?
Because if you have, we have a BIG BOOK for you . . .

and that was the winner. We didn't bother transmuting the copy appeal to a circular, we just mailed out those cards. Nearly a million of them, and the only reason we didn't mail more was that we ran out of books.

(Fred Pohl's friend, Cyril Kornbluth, once wrote a story entitled "The Marching Morons." I'm morally certain Pohl's experiences in advertising influenced the title.)

I love this story because it so perfectly illustrates the point (actually a number of points, but we'll get into them later). It is hard to imagine a more banal question than "Have You Got a Big Bookcase?" There is *no* excitement, *no* sex appeal in that question—but it worked! And it worked for one simple reason: People who read that question either had a big bookcase or they didn't. If they did, their response was, "Yes. I do. I guess they're talking about me," and they turned off the indifference filters. They listened, heard, and bought. Here are a few other examples.

- One of the most successful direct-response ads of all time ran unchanged for years. Its headline was: "Do You Make These Common Mistakes in English?" The first paragraphs illustrated some common grammatical mistakes. A pointed question and a clear scenario; within 30 seconds the real prospect was saying, "They're talking about me!"

- Dr. John, the chiropractor, has a Yellow Pages ad with a nice picture of him smiling warmly next to a large-type question: "Do You Want to Be Free of Pain and Discomfort?" It's a very good bet that anyone reading it will say, "Yes!" (Why else would they be looking in the Yellow Pages under "Chiropractors?")

- For years I have sent out a four-page letter promoting my two-day workshop. The headline is the same every year with only one change. This year it reads: "Will 1990 Be The Year You Finally Get Serious About Marketing?" People who have not been putting serious effort into their marketing recognize that this letter is about them. Many people who claim they never read mailers have told me that they read my letter through word for word.

_____ **WORKWORK: THE POINTED QUESTION** _____

Would a good pointed question help *your* marketing communications? If it would, let's create one for you.

In stating your mission (Chapter 3, remember?) you identified the benefit of your services from your customers' point of view. That benefit takes one of four forms when you address your customers:

- "I help you solve this problem."

- "I help you make the most of this opportunity."

- "I help you achieve this desirable outcome."

- "This is your situation, and I help you with it."

Which form best describes your benefit? Your pointed question should then, simply and clearly, evoke the benefit.

Problem

If your benefit is seen by your market as solving a problem, begin by asking if they have this problem. Start the question with "Do you . . ." or "Are you . . ." or "Is your . . ." or "Does your . . . ."

- "Do you make these common mistakes in English?"

- "Are you struggling to make payroll each month?"

- "Is your appearance holding you back from promotion?"

- "Does your car hibernate every winter?"

Opportunity

If your benefit is making the most of an opportunity, ask if they *are* making or *want to* make the most of the opportunity.

- "Are you just sitting on a mailing-list goldmine?"
- "Is your manufacturing operation working at its maximum potential?"
- "Do you want to use your skills in a more rewarding job?"

Outcome

If you can state the desirable outcome clearly, it can be very effective. The question begins with "Do you want . . . ."

- "Do you want to live your life free of pain and discomfort?"
- "Do you want a rewarding career in data processing?"
- "Do you want to lose 15 pounds without going hungry?"

Situation

There is something distinctively powerful about a pointed question that nails down the prospect's situation exactly.

- "Will 1990 be the year you finally get serious about marketing?"
- "Are you tired of waiting for 'Mr. Right?'"
- "Do you have a burning desire to write?"
- "Do you have a BIG BOOKCASE?"

Write down a first draft of your pointed question. Try it several different ways if you like. Keep going until you have something that seems to work.

But remember, that's a *first* draft. Try it out on friends and customers; listen to their feedback and suggestions. Better yet, try out several different versions; one of the important points of Pohl's little story is that he was as surprised as anyone at which "copy appeal" actually worked! Be ready to find out instead of needing to know in advance.

One last point. Unless you are a professional copywriter, your version of the pointed question will probably be like a dull razor: basically sound, but in need of sharpening before you use it. Take your mission and your draft to a free-lancer who has experience in direct-response copywriting. (Try the Yellow Pages, to begin with.) Hire him or her for an hour to rewrite your question so that it sings; it should cost you less than $100. ("What! Fifty dollars for one lousy question! So much!" Wrong understanding, friend. Try: "What! Fifty dollars to make sure people will pay attention to my marketing materials! What a bargain!")

Situation Description

Whether you use a pointed question or not, you will need to nail down the prospects' attention by describing their own situation to them in terms they will recognize. This situation description approach requires you to be quite explicit and exact in describing the situations in which your prospects find themselves. (I said "situations" because it usually takes more than one to do the job.) This powerful and absolutely crucial step (again, one that is often overlooked) accomplishes two important things at once:

1. Like the pointed question, it brings down the indifference filters;

2. It gives you some initial credibility, because you have stated concisely and accurately an important fact about the prospect. ("Got that one right!")

Situation description takes two basic forms: assumptions and scenarios. Flip back to the section at the beginning entitled PLEASE READ BEFORE BUYING THIS BOOK. Notice the three assumptions stated there. These are clear, simple assumptions that work well because they clearly define a market segment. They are neither so global that they lose credibility ("I assume you want your business to succeed." "Sure, but who doesn't?") nor so narrow or technical that they exclude people who ought to be paying attention ("I assume you need to improve your alignment with your market." Until you had read a few chapters, you didn't know whether that was true, so the assumption probably would have missed you.).

Scenarios are both more powerful and riskier than assumptions as a means of situation description. A scenario is a quick "slice of life" that shows rather than tells. If it is well-chosen (and well-written) it seems to the Prospects as if you have been listening in on their lives. They experience a jolt that nails down their attention: "Wow! That's exactly my situation!"

For example, a manufacturing consultant began his marketing communications with these scenarios:

Walk through the modern manufacturing plant. Listen in on staff meetings. What do you hear?

- "The production line is down again! That's the fifth time this week!"
- "We had to reject the whole batch this time."
- "This quality problem is hurting us, and our customers aren't going to put up with it much longer."
- "Looks like we've got more people working on repairs than on the line."

- "Overtime is killing us—but we can't make schedule without it."
- "Doesn't anybody on the line care about getting the job done?"

Any of this sound familiar? If so, you've got plenty of company. You can hear things like this in just about every manufacturing plant in the country. Getting the most out of your manufacturing process is a hard, unending job. It takes a strong boss, good people, and all the help you can get.

In less than 30 seconds, the real prospect for this consultant's services is paying close attention.

Scenarios are riskier because it's easy to miss a lot of real prospects if you're not careful in your selection. (Or else you wind up with so many scenarios that nobody will wade through them all!) Look for "generic" scenarios that almost everybody can relate to, and then make them seem very real. Again this implies excellent writing; unless you are a published novelist or earning your living as a copywriter, pay a professional to polish your rough draft.

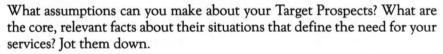

_____ **WORKWORK: ASSUMPTIONS AND SCENARIOS** _____

What assumptions can you make about your Target Prospects? What are the core, relevant facts about their situations that define the need for your services? Jot them down.

_____

Do they seem to form a clear picture? Do these few (three or less) facts pinpoint their situation? Ask yourself:

- Are these assumptions too global to be credible? Can I make them more focused?
- Am I leaving out some important prospects in these assumptions?
- Most important: Will my prospects immediately recognize themselves in these assumptions?
- Would it work better to just list the assumptions, or do they go together into a quick, clear story?
- In summary, do I have a good set of assumptions to use?

Now look for possible scenarios. Is the common thread in your customers' situations usually invisible to them? Do they tend to see their specific "tree" instead of the forest you can see? Perhaps you need to describe the various trees so they can recognize theirs, and then tell them about the forest.

Make a list of the situations that your customers find themselves in when they need your services. ("Neck and back pain; stiffness; chronic pain or headaches; . . . .") Keep going until your list covers the major possibilities.

How many do you have? More than about six or seven may overwhelm your prospects. Can you get your list down to that size?

Take a stab at writing a crisp, real example for each situation. ("Jane wakes up each morning with pain in her back. It gets better as the day goes on, but never really goes away.")

Now look at what you have. Ask yourself:

- Would prospects recognize themselves in these scenarios?

- Have I left something important out?

- Are these in roughly the right order? (Most frequent and important first.)

- In summary, do I have a good first draft set of scenarios?

Where are we? We are working on the critical task of converting Target Prospects to Qualified Prospects. Recall that there are three inviolable rules in creating communications to accomplish that. You now know how to follow the first rule. Let's look at the second.

The Second Critical Step: Communicating the Benefit

You've got my attention. I know you're talking about me. Great!
Now what?

The second thing you must do in a marketing communication is to get me to see the benefit of your services.

Sounds pretty obvious and straightforward, doesn't it? It is, but you would be amazed (and dismayed and horrified) at how many marketing pieces do not accomplish this simple task. Notice that the rule says, "Get me to *see* the benefit." It does *not* say, "Allude to the benefit in a clever play-on-words headline." If that's all you do—and once you start looking for them, you'll be amazed at how many print ads do nothing more than that—you are wasting your money. Your task is to lay out that benefit so clearly and exactly that your prospects *see* it for themselves. And since it's an initial communication, you don't have all day to do it.

Fortunately, Chapter 3 left you well-prepared. This is another of those "moments of truth" that your mission statement will get you through. There are three key links in getting prospects to see your benefit. They must see:

1. *What* the benefit is

2. *How* you go about making that beneficial difference in their life

3. *Why you* would be able to do it successfully

Because the first point, what the benefit is, is strongly implied in the "situation description," you may be tempted to leave the obvious implication unstated. Resist that temptation. As soon as you have the prospects' unfiltered attention, tell them the benefit you provide in a crystal-clear sentence—the mission sentence you worked so hard to create in Chapter 3.

Telling them how you do it takes more time. Chances are very good that your current ways of describing your services need polishing. We'll work on that in Chapters 10 and 11. For now, notice that merely claiming you make a difference won't be enough; you have to show plausible means by which you do it.

Why you would be successful is a simple matter of credibility. Much of that is handled by the relationship-building nature of how you approach any communication; we went over that in detail in Chapter 5. The best evidence you can offer of your competence is to do a good job of what you are doing *right now,* that is, getting them to see what you have to offer. In addition, some background on you and your firm is called for ("Ten years' experience . . . hundreds of satisfied customers, including . . ."), and perhaps a few well-chosen testimonials. Watch out for overkill. At this stage a few simple but impressive points will probably be enough to get you past the first cut; too many credentials may leave the prospect wondering, "What are they trying to prove?"

The Third Critical Step: Getting a Response

This is the payoff step. Remember that this part of your marketing machine has one specific purpose: to make Target Prospects into Qualified Prospects. You have to get them to do or say something that shows they are interested in your services. And that means you have to do two simple things:

Make me an offer, and then show me how to respond.

Exactly what offer you make is a little tricky and calls for some hard-nosed decisions on your part. You have to decide whether to go for a "weak" qualification or a "strong" qualification. To be more exact, where on the "weak-to-strong" spectrum do you want this offer to fall?

A weak qualification calls for very little effort or commitment on your prospects' part. It's like a net with very fine mesh; many fish will be caught in it. A strong qualification commits the prospect to taking a next step, essentially becoming a Tryer. This net has bigger mesh; only the largest fish will be caught.

Here are some examples of weak qualifications:

- "For further information call . . ."
- "If you want to be informed of our next offering, fill out the mailing list card."
- "For a free brochure call toll-free . . ."
- "Everybody who hates mowing your lawn, raise your hand."

Strong qualifications include:

- "Call 555-1515 to ask for your free, no-obligation estimate."
- "Bring your car in for a free alignment check today!"
- "If you are interested in attending our free introductory program, fill out the registration card."
- "Everybody who wants to take advantage of our offer of a free manicure, raise your hand."

The trade-off is obvious. If you ask for a weak qualification, 70 prospects may respond. You may get only 30 responses to a strong qualification. Those 30 are obviously further down the funnel than the 70; a strong qualification demonstrates more interest. Your activation rate (the percentage of Qualified Prospects you turn into Tryers) will be higher with a strong qualification. But your pool of Qualified Prospects will be smaller, because 40 people whose interest was enough to get a response to a weak qualification did not respond to the stronger qualification. Even with a lower activation rate, if your pool of Qualified Prospects is bigger, you may wind up with more customers.

Which way should you go? It depends on your circumstances. Salespeople believe strongly in ABC (Always Be Closing) so they would advise you to go for the strongest qualification you can. But that's sales; we're doing marketing. Your final goal is to create customers, of course, but the specific task of this part of your marketing machine is to create Qualified Prospects. Once they are qualified, you can afford to try many times, if necessary, to activate their trying and buying. But you can't do anything with them if your qualification called for more commitment than they were ready to make.

I recommend using a weak qualification, to get you a large pool of Qualified Prospects. Count on your follow-on materials to activate and convert your prospects into customers. However, note two exceptions to this recommendation:

1. If your average customer doesn't pay a lot for your services—say, less than $50 per year—it may not be economically feasible to keep making many follow-up offers. In that case, it would make sense to use a strong qualifier.

2. If the qualification offer takes place after a substantial persuasive communication—you have given a talk to a group in which your services and their benefit have been thoroughly described, or you are sending out a several-page direct-mail letter that tells your story persuasively and well—you can afford to go for a stronger qualification. (Indeed, in direct mail you usually try to move people all the way down to Tryers or Customers with a single communication.)

Strong or weak, qualification requires an offer. Be sure that the offer is both attractive to your prospects and directly relevant to your service. One technical writing firm did a very nice mailer that described their services and benefit quite well. But their offer was: "Send for a free booklet on 25 Mistakes in Writing Documentation." They got horrendously poor results, because the kind of people who are interested in hiring technical writers are not interested in that booklet. Worse yet, the booklet did nothing to move people further down the funnel. Your qualification offer should lead directly to either a thorough, attractive presentation of your services capped by an offer of a trial, or else some kind of trial capped by a conversion to customer.

And don't forget to tell how to respond! Make responding as easy as possible: give the option of either calling or writing, and make the phone number and address crystal-clear. Here are a few common-sense tips:

- If your target market includes people who will be calling long-distance, make an 800 number available. (Yes, you *can* afford it. It's much cheaper than losing Qualified Prospects who can't or won't spring for a long-distance call to take you up on your offer.)

- Be sure to include hours when they can call, or else be prepared to answer the phones 24 hours a day.

- If your offer is made by mail, include a preprinted, self-addressed response card with no postage necessary. (You can afford that too.

Talk to your local Postmaster about no-postage replies.) Design it so that all that's needed is to check a box or two, perhaps transfer a mailing label to the card, and drop it in the mail. If they have to hunt up a stamp, some people won't get around to the card.

- If your offer is made during a talk or speech, consider this approach: "We have prepared an in-depth report on this topic. If you would like a copy, please take out your business card and write on the back of it: In-Depth Report. Give it to me after the talk and I will see that you get a copy." (Other offers: If you want to be informed of our next seminar; if you would like to receive our catalog; and so on.)

Let's summarize qualification. This part of your marketing machine is designed to turn Target Prospects into Qualified Prospects. You have to get them to say or do something that demonstrates interest in your services. You do that by communicating with them in some way—via mail, magazine or newspaper, telephone, speech or talk, personal contact, radio or television ads—and making them an offer to which they can easily say "Yes!" The three inviolable rules of qualification are:

1. Get prospects to recognize, "They are talking to me!"

2. Get them to see the benefit.

3. Make them an offer and show them how to respond.

You now have the names and addresses of a pool of Qualified Prospects. The next task for your marketing machine is to activate the interest of these Qualified Prospects and turn them into Tryers.

Activation

Activation is a good new word for an ancient idea. (I took the word from Stan Rapp and Tom Collins's intriguing book, *MaxiMarketing*.) You have an expression of interest; now you need to activate that interest. You have to turn *interest* into *action*. Time for your big guns.

We assume your service is good and valuable (if it's not, change it so it is good and valuable). Experience shows that if you can get people to try your services once, you will be able to turn a high percentage of them into customers. That goal is worth your best efforts: your most powerful presentations, your most telling examples, your first-class brochures, your persuasive testimonies, your most irresistible offers. In other words, this is when you tell your full story as well as you can.

There are basically two ways to tell your story at this point: in person, or through prepared "tangible" materials such as brochures, letters, videotapes, and so on. Your choice depends primarily on the size and scope of your services. A firm that sells services in very large packages, such as an auditing firm or any consulting firm, should almost certainly activate through in-person presentation augmented with good-quality tangible materials. If your service comes in smaller packages, and the sheer number of your Qualified Prospects makes personal activation impractical, then you need outstanding tangibles that do as good a job of telling your story as you could do in person.

In either case your activation methods must meet three tests:

1. They must be *prepared* and *practiced*.

2. They must show/tell/demonstrate to the Qualified Prospects exactly what they are buying.

3. They must make an offer that is simply too good to turn down.

Your marketing machine will work only if your activation methods are prepared and practiced. If you have to make up parts as you go along, you're out there trying to catch the rabbit when you should be popping rabbit stew into the microwave.

You cannot afford to leave anything unclear or not covered in activation materials. Your Qualified Prospects have said they are interested; they have asked to hear more. Tell them! Show them! Demonstrate to them if you can! The easiest way to lose when activating interest into action is to leave something unclear.

What materials do you need to prepare? And how do you make sure they are clear and complete? We will answer these questions thoroughly and completely in Chapters 10 and 11, which cover packaging and presentation. For now, ask yourself: Do I have activation materials that meet these first two tests? (Are you *sure?*) Filling the holes in your activation methods is one of the best investments in time and money you can make.

The third test, the offer, is crucial, so let's nail it down. At this stage it can't be an offer of further information. You must get Qualified Prospects to step up and try your services. Your offer should be as easy to accept as an offer of a free taste of frozen yogurt. All details aside, three basic types of offer turn Prospects into Tryers:

1. The free sample

2. The introductory great deal

3. The no-risk first session

The Free Sample

It's hard to turn down a free sample.

It's especially hard to turn it down when it's a small sample of something you're already considering buying.

The free sample works beautifully if you can legitimately package your services in a small portion. I keep mentioning the frozen yogurt sample because it's the perfect example: a tiny dish that tastes and even looks exactly like the bigger one you're considering buying. Can you offer a free sample? Here are some businesses that do:

- A housecleaning service offers to "clean your dirtiest room—free." As a neat twist, they ask the Tryers to time them. They present an invoice, stamped "Complimentary," based on the time it took. The quality, speed, and good value of the service impress the Tryers. "Such a good job, so fast!"

- A computer software company offers free "Trial Versions" of its word-processing package. The Trial Version does everything the real version does, but with one small difference: it will only "save" the first 10 lines of what has been written.

- A training company offers a free admission to its public seminars to every company that has expressed an interest in having the seminar done "in-house."

- A free-lance writer offers to rewrite a one-page business letter free.

Frugal money-managers often object at this point: "How can I afford to give away all this free service? What's to keep people from just taking the sample and leaving?" The answer is: Remember where you are in the marketing process. You are offering free samples to Qualified Prospects. You can afford to do that because a higher percentage of them in fact will become customers. It may not be cost-effective to offer free samples to prospects in general, so don't. Wait until they are Qualified.

Be careful here. Don't offer a free sample unless it is a legitimate sample of your service and will give an accurate "taste" of the benefit. In particular, don't make the mistake of offering a "free diagnosis" or esti-mate and thinking you are offering a free sample. You aren't, unless your mission is to provide people with good estimates or diagnoses. (Hard to see a lot of benefit in that, but it's your business . . .). In my experience, "free diagnosis" is not seen by most prospects as a valuable sample, or even as a great deal; it's seen as a way of getting them in the door for a sales pitch. At best, you are seen as saying, "We don't charge you for telling you what's wrong; we just charge for fixing it." More typically, a "free diagnosis" offer is viewed rather cynically: "Gee, I wonder if they will decide I need their services. I bet I can guess."

The Introductory Great Deal

Some services can't be repackaged into small enough portions to make a sensible free sample. Sometimes qualification and activation take place in the same communication (direct-mail marketing usually does that). In those cases, you might try the introductory great deal.

"Bring this coupon with you for 50% off on your first custom-tailored dress shirt." That introductory great deal brought me in; I figured at 50 percent off I was getting a custom-tailored shirt for less than a ready-made. And it worked the way it was supposed to: I found that custom shirt so much more comfortable that I've never bought a ready-made dress shirt since.

An introductory great deal is like a strong qualification: some people whom you want to try it won't, because their interest is not strong enough to make that kind of commitment. But it has distinct advantages. Anyone who takes you up on it is a strong Tryer: your conversion rate will be high. Most important, if you price it right, it won't cost you much (if anything) out-of-pocket. If you price the great deal essentially at your bare-bones cost, it's like "free marketing."

But make sure it really *is*, and will be seen by your prospects as, a great deal. The custom-tailored shirt was cheaper than a ready-made; it wasn't hard to see the value in that offer. But the real value in many services can only be seen *after* they have been experienced—many types of consulting, "body work," and therapy come immediately to mind. Half-price may still seem an outrageous amount because the prospect can't see the value.

The No-Risk First Session

OK, you can't package your services small enough to offer a free sample and prospects probably won't *really* see the value until they've tried the services anyway. What do you do? Offer a no-risk first session.

Better yet, offer a no-risk first session as part of an introductory great deal. Direct-mail newsletter and magazine marketers have raised this combination to a high art. "Send today for your special half-price subscription to our award-winning newsletter." (That's the great deal.) "If at any time during the first 90 days you feel you are not getting the best investment advice ever, we will refund your money—every penny of it!" (That's the no-risk first session.)

Almost any service business can offer a no-risk first session. Your offer is straightforward: Try us once at no risk to you. If you don't see the value, you don't pay. Of course, you know that most of these Tryers will in fact see the value and become Customers. As a rough rule of thumb, about

5 percent of these Tryers will ask for their money back. If you've done your qualifying well, that percentage can be even lower. But even if you're only average, that means that for every free session you do, you get 19 new paying Customers! That's what I call a good return on your investment.

Many Qualified Prospects, however, will not be able to make the leap to signing up for a first session:

- Some aren't interested enough. Not much to do about them, although you may be able to pick them up with later offers.

- Some are interested enough but they doubt your money-back offer. Not all people feel comfortable asking for their money back; they would rather avoid the entire situation. (You might be surprised at how many people feel that way.) You can activate some of these by making a very clear no-risk but not money-back offer: "Try it and only pay if you see the value." The down side of this approach is that your refund rate will probably increase somewhat.

- Some are interested but need a push to overcome lethargy. You can activate some of these by combining your no-risk first session with a limited-time introductory great deal: "Call for your appointment before July 31 and get a 50% discount on your first session." It's a powerful combination.

Conversion

Your prospects have taken you up on your offer and tried your services. The customer creation process is almost complete. All that's left is that last, critical process in your marketing machine: converting Tryers into Customers. If they've tried the service, shouldn't converting them into Customers pretty much take care of itself? It *should*, but it *doesn't*. Your marketing machine has to make sure it happens.

Salespeople call this "closing the sale" and it's widely acknowledged as the trickiest part of selling. The specific relationship tasks required for successful conversion will be covered in Chapter 14.

The materials required for converting a Tryer into a Customer are essentially the ones you used in activation, with one addition: you need a well-developed Summary Sheet to guide you through the relationship tasks of conversion. We will design a Summary Sheet for you in Chapter 14.

Completing the Customer Creation System

You are finally at the end point of a long journey: you have seen all the customer-creating parts of your marketing machine. If you're like most people in my experience, you probably will leave this chapter with two strong insights:

1. There is no mystery to creating customers. You need only to put the right pieces into place, and make sure they are used routinely.

2. You have a lot of work to do because you do not already have all the pieces in place.

At this point you may be feeling like the farmer with the leaky bucket. Every day the farmer had to haul water from the pump to the watering troughs. He would fill the bucket at the pump and start carrying it. But the bucket was full of holes; by the time he got to the watering trough most of the water had leaked out. Back and forth he went, day after day, hauling water in his leaky bucket.

Finally his wife couldn't stand it any longer. "Your bucket is leaking!"

"I know."

"So why don't you fix it?"

"Don't have time."

"Why don't you have time to fix the bucket?"

"Too busy hauling water."

Are you too busy keeping your business going to fix your marketing machine? Please don't be like the farmer. Taking the time you need to get all the parts in place and using them will be the best investment of time and resources you can make.

Chapters 10 and 11 will help you fill the gaps you may have found in your materials. But before you charge off to work on those, we have one more part of your marketing machine to build: the Marketing Information System. It can tell you exactly where to apply your efforts for best return, and how well you are doing. We will deal with it in the next chapter.

9 | **Building Your Marketing Machine—II**

Your Marketing Information System

It hurts to watch a business die and know you could have saved it, if only . . . .

I've known Red since we were kids together, more years ago than either of us cares to remember. His father was the top mechanic in town. Pops owned the local service station; then, as self-service gas pumps took over, he went out and built a small but thriving independent garage. Red worked alongside him for years and learned the business; when it came time for Pops to retire, he proudly turned the Oak Bluffs Garage over to his son.

But time changes things; "rust never sleeps." The economy in that part of the country collapsed; and instead of getting better after a while, things got worse. People didn't have money to get their cars fixed. And new cars were getting more and more complex; every year Red needed more expensive equipment to keep up in the repair business. He had to lay people off. Finally it was just Red and the building, and the overhead was eating him alive.

About that time I went back for a visit. Over coffee Red told me what was happening, so I plunged in. What good is being a marketing consultant if you can't help your friends?

"OK, Red, here's how much you need to make each month." I wrote it down on a napkin. "Roughly how much do you make off each job?" He told me that and I wrote it down. A quick division. "So you need this many customers a month to make it, right?"

Red nodded.

"Oak Bluffs Garage has been in business a long time in this town, Red. How many satisfied customers would you say you've had?"

"Oh, I don't know—eight, nine thousand, easy."

117

"OK. Now let's do some figuring here. . . ." I thought quickly to myself, "Maybe a direct-mail campaign—free inspection or something like that. These are all customers, so assume this activation rate; and this conversion rate. We need to send out how many mailers to get that many customers. At a cost per piece of—hmmmm. . . ."

"Red, I think you've got a good chance of turning this around. We need to get you started sending out about 500 mailers per month to your former customers, with an offer . . . what's wrong?"

Red looked very unhappy. "Tony, we didn't keep track of those old customers. We keep the work orders for a few months just in case there's a problem, but then we throw them out."

And that was it. There was no way to reconstruct the customer list, and the "hit-rate" for mass mailing was too low to pay off. Business kept getting worse, and we couldn't think of a thing to stop the slide. A few months later, despite his best efforts, Red had to close the doors of the Oak Bluffs Garage for the last time.

Marketing Information Systems are boring. It takes work to put one together and to keep it up. Most people treat it like flossing their teeth: something they know they should do, but never actually get around to doing. And then when, like Red, they *need* that information *now*, it isn't there.

Please don't skip this chapter. Read it and work at it. I don't want your business to wind up like the Oak Bluffs Garage.

Your Marketing Information System

A Marketing Information System is an indispensable part of your marketing machine. The Customer Creation System we looked at in Chapter 8 does the job of moving people routinely from being Prospects to being Customers. The Marketing Information System makes it possible for your Customer Creation System to do its job. It tells you:

- Where people are in the process.

- How you can communicate with each individual.

- What you have done with them already, and what you should do next.

- What kind of performance you are getting from each part of your marketing machine.

- What kind of performance you *need* from each part of your marketing machine.

Think of your customers as buried treasure. The Customer Creation System gives you the tools to dig up the treasure. The Marketing Information System shows you where to dig.

You know what a business looks like without a Marketing Information System; the Oak Bluffs Garage is typical. Here's what a business looks like *with* a Marketing Information System. Rob is a very successful electrical contractor. He has aligned himself skillfully with a terrific high-opportunity segment: office building owners whose buildings have been found by the building inspectors to have substandard wiring. Rob gives most of his time and attention to overseeing the current sites his company is rewiring. But once a month Rob sits down at his PC and starts cranking his marketing machine.

First Rob looks at his calendar to see how far in advance he has scheduled projects. He projects his revenues, expenses, and cash flow to see how much more money he needs to generate, and when. He figures out how many more customers he needs, and how long he has to get them. This standard financial stuff takes only a few minutes on his computer; his coffee is still steaming in his cup when he finishes.

But now Rob turns to his Marketing Information System. He runs a quick little program that looks over his past results and tells him how many Qualified Prospects are required to get the number of customers he needs. Another quick pass tells him how many Prospects he will need, to get that many Qualified Prospects. That sets the task for Rob: Get that many Prospects to put into the top of the funnel.

The next morning Rob is at the City Clerk's office when it opens, poring over the building inspectors' reports for the previous month (these are public records, so it's perfectly legal). When he closes his briefcase to go back to his office, he has the names and addresses of at least the number of Prospects he needs (usually a few extras for good measure because Rob likes to give himself a lot of margin for error). When he returns to the office, his secretary puts the new names and addresses into the computer database, types in a couple of simple commands, and out come personalized qualifying letters to each Prospect, politely offering them a free estimate on their job. Rob knows from previous experience the approximate percentage who will ask for the estimate; of these, a known percentage will hire Rob to do the job. From this point on, Rob uses his well-aligned presentation materials and relationship-building tactics to move people through the process of becoming Customers. Marketing for Rob is routine, predictable, and highly effective.

Would you like your marketing to be as easy as Rob's? You need a Marketing Information System to make the whole thing work. It gives you access to the three "R's" of business:

- Records
- Rates
- Results

Let's start designing your Marketing Information System at the bottom. The word on the bottom line is *results*.

Marketing for Results

What kind of performance do you need from your marketing machine? How many Target Prospects do you need? How many do you need to qualify each month? Basic questions like these seem to baffle many business owners. The answers are as simple as the farmer's answer to the traveler's question. A traveler was walking through the countryside on a long journey. He was impatient to get to his destination, so when he spotted a farmer in a field he stopped and called out, "Good morning, friend! Can you tell me how long it will take me to get to the city from here?"

The farmer looked up from his furrow, mopped his brow, and looked at the traveler without saying a word.

The traveler tried again. "I'm sorry to trouble you, but I'm a stranger and I don't know this road. How long will it take me to get to the city?"

Again the farmer looked at the traveler without saying a word. The traveler was furious at the farmer's rudeness. He turned away and began walking down the road again.

He had gone only a few steps when he heard the farmer call out, "You'll get to the city late tomorrow morning."

The traveler stopped in amazement. He turned back to the farmer and said, "But why didn't you answer me the first two times I asked?"

The farmer shrugged. "First I had to see how fast you were walking."

How many letters should you send out? First let's see how fast your services are generating money—how fast *you* are walking.

WORKWORK: AVERAGE PER CUSTOMER

Take this quick pop quiz to find out what kind of shape your Marketing Information System is in:

How much does *your* average customer spend for your services?

You should know that figure to the penny. OK, so you don't. Most people don't. Let's figure it out. There's an easy way and an accurate way.

- *The accurate way.* Gather your customer billing records for the past two years. Find out the number of customers you had in each year. Now enter in two columns, headed "This Year" and "Last Year," the total amount each customer spent for your services in each year. Add up the "This Year" column and divide the sum by the number of customers, then do the same for "Last Year." You now have two averages, this year's and last year's. Do you sense your trend is up? Down? Steady?

- *The easy way.* Determine your total business income from last year. If any of that income was from accounting or financial windfalls (interest, royalties, tax refund, and so on), deduct it, leaving only the income you were paid for your services. Divide that figure by the number of your customers to get your average per customer.

How hard was that? Were you able to do it the accurate way in a few minutes on your computer? Great! That's how it's supposed to work. Didn't have the information your needed? Took a long time to dig it out? What's that—*you don't have a computer?* This is just the tip of the iceberg, friend. You have some work to do; you can't hope to run your marketing machine without good information to guide it. We'll look at putting together your Marketing Information System a little later. For now, we need that Average Per Customer, so do the best job you can to figure it out.

You may need to do a little adjusting before we move on. Your Average Per Customer reflects what you have charged for your services in the past. If you are like most people, Chapter 7 may have caused you to reexamine your rates for future work. You should adjust your Average Per Customer to reflect what your customers would have paid at your new rates. (For example, if your rates are 20 percent higher, multiply the Average Per Customer by 1.2.)

On your Pricing Worksheet in Chapter 7, you figured out how much income you needed to just break even. We called it "My Breakeven Figure." Divide that income by the Average Per Customer you just calculated, and round up to the nearest customer. That's the number of customers you would need next year just to break even. Multiply that by 1.5 to get a quick, close estimate of how many customers you need to *succeed* next year. (Margins, remember? Don't forget margins!)

Your marketing machine must easily and routinely generate that many customers.

It is possible, of course, to decrease the number of customers you need by increasing your Average Per Customer. You can do that by more effective packaging, by better selling, or by marketing new follow-on services to established customers. But you would be unwise to bet your business on *assuming* that you will succeed at increasing your Average Per Customer. Instead, set up your marketing machine so that you can succeed at the current Average Per Customer; any increase will then give you the outstanding success we all hope for.

You need *that many* new customers next year. That's the Big Result. Achieving it depends on all your other results, which are reflected in your rates and your records. We'll look at your rates next.

Tuning the Marketing Machine

Back in the days of the gargantuan dinosaur automobile, I had one that died a slow and very instructive death.

It was a 1950 Buick, the one with the four "portholes" in the side of the hood, and it had the biggest engine I have ever seen. I put massive amounts of fuel into that engine, and it generated enormous power. When the car was new, that power propelled it down the road like a rocket. As it got older, things began to get loose. All those gears and joints and differentials that connected the engine to the road began to slip; more and more of that massive power was wasted in the transitions. By the time I put the old beast out of its misery, it took 10 gallons of gasoline to cover *slowly* the distance a new car could zip through on one gallon.

Is your marketing machine like my old Buick? If so, we need to tighten up the transitions. Recall that there are three main tasks in creating customers: qualification, activation, and conversion. Each of these is a transition, in which a certain amount of slippage is unavoidable. Exactly how much slippage do you have at each stage? How can you reduce the slippage? Answering these questions can make a huge difference in the performance of your marketing machine.

To answer these questions you need to calculate three simple rates:

- *Qualification rate.* One hundred Target Prospects hear your story and your qualifying offer. Three respond to the offer. Your qualification rate for that communication was 3 percent—the percentage of people who respond to a qualification offer and become Qualified Prospects.

- *Activation rate.* This is the percentage of Qualified Prospects who become Tryers. If you send detailed materials to 100 Qualified Prospects and 25 of them come in for their free sample, your Activation Rate is 25 percent.

- *Conversion rate.* Once they have tried, how many Tryers have become Customers? Out of 10 Tryers, if you get six Customers, your conversion rate is 60 percent.

At this point many people get a somewhat itchy, uncomfortable feeling. "What's all this percentages stuff? That's for accountants and bookkeepers. Who needs all these rates?"

You do. You can't get good performance from any system unless you fine-tune it, and you can't fine-tune anything unless you know very accurately how it's performing now. Gut feel and ball-park guesses won't do the job. You have to *know*.

The first and most important step in *improving* performance is keeping track of *current* performance.

Want proof? Try this: Someone did a study of diets to see which ones worked and why. They found that some diets do work—people actually lose weight and keep it off—and some don't. No surprise there. But when the diets that work were analyzed to find out what they have in common, researchers found that every diet that worked included one common factor: It was *not* goal setting or group support or even increasing exercise. The single factor that all successful diets have in common is: writing down what you eat. Just that. Keeping track of all the food you put in your mouth.

Don't misunderstand: Writing down what you eat doesn't *cause* you to lose weight. Eating less food than you need causes you to lose weight. Writing down what you eat *enables* you to lose weight, by letting you see exactly how much you are actually eating.

The qualification rate, activation rate, and conversion rate help you to keep track of how your marketing machine is currently performing. They don't *cause* you to improve your marketing results; they *enable* you to improve your marketing results. Without them you are like an archer who can't see the target; if you can't see where your last arrow landed, how can you improve your aim?

How important are these rates? Consider this: perhaps with your current methods two out of 10 Qualified Prospects become Tryers. With a little focused attention on packaging and presentation, you manage to increase that to three out of 10, an easily attainable result. You don't change anything else; everything else stays as it was before.

Congratulations. You have just increased your income by 50 percent!

Work on your Customer Creation System. Keep your eye on your rates to tell you how well you are doing.

All of this assumes, of course, that you have kept track, carefully and routinely, of who your prospects are, what you have done with them, and how they have responded. If you have, you are far ahead of the game. If you haven't (like Red) we need to take a close look at the third "R" of business: Records.

Your Most Valuable Tangible Asset

The hot new buzzword in marketing circles is *database marketing*. Using a potent mix of computers, demographics, and mailing lists, the new "rocket scientists" of marketing are making a breathtaking leap into the future—and in the process, taking business *back* to its roots in personalized, hand-crafted service. The day is quickly coming, say the advocates of database marketing, in which smart businesses of all sizes will offer customers exactly what suits a particular customer best.

In other words, marketers in big companies are trying to become more and more like you. If you keep your wits about you, they aren't likely to catch up. But you will lose your advantage unless you learn a simple lesson from the "database marketers":

Your most valuable tangible asset is your customer database.

I can hear you now: "Database? What database?" Your database is your list of Prospects, Qualified Prospects, Tryers, and Customers, along with your records of how and when you have communicated with them, and how they responded. You have put very substantial time, effort, and money into creating this information; you should consider it like uncut diamonds. A little discipline and skill will turn it into wealth.

Technically, you probably don't have a database yet. You have the ingredients for a database, the raw information. To turn it into a database you have to do three things: organize it, store it, and access it.

Organizing your information means that you have to decide what information you are going to keep track of, and then create a standard format for keeping track of it. These "records," the tangible substance of the database, fall into three basic categories:

1. *Individuals.*
The name and identifying particulars of each individual in your database—Target Prospects, Qualified Prospects, Tryers, and Customers—and of anyone else you want to keep track of—referral sources, suppliers, and so on. Usually these records contain only the minimal information you need to get in touch with each prospect: name, title, company, address, phone number, perhaps special numbers like fax or electronic mail codes, and a unique identification number that you have assigned to this person.

2. *Communications.*
All contacts, messages, and presentations you originate to a person in your database. Each time you send a mailing, for example, your records should show what was sent (standard letter, personal note, brochure,

and so on), when, and to whom. If you use telephone calls to qualify or activate, record details of each call. Conferences or talks from which you received Qualified Prospects should be treated the same way.

3. *Transactions.*

All actions taken by someone in your database: request for information, free sample, purchase, complaint, and so on.

Storing means you have to buy a computer. I'll break it to you gently: *You don't have the proverbial snowball's chance of keeping track of all these records without computer support.* What's more, without computer support, every letter you send out has to be done by hand—reasonable for 10 letters, possible for 30, unthinkable for 500.

Accessing means you have to decide what reports you will need (start with the three rates, above) and to what use you will put the information gathered (to drive your Customer Creation System, for example).

That's really all there is to it, except for fleshing out the details. Let's finish this chapter by designing *your* Marketing Information System.

_____ **WORKWORK: YOUR MARKETING INFORMATION SYSTEM** _____

For your Marketing Information System, besides a computer, you need:

- Forms to keep track of individuals.

- Forms to keep track of communications and transactions.

- Computer software to keep track of what has happened and what needs to happen, and to drive your Customer Creation System.

Let's look at them one at a time.

Forms for Individuals

You will need a Basic Customer Information form to keep track of each individual and how to communicate with him or her. In addition, you will probably need some other forms to record important things you find out over time—height, weight, diagnosis, hat size, tax bracket, or whatever other information you need, to give the individual the best possible service. Many people make the mistake of trying to cram all of this onto one form. Trust me: You will be happier with several small forms than with one big one, and your computer will be a *lot* happier if you don't stick everything onto one form.

Grab some paper and let's draw up your Basic Customer Information form. (You might also grab a good example, like a Federal Express airbill; no sense in reinventing the wheel.) Start with the five essentials:

1. *Customer's name.* First, middle, last; or last, first, middle; whichever you prefer is fine. Make sure you leave enough space for long names like Kristin Schmichealklein, or the increasingly common hyphenated last names like Levin-Koopman. If your customers have Hispanic or Oriental names, make sure you learn which of their names they consider their last name.

2. *Title.* Never leave it off, if you know it.

3. *Organization.* Leave two or even three lines, to identify the department or the division of the organization the person works for. Leave these off, and your mail may never make it through that organization's internal mail system.

4. *Address.* Street number and name, suite or apartment number, box number, city, state, zip code.

5. Telephone number, area code first; if available, fax number, electronic mail codes, telex number, and assistant's name and extension.

Finally, make a space for the unique customer identification number by which you will uniquely identify this individual. This is important, because it quickly gets awkward to keep copying and recopying the same name-address-etc. information; it's also guaranteed to introduce errors. So it is standard practice to assign each person a unique identification number when you first start keeping track of them. The ID number tags for recall each communication or transaction with that particular person.

(An easy method of creating unique ID numbers is to use a nine-digit number, made up of two-digit units for month, date, and year, followed by a three-digit sequence number for that day. In other words, on January 25, 1990, the sixteenth *new* person you sent a letter to got ID number 01-25-90-016, or 012590016. That person will have that same ID number on your database forever. (This coding also gives you a way of telling at a glance when you first made the contact with this person.) Needless to say, your ID numbers are for internal use only; unless you are in heavy-duty direct-mail marketing, your customers should *never* see themselves referred to by number.)

And that's all, for the basic form. If you think of other important information you absolutely must store, make another form for it and connect it to your basic form by means of the customer ID number. Your computer will be able to find the information when you need it: that sort of thing is easy for computers.

(If you don't have a computer yet, make up one neat copy of your form on paper or on a $3 \times 5''$ card and then Xerox it. Keeping track of your customers by hand is better than not keeping track of them at all, and I can't think of a quicker way to convince yourself that you really have to get that computer.)

Forms for Communications and Transactions

Remember the three rates: qualification, activation, conversion? Remember how important they are? To figure out those rates, you have to keep records of every communication and transaction you have with your market. Picky, unnecessary work? No; simple and easy, once you get organized for it.

You need to keep records of four categories of communications.

1. *Public presentations.*

You describe your services in a talk to the local Kiwanis. The group provides you with a list of people in attendance, along with their business addresses and phone numbers. You consider each of these individuals to be in your target market, so you want to record them as Prospects. When you return to your office, you create two records for each person in attendance: the Basic Customer Information form you designed above, and the following communication record:

4-25-90
Presentation: "How to Improve Your Profit Picture"
Central City Kiwanis
042590001

Four facts are recorded here: the person referred to by customer number 042590001 heard you give that talk to the Central City Kiwanis on April 25, 1990. Over time, those entries will help you find out exactly how much future business you can expect from giving this talk to similar groups. (The talk may be a waste of time or it may be a gold mine. You can't *know* unless you keep track.)

And actually it's even easier than it looks; you can set up your software so that the communication record is generated automatically.

2. *Mailings.*

For every piece of mail (or fax or Fed Ex or whatever) some record must be created saying when, what, and to whom. This example is typical:

1-22-90
Brochure A plus cover letter 1
012290045

If you have been careful and lucky in your choice of software, you can create this record automatically while you are telling your computer to print the cover letter.

3. *Proposals.*
This is a special category of mailings. In addition to when, what, and to whom, other information pertinent to your business should be stored.

4. *Sales calls.*
Who? When? What offer did you make?

Before we go on, take a few minutes and draw up rough forms for keeping track of all the communications you send to your market. These forms will guide you (or your consultant) in setting up your computer to keep track for you.

Transactions are actions taken by the prospect or customer. They also fall into four categories:

1. *Requests for information.*
When someone calls or writes for information about your services, obviously you want to be able to fill out a Basic Customer Information form. You also want to record the transaction, including who, when, and how they heard about you:

2-17-90
021790003
Request for schedule
Yellow Pages (or "Free Press Ad" or "Flyer" or "Jane Lippitt")

2. *Accepting a trial offer.*
Who, when, which offer, where they saw it.

3. *Sales.*
This is the one transaction for which almost everybody already has good forms. Be sure to add the customer identification number, and store these records permanently on your computer. Don't throw them away like Red did; you're throwing away uncut diamonds.

4. *Complaints and kudos.*
In Chinese, the word *crisis* is represented by a combination of two symbols: danger and opportunity. In a service business, the same two symbols could represent *complaint*. The danger is that a dissatisfied customer will not remain a customer and can be counted on to tell other people about the dissatisfaction. The opportunity is twofold: (1) A way to bring

your services even further into alignment with your market may be revealed, and (2) You have the opportunity to make this customer a customer for life, by your response to their complaint. So keep track of complaints: who, when, what complaint, what response. And while you're at it, keep track of those occasional "pats on the back" people send you. They make great copy for ads and mailers.

Before we go on, take a few minutes and rough out forms for keeping track of your transactions—*all* of them.

Software and Hardware

Deciding which software and hardware to purchase for your Marketing Information System is not easy. Unless you are very confident of your ability to navigate the waters of RAM and megabytes, you will be well advised to seek out a good consultant before making these decisions. The best consultants are often people who have had practical experience in using computers in their service business. Call some of the local "users' groups" and explain what you're after. They can usually help you connect with someone who can advise you.

Before you look at specific packages, it is absolutely imperative that you know what you want the system to do for you. You may have specific needs stemming from the nature of your business; if so, you probably already have a good idea of what they are. Be sure to add them into your "shopping list." For your marketing machine, these are the features you need:

1. *A database program that will enable you to store and access your customer records easily.*

You need a "relational database." You could start with a less powerful program, but you will regret it soon when you discover it won't do what you want.

2. *Forms for entering all your records.*

You should be able to quickly and easily tell your system that you want to enter a new Basic Customer Information form, or a particular kind of communication record, or whatever, and it should instantly give you the correct fill-in-the-blank master form that is easy to follow and foolproof. Your forms will either be pre-made, if you get a customized system, or very easy for you to make up yourself without any programming at all.

3. *A word-processing program that will enable you to make up standard letters that can be customized automatically.*

This program must work seamlessly with your database. Here's a critical test: You want to tell your system to send a personalized copy of a standard letter to a certain group of prospects. With one or two very obvious instructions you should be able to say: "Send this letter to these people." In response, the computer would then print out a copy of the letter for each person, enter each name and address in the right places, and address the envelopes (or mailing labels) for you. All you should have to do is sign, fold, seal, and stamp. Do not settle for a system that requires you to tell the computer about the letters one at a time, or to create some file from the database that would then be transferred to the word-processing program. The system should do all this for you.

4. *Reports that will tell you how you are doing.*

Your system must be able to handle simple percentages and arithmetic; nothing fancy, but you do need those rates and results, and you don't want to do them by hand. Your database program should enable you to ask for and get essentially whatever report you need without having to do any programming to get it.

Do not let someone talk you into a system that does not meet every one of these specifications. You will wind up with a two-legged tripod.

Two key decisions remain: (1) Do you get a custom system, or buy off-the-shelf? (2) What kind of computer do you get? These are hard decisions, and any specific advice I could offer would be badly outdated before you read it, but here are some pointers.

The "custom vs. off-the-shelf" trade-off is essentially a matter of what you value most. A custom system will save you time and frustration; you will get what you need quicker, with less effort, and with more support. However, it will cost you quite a bit more money, and you can count on an ongoing outlay for future revisions, trouble-shooting, and so on.

Off-the-shelf software is a lot less expensive and, if it meets all the specifications mentioned above, gives you a great deal of flexibility. Its drawback is the very significant amount of time you will spend getting it up and running, along with the wear and tear on your nerves when the blasted system starts doing crazy things.

Which to choose? If you are already very busy, and have access to the money, and never *did* figure out how to get your VCR to record the opera while you watched the NBA playoffs, consider the custom solution. If you are operating on a shoestring, and don't mind taking the time to learn, and *hate* taking anyone else's word for how gadgets work, go for the best off-the-shelf package you can get.

Which computer should you buy? The big decision is choosing between the Macintosh world and the PC world. Macintosh is much easier to learn, a lot more fun to use, and it has plenty of good, useful software available. If your business involves lots of newsletters or graphics, Macintosh is the definite favorite. But Macintosh is much more expensive for what you get. Again, is it really cheaper to buy a less expensive system that you won't or can't use?

PCs (IBM and all the rest) give you much more bang for the buck. If you need massive amounts of storage for your records, or if your business involves a great deal of number-crunching, the PC world offers great value. If you decide to buy a PC, look at the AT or 286 models for the best price-to-performance ratio.

If you are essentially a novice in computing, get a Macintosh if you can possibly afford it. People actually use their Macs—that's the final test. (This is not personal bias; I happen to use a PC.)

Either way, be sure to get the largest hard-disk drive you can afford. You're going to fill it up more rapidly than you imagine possible, with a database that will drive your business to marketing success.

10 | Packaging for Maximum Benefit

What to Do Before *You Print the Brochures*

One thing about Roger: he knows and appreciates good food. The new restaurant he had invited me to was a real winner. I hated to ruin the meal for him, but it couldn't be helped. After all, that's what he was paying me for.

"My marketing has really improved these last few months, Tony, and so have the results. It feels to me like I'm almost where I want to be with marketing. Almost, but not quite. It's still harder than it ought to be to get that final OK to start work. What's missing?"

I took another bite of the Sacher torte before replying. "Sounds like we need to work on your packaging, Roger."

Roger looked as if he had bit into a sour cherry. He put his fork down and looked at me. Finally, he sighed. "OK. You know I have a real problem with that. Every client of mine has a different situation; I have a serious ethical problem with people who come in with canned programs that are supposed to work for everybody. They don't work, and I won't do business that way."

"Commendable, Roger. That's part of what makes you such an outstanding professional. Your services are much too complex to be put into a canned program. I agree."

Roger nodded warily. "So?"

"So we still need to work on your packaging. Look, Roger. You are trying to sell a benefit and a relationship. That's fine, except for one thing: People don't ordinarily *buy* benefits and relationships. They buy packages of services. They buy packages that look to them like the sort of thing that will deliver the benefit they are after. And they buy *your* package mostly because of the relationship you have created with them.

"We need to work on your packaging. And we will start by changing your idea of what packaging is."

Roger chuckled. "By now I should have guessed. So tell me, what *is* packaging?"

What Is Packaging?

Packaging is essential if you hope to market effectively. Let me repeat what I told Roger: Ordinarily people don't buy relationships or even benefits:

People buy packages.

So how's *your* packaging?

Packaging is a stumbling block for most service providers. Some, like Roger, find the whole notion of packaging distasteful. They object to the glitz and flash they associate with packaging; in their minds packaging is the triumph of style over substance. Even people who don't share Roger's objections to packaging in principle find packaging difficult in practice.

You may already be eager to come up with a great package, but do you know how? This chapter will help you see how, in detail. Along the way we will clear up some very common misconceptions about packaging and its role in service marketing.

The first problem we have to deal with is the word itself: *packaging*. We read about packaging every day; it's one of those hot words that the media love. At least four distinct meanings of the word packaging are in common use; three of them will lead you in the wrong direction in your marketing. Let's sort them out.

Putting the Box Around the Cereal

The most common notion of packaging comes from service providers' first cousin, consumer products marketing. The basic notion is this: You have a perfectly good and useful product—say, corn flakes—that you want to sell to consumers. You could put your product in a big barrel labeled Corn Flakes, alongside a scoop and a scale, and invite consumers to help themselves. Bulk food stores in fact do that, and it's a perfectly reasonable way to sell cereal. But you won't sell many corn flakes that way. If you want to sell a product to the mass market you have to put it in a convenient, attractive package. You have to take those corn flakes and wrap a box around them. The better the box, the better the sales.

This is *not* the kind of packaging you need for your services. The problem is obvious when you think about it. Products are tangible *things*. You can put your hands on them, so you can put them in a box or a blisterpack or a four-ounce spray bottle, or color them purple, if that's what will attract the attention and interest of your customers. Services are intangible; you can't put your hands on them so you can't put them into anything.

Don't get me wrong. I'm not saying you don't need attractive, well-designed materials. You do. I'm just pointing out something very obvious:

Services don't come in boxes.

Packaging the Candidate

A rather cynical image of packaging has emerged from politics in the TV age. The basic approach in modern election campaigns is that candidates have to be sold, like beer or cigarettes. Image is the *only* thing that counts. People get their information from TV, and TV deals in quick, vivid images and "sound bites." It's not what is said, but how it looks and sounds in a 20-second film clip that wins an election.

Accordingly, modern would-be kingmakers look for raw material around which to create a "package." They start with a candidate who looks and sounds like a film star or a TV newscaster, make sure he or she has no terrible secrets that would interest journalists, and then add ingredients: one exemplary spouse, good-looking kids, and a dog; a few memberships and credentials, for show; and one or two "positions" that are pretested in the polls and play well in sound bites. Keep crafting the positions to fit the polls, avoid saying or doing anything that could offend the public or might sound bad in the opposition's commercials, and— who knows?—you might even become Vice President.

Is this how politics really works these days? Beats me. For all I know you can fool enough of the people all the time that the rest can be safely ignored. But I do know this for a fact:

You can't fool your customers.

More accurately, you *can* fool your customers but you won't fool them for long and they won't remain your customers. People don't have to rely on mere image to make buying decisions; they expect and get a great deal of solid information before they hire you. And once they have hired you, you had better deliver the benefit you promised or you won't be able to "maintain the relationship of customer."

The TV-commercial kind of packaging is the Mercenary position again: "Give them what they think they want." This is *not* the kind of packaging you need to do for your services.

"Available Now in Book, Videotape, CD, and Comic Book Versions"

Modern media businesses practice a particularly intricate form of "packaging." For example, Jeff is pretty handy around the house, and he has collected some nifty tips on how to get things done. He approaches an agent with an idea for a book. Fortune smiles on Jeff; domesticity and getting your house in order are the hot new emerging topics in the national consciousness, and he has a great agent. In short order Jeff has his book contract, with serial rights presold to several magazines; he also has a syndicated column, a lecture tour, a weekly spot on cable, and Jeff Handyman's Workout Video ("Aerobic Sawing!"). Jeff has been "packaged."

This kind of packaging looks for as many different bottles as possible into which to pour the same wine. Nothing wrong with that: it's "nice work if you can get it." The material in this book, for example, was originally offered in the form of workshops and year-long courses; it has also been adapted as a Computer-based Coach for personal computers (see the Resources section at the end of the book). Different forms for different purposes.

But this kind of packaging, if it is appropriate for you at all, is a second step. First you have to package the primary form in which your services will be delivered. Once you have succeeded at marketing that, you might begin to think about creating new packages. (Chapter 16 will give you some help.)

Don't try to do two things at once. Package and market your services in one form first. Leave the Workout Video for later.

The "Tahiti Getaway"

If you're not wrapping a box around your services, manufacturing an image, or becoming a multimedia phenomenon, how *do* you package your services? I recommend you think like a good travel agent and create a Tahiti Getaway.

This is my favorite image of the ideal service package. When the world is too much with you late and soon, you visit your friendly travel agent who, after some sympathetic sizing-up, offers you the Tahiti Getaway! "Two weeks of total relaxation in the tropical paradise! No phones, no kids, no pressure to get anything done. The climate is ideal and the people are friendly. The package is all-inclusive for airfare, hotel, and all taxes, visas, and fees. You can choose from among these five hotels; the two listed with three stars are available for an additional charge of $500. Would you like meals included as well? I thought not, you seem like the sort who likes to pick his own restaurants. The hotel is right on the beach; you can swim, sail, surf . . . here's a list of all the activities available. Or you can just sit under a palm tree and do nothing at all. As optional extras you can include a side jaunt to Bora Bora, or a two-day stopover in Hawaii. You can leave any Wednesday; we will pick you up at your home, and take care of your luggage from door to door. The total cost comes to $3500 coach, $4200 first class, and of course we can charge it to your MasterCard. When would you like to leave?"

Now *that's* a package!

We will examine the Tahiti Getaway in detail through the remainder of this chapter. We will look at what makes it such a powerful package; more importantly, we will look at what *you* can do to make your service package as powerful as the Tahiti Getaway.

Anchoring in the Core Benefit

Designing a package of services is an advanced exercise in alignment. You have already defined your mission; that's the starting place. You have also defined your target market segment. Now let's take it a step further, and look at your target market's circumstances. We are looking for the Core Benefit of your services.

A Core Benefit is a further refinement and elaboration of your mission. It is your mission as seen through the eyes of a particular group of people in your target segment, all of whom share some common, definable circumstances. (In more technical terms, they define a subsegment within your target segment.) Most importantly, a Core Benefit defines a package of services.

Always package your services to deliver a specific Core Benefit.

My travel agent, Cooper Travel, has a clear mission: to support travelers in getting exactly the travel arrangements that suit them best. They have cleverly set up a division, with separate phones and personnel, to support a specific subsegment that has common, definable circumstances: people traveling on business. From the point of view of business travelers, Cooper Travel's mission boils down to one simple thing: trouble-free travel arrangements. Business travelers, above all, want to be able to tell somebody quickly where and when they want to travel, and then be certain that the arrangements will be made exactly as they want them, with no further effort on their part. That's the Core Benefit for the business traveler.

To deliver this Core Benefit, Cooper Travel has created a superb package of services which they vigorously market to the business community. Business travelers are given a separate phone number that automatically connects them to the "Executive Accounts" agents; they almost never are put on hold to wait for "the next available agent." As soon as callers give their name, the agent brings up their file on a computer screen. When they say, "About that Denver flight . . .," the agent can say, "The one on September 21?" The file contains all the relevant information: airline, hotel and rental car preferences, seating and special meal preferences, frequent flyer numbers, and so on; all those details are handled automatically. The agent efficiently locates the flights that best suit the travelers' circumstances, makes and confirms the arrangements, double-checks them on the spot, and has the tickets delivered to the travelers' office. Cooper even makes sure its customers get the right frequent flyer credit. Most importantly, this is all done courteously and quickly, and they almost never foul up. (They have a 24-hour 800 number for when things do go wrong.)

They also offer that Tahiti Getaway. Cooper Travel's mission, remember, is to support travelers in getting exactly the travel arrangements they want. Look at that from the point of view of another group: businesspeople who want a totally relaxing, change-of-pace vacation. Same segment, but different circumstances; and therefore a different Core Benefit around which the package is created. What is that Core Benefit? Exactly what they tell you in the first sentence of the brochure: "Two weeks of total relaxation in the tropical paradise."

Once you have defined the Core Benefit of your services to a specific group, you can create a terrific package of services to deliver that benefit.

_____ **WORKWORK: CORE BENEFITS** _____

Let's pin down the Core Benefits of your services. Notice I said benefits. Unless your situation is very unusual, you will find that you must package your services in more than one way to best serve your target market. Within your target segment, you will find subsegments that have common circumstances. These circumstances create the need for different services to fulfill your mission. Figure 3 illustrates this.

Let's reinforce this with a few examples. Chris consults to complex organizations. Her mission is "to help my clients create a shared image of the future that will enable them to thrive." After a good deal of reflection and hard work, Chris realized that her clients fall into three basic subsegments defined by their circumstances:

1. Organizations facing installation of a complex new technology or system with which they have little experience;

2. Organizations that have gone through major "cultural change" as the result of merger, acquisition, or the like;

3. Organizations wishing to improve performance by increasing involvement and participation at all levels.

Chris helps the organizations in each subsegment to "create a shared image of the future that will enable them to thrive," but few of her clients would immediately recognize the full value of her services as stated in her

X

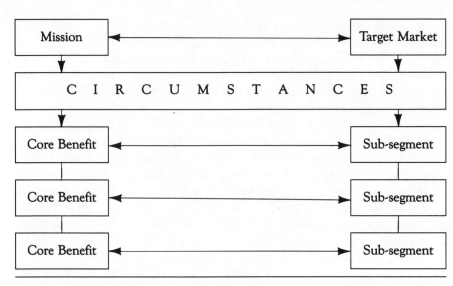

Figure 3

mission statement. Each subsegment sees the Core Benefit of her services according to its circumstances:

1. Successful implementation and acceptance of the system with minimal disruption of operations.

2. Creation of a new, integrated "culture" that supports the success of the new organization.

3. Having an employee involvement program that actually works.

One mission, three circumstances; three quite distinct Core Benefits. Not surprisingly, three quite distinct service packages as well.

Remember Dr. John, the chiropractor? His patients divide into two groups: those who have had a recent fall or other traumatic injury, and those who simply experience pain or discomfort. Both groups want to lead a life free of pain and discomfort, which matches Dr. John's mission. His mission statement works quite well as a Core Benefit for the second group, but the first group is looking for successful treatment of their injury; that's their Core Benefit. The two different groups, accordingly, require different service packages built around their Core Benefit.

One more example: The Putman Marketing Group. My mission is to help the owners of small-to-medium size service businesses market their services effectively. My customers fall into three basic subsegments:

1. People who really do not understand how to market their services effectively (the large majority);

2. People who see the need to develop a high-performance marketing organization;

3. People who need some great marketing *now* (a small but sometimes desperate minority; see Chapter 15 if this describes you).

My mission looks different to each of these groups. The Core Benefit each sees is:

1. Becoming an effective marketer of your services.

2. Creating a high-performance marketing organization.

3. Putting in place a marketing program that gets the customers needed for survival.

Need I say that the service packages that deliver these Core Benefits are quite different?

Got the picture? Your turn now. I know from experience that the Core Benefit search may not be easy for you. It's like solving a puzzle or a riddle; once you see it, it's obvious, but it can be extremely frustrating while you're still working on it. *Hang in there.* The result is worth the effort.

Start by listing your customers. Include all of them if you only have a few customers at a time, or the last six-months' worth if you usually have several new customers a week. Look at the list and reflect on exactly what their situation was when they first became your customers, and what you did for them. Don't try to define this in exact words yet; just get a sense of it.

Now start making connections. Without being too analytical, notice the customers that seem somehow similar. Maybe they were in similar situations when they first became customers, or perhaps what you did for them was similar. "Let's see, this one is sort of like that one, but definitely not like this other one, it's more like . . . ." Put the same notation (a number or letter, say) beside the customers that seem somehow similar; do this until each customer has a notation beside it.

How many different symbols did you use? If you used more than six, do you really have that many separate service packages? Can you see ways of clustering the clusters to bring the total down to three, four, or five?

Pick one grouping of customers. Back off a bit and ask yourself. What do these customers really have in common? What common description of their circumstances can you give? Jot down whatever comes to mind. If it forms a clear pattern, fine; if not, just keep jotting down the obvious similarities until the pattern clicks into place for you.

Now look at the next group of customers. What circumstances do they have in common? Describe their circumstances until you have a pattern for them. Do this for each grouping of customers. If you are having difficulty seeing the pattern for some of the groups, show what you have to a friend. Talking it out may help you see the obvious.

You now have identified a number of subsegments within your customer base. Do you intend to market to all of these in the future? In other words, do all of these fall within your target market? Prune the list until only subsegments of your target market remain.

Here comes the payoff. For each subsegment in turn, ask yourself: "What does my mission look like in their eyes? I am in business to make a specific beneficial difference in the lives of my customers. What does that beneficial difference look like to this subsegment? What words would they use to describe it?" Jot down your answer: it is the Core Benefit of your services to that group of customers. That's what you will use to anchor your packaging.

If you find it difficult to state clearly the Core Benefit for a group, ask some of its members for help. What do they see as the primary benefit of your services? Listen carefully and wait for the Aha!

Packaging for Maximum Benefit

Now that you know the Core Benefit of your services, you can proceed directly to build a service package around it. The principle is simple: Create a package that includes *everything* your customer will need in order to experience the Core Benefit of your services. Don't leave anything out. Allow for individual preference and choice as much as possible, and if there are some nice options ("nice to have," not "need to have") put them in as options. At each step along the way, make sure the relationship is clear between each piece of the package and the overall Core Benefit. The customer's reaction to each piece should be, "Yes, I can see how that is needed." Figure 4 illustrates how packaging works.

Take the Tahiti Getaway as an example: "Two weeks of total relaxation in the tropical paradise." What package of services is needed to produce that benefit? Obviously you have to get there and you have to have a place to stay, so "air transportation" and "hotel accommodations" are the first two pieces. Once you're there, you have to eat, so "food" is the third piece. What will you do once you're there? "Activities" is the fourth piece. Nobody wants to hassle with foreign regulations and taxes on a relaxing vacation, so "fees and visas" are piece five. The relaxation should start as soon as you step out of your door, so "luggage and limo" are the sixth piece, a nice touch. Since you've gone so far, you might want to drop in on some sights in that part of the world, so piece

Service Package

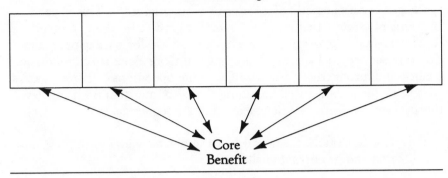

Figure 4

seven is "optional side jaunts." Finally, you have to have some way of paying for all this, so "pricing and terms" are piece eight.

Eight pieces, one comprehensive package: all oriented toward the Core Benefit, "Two weeks of total relaxation in the tropical paradise."

Notice that some pieces leave little room for choice. The travel agent has to make a deal for a block of seats, so "air transportation" is fixed. Your only real choice is which Wednesday you want to leave. "Fees and visas" and "luggage and limos" are also fixed. "Pricing and terms" are fixed, in the sense that they are determined by the other choices the customer makes.

But different people have different preferences for food and hotel accommodations, so the travel agent offers options in how these are handled. Side jaunts and activities are classic "cafeteria" pieces: here are the possibilities, take your pick. Again, the principle is: Include everything that is needed, plus all the options you can reasonably handle.

_____ WORKWORK: ASSEMBLING THE PACKAGE _____

Your turn again. From your list of customers, pick one group, with its Core Benefit, for which you want to create a package of services. Ask yourself: What services are essential, in order to deliver that Core Benefit? Jot them down as they occur to you. Don't overlook the very obvious.

Review the list and ask yourself "what other services do I or might I offer as part of this package in special circumstances?" (What are those circumstances?) "What pieces might I offer as nice to have options?" Jot these down too.

Is your list complete? Is this really all it takes to get that Core Benefit? Were any optional pieces overlooked? Jot down what is needed to complete the list.

Having trouble? Some examples may be helpful. Sometimes the "package" consists mostly of a series of sequential steps. This is particularly true of services that require a complex process for their completion. Roger, for example, once he got over his distaste for packaging, realized that one service package he offers has the Core Benefit of "increasing quality and productivity in manufacturing operations." (Roger works with some *huge* companies, including the auto industry.) As he analyzed this package, he identified five pieces that are sequential steps:

1. Create a public "databank" of the diverse views of the organization and its current challenges.

2. Create a shared image of the desired future for the organization.

3. Identify and prioritize barriers to achieving the desired future.

4. Organize and support "work teams" to eliminate these barriers.

5. Implement these "work team" methods as standard practice throughout the organization.

Roger found that these five sequential services were both necessary to accomplish the Core Benefit and, even better, were credible with his prospective customers ("Yes, I can see how you would need to do each of those to improve quality and productivity."). He also found that he had to break each of these steps down into substeps in order to explain the package adequately; by the time he had finished, he really needed Chapter 11's material on presentation. (You probably will too.)

As another illustration, my "High Performance Marketing Group" package was designed to support owners of service businesses in creating a high performance marketing organization (package names don't have to be clever if they are well-aligned). It consists of the following pieces: attendance at my two-day workshop on "Marketing Your Services" and then at 20 half-day sessions (one every two weeks for 10 months) with me and five other participants. Each half-day session is divided into half free-form consultation "in-the-round," and half planned "process" that forces participants to strengthen one building block of their marketing organization. Participants are also entitled to telephone consultation between sessions (weekdays, between 5:00 and 6:00 P.M., first come, first served). All this for a package price designed to represent excellent value. (If you *work* your way through this book, you will get the same benefit, minus those bits of fine-tuning that only individual consultation can give. The Computer-based Coach closes even most of that gap.)

Getting the hang of this packaging stuff? Look at your list again and ask yourself: Which of these pieces are required? Which are optional, depending on circumstances? What are the circumstances? Which allow a range of choices by the customer, and what are the choices available? Write down a description of the package, defining its pieces and options.

One last step: as you look at each piece of your package, refer back to the Core Benefit. Is the relation between each piece and the Core Benefit obvious? Would it be obvious to the customer? If not, what do you need to do to make it obvious?

Filling in the Gaps

Now you need to field-test your packaging. Use the classic test of a marketing program: when you show qualified prospects the package, do they buy? If not, why not? What do you have to add or elaborate to get them to buy? In "sales talk," what are their objections and how do you turn the objections into closings? Good salespeople love objections because they give an immediate opportunity to close the sale. "It's great but I hate the color." "I agree, it's a terrible color for you. We also have it in blue, red, or purple. Which do you prefer?" Marketing people (that's you) have to make sure that the salespeople (also you) have what they need to respond to objections. In other words, this is where you fill in the gaps of your package.

You may be missing an entire piece of your package. Listen carefully to people's objections: they will tell you what's missing, although not always directly. More likely, the gaps will be found in one of three places: pricing and terms, scheduling, or features. Let's take a quick look at each.

Pricing and Terms

Follow these two simple principles:

1. Offer a package price.

2. Work with the customers to help them afford it.

It's surprising how many service professionals violate the first principle. Their reasoning goes something like this: "Look, I don't know for sure how long this job will take. I can give you an estimate, but you can never be sure _____" (fill in the blank for your particular type of service: "what unforeseen problems will come up"; "how well they will respond to treatment"; "what the weather will be like"; "how long it will take to . . .").

"I want to be paid for my work; if I give a package price, I will wind up having to work for nothing to complete some jobs, and that's bad business." Is this your basic position? Reasonable, but now look at it from the customer's point of view: "Your services look good to me, but how much is all this going to cost me in fact? No offense; you seem like a terrific person. But you're asking me to sign a blank check when you tell me you will bill me for services as we go. Just tell me what this is going to cost."

Two different points of view; both reasonable; but in this case your reasonable position may put you out of business. Wake up! That's your customer talking to you, friend, and you're not listening. For proper alignment:

When you and your market see things differently, *you* change.

Without alignment, you can't market successfully, and alignment in this case means acknowledging and acting on a simple fact: Customers want a package price.

Some apparent exceptions to this rule actually show how universal it is. The practice in the traditional "professions"—physician, lawyer, accountant, to take three obvious examples—has been to charge on a "fee for service" basis. You pay for each office visit to your cardiologist and for each "procedure"; you pay your lawyer for each minute of her time; and so on. This has been going on for generations. Doesn't that disprove the rule?

No. These professions not only have been horrible marketers, they actually had professional canons that prohibited marketing (a Supreme Court ruling in 1978 struck down these canons as being in restraint of trade). They were able to stick to their "no packaging" guns because they had a monopoly on a necessary service. As soon as the restrictions on marketing were lifted (and the professions began to be overstocked; what are we going to *do* with all these lawyers?) the "no packaging" stance went out the window. Today you can get a package price on a will, a divorce, even a kidney transplant. And if your accountant doesn't quote you a package price for doing your business taxes, consider finding another accountant.

So sharpen up your pencil, keep better records so you can progressively improve the estimates on which you base your pricing, take a deep breath, and come up with a firm price for your package. A *firm* price.

Now, however, you may need the second principle: helping people to afford your services. It may be straightforward—it's a rare dentist these days who doesn't take MasterCard or Visa. Most body shops can recommend a bank that will lend you the money to get a new fender for your Corvette. My son's orthodontist even provides a coupon book, spreading the financial damage over the full 18 months of the treatment.

But terms may be a little more complex, and you need to be ready to work with your customers a little. Dr. John, for example, found it frequently difficult to get patients to complete the course of treatment he prescribed for them. The problem was not with Dr. John's treatments; the problem was a gap in his packaging. For many patients, insurance covered some but not all of the necessary treatments. When the insurance coverage stopped, the patients were suddenly faced with paying for treatments that had to that point been "free"; many said, "The original problem is taken care of. I really can do without this last stabilization bit."

Dr. John had complacently gone along with the prevailing practice in medicine ("How much will this cost?" "Don't worry, it's covered by insurance.") and was now paying the price. His first step was to stop his "come in for a treatment and pay as you go" relationship; now every patient has a specific treatment package, including a package price. His next step was to recognize the psychological hump the sudden end of insurance payments created, and to work around it. His staff now finds out what insurance the patient has; they have made it their business to know exactly how much each insurer will pay for chiropractic treatment, and for how long. The staff deducts the total insurance payment from the package price, divides what's left by the total number of months in the treatment plan, and sets up a monthly coupon book spreading the payments over the time of treatment. Legally, in effect, the patient is prepaying for the treatments received after the insurance runs out; the patient sees it as simply paying a certain amount each month for a badly needed service.

Listen to your customers. If they seem to be telling you, "I don't see how I can afford all this," make it your responsibility to help them afford it. Make that part of your service package.

Scheduling

Ann Arbor is a brutal town for dentists. It has one of the best dental schools in the country, and it's a pretty nice place to live, so the supply of really fine dentists far outstrips the demand. Starting a dental practice there is very difficult.

My dentist succeeded at it, though. He filled a gap in packaging that most of his competitors hadn't even noticed—scheduling. Gordon does something startlingly different: his office hours are from 5:00 P.M. to 11:00 P.M. You can get your teeth cleaned and fixed without missing work! In a town full of overworked professionals, that's like a license to print money.

I asked Gordon how he came up with this brilliant breakthrough in packaging. He laughed. "I wish I could take credit for marketing smarts, Tony. Actually, I backed into it through necessity. When I first started here, I couldn't afford my own office, so I worked out a deal with another dentist to use his facilities when he wasn't using them. He worked standard hours, so I couldn't start until 5:00 P.M. I'm a night person anyway, so I didn't mind the hours. Turns out a lot of people wanted a good dentist who would see them in the evenings."

Scheduling can be a matter of "when." Domino's and Lenscrafters made it a matter of "how quickly." Both these companies spotted the same hole in the service package: people want their goods quickly. Domino's Pizza offered "Delivery in thirty minutes or it's free" (they've since backed down from that a bit). Lenscrafters offered to make "glasses in an hour while you wait," and since they are located in malls, waiting an hour is no big hardship. If customers have to wait too long for something, they might decide not to buy it.

The last part of scheduling is "where." Too busy (or lazy) to go to the gym? Fine—we'll send a "personal trainer" to your house to make sure you get your workout. Bored with the idea of an investment seminar in Chicago? No problem—how about an investment seminar on a cruise ship in the Caribbean? If you don't want to come to our place, why don't we come to yours?

Features

Salespeople love features. In a classic sales closing, the prospect voices an objection: "I like it, but . . . ." The salesperson smiles and responds by pointing out a feature of the package which handles the objection, then goes on to ask for the order. This is called "closing on the objection" and it's the salespersons' bread and butter. The more features you have, the more objections you can close on. (If you like selling you already know this; if you don't, you probably couldn't close on an objection if your life depended on it. Don't worry. You can succeed without it.)

Marketing people need to provide features, but which ones? Why, the ones that handle the objections, of course! When an objection points out a gap in your packaging, you should adjust your packaging accordingly. In other words:

> If you find a gap in your packaging, fill it with a feature.

A feature is *anything* about your services that can be made visible to the prospect. As we will see in the next chapter, the more concrete and tangible you can make the feature, the better. For now, just realize that you need to listen carefully to your prospective customers' objections in order to identify the features they want.

- "I hate this software! Every time my fingers slip it takes forever to get back to where I made the mistake!" A classic objection, for which a classic feature was invented: the "Undo" key that lets you take back your last move.

- "I'm not sure Rolfing is really for me." A rephrased classic objection—"I can't be sure until I've tried it"—for which the classic feature is the "no-risk first session": "If the first session doesn't convince you, there's no charge."

- "I'm not sure these group sessions will give me enough personal attention." "No problem. The package includes free telephone consultation any weekday between the hours of 5:00 P.M. and 6:00 P.M. Plenty of time to get the individual attention you need."

- "The paperwork is such a hassle." "We fill out and file all the necessary forms for you."

- "I'm not sure which session to attend." "We allow you to enroll in a session and transfer to a later session at no charge."

- "I'm not convinced I really need the second day of this workshop." "Then sign up for the first day. You can apply the cost to a two-day registration at the end of the first day if you change your mind."

―――― **WORKWORK: YOUR COMPLETE PACKAGE** ――――

Let's round out your packaging. Look over everything you have included in your package, leaving the options aside for the moment. How much are you going to charge for that package? *Firm price*, not an estimate.

If your package price includes phrases like "per hour" or "per day" you have missed the point. Those are blank checks issued to you by the customer. Figure it out. How many hours will it take? How many days? You say the best you can do is a range, "between 50 and 70 hours?" Fine. Then pick a conservative midpoint—say, 62 hours—as the standard you use to come up with the package price. (Keep these estimates to yourself. The upside of offering a package price is that it's really nobody else's business how you got to that figure. They know up front what they will have to pay, and on what schedule. That's all they need to know.)

That's your basic package. Now consider the options. Make them "no-extra-cost" options if you possibly can. If not, how much will each cost?

Now look at payment terms:

- Is cash in advance realistic for these customers?

- Will they be paying it out of their own pockets, or will someone else be paying all or part of the cost?

- Will they need help with figuring out a payment schedule? With filling out and filing forms? With arranging financing?

Jot down any payment terms you need to add to your package. Then move on to scheduling:

- When will your services be delivered?

- Is this when the customers most prefer to get them?

- If not, how can you deliver the services when the customers want them?

- How quickly do the customers want response? Will they be willing to pay a little extra for the speed? Can you gear up to meet their preferences?

- Where will the services be delivered? Can you offer options in this? Where do your customers really want the services delivered?

Again, jot down any scheduling items for your package. Finally, work on features:

- What common objections to buying your package do you encounter?

- What features can you add or emphasize that overcome these objections?

- What features can you use to ask for the order? ("You can leave for Tahiti any Wednesday. What date looks best to you?")

Jot down the features you need to round out your packaging.

You now have pieces and gap-fillers. This is your complete package, your Tahiti Getaway, to be sold to your Qualified Prospects with some confidence they will buy.

The Name's the Thing . . .

You need one last piece—a name. A package name serves several purposes. Among them are:

1. It lets you refer to the package directly and succinctly, as in, "Do you want the Tahiti Getaway or the Rio Blowout?"

2. It reminds your customers (and you) that they are getting a full package for their money.

3. It serves as a mental handle for your customers to distinguish your package from your competitors'.

Naming things is an art. If you're not good at it, enlist the help of someone who is. The name doesn't have to be cute or snappy—in fact, it probably shouldn't be—but it does have to meet three tests:

1. It should describe or evoke the Core Benefit.

2. It should be distinctive and easy to remember.

3. It should *not* be currently in use by one of your competitors.

Once you have a package name that works (you will field-test it with customers before you pledge your life and fortune to it, won't you? Please?), I recommend you go ahead and protect it legally. You want this name to be a servicemark of your company. Talk to your lawyer for details. Then you can safely invest time and money in promoting this package by name, without worrying that someone else will reap your harvest.

A Personal Note on Packaging

Having spent so much time describing the glories of the Tahiti Getaway, I feel I should clarify something: I have never been to Tahiti. I have no professional affiliation with the travel industry or the South Sea islands. The only Tahiti I have visited is the one in the back of my mind, which I visit occasionally for brief but refreshing moments. But then nobody has ever offered me a Tahiti Getaway package. Perhaps someday a good travel agent will make me an offer I can't refuse. I think I'll include the side jaunt to Bora Bora.

11 | Presentation

"What exactly is the sizzle in actuarial auditing?"

The meeting with the ad agency must not have gone well.

Dan's a software engineer, normally a calm and competent type with an easygoing style. But he was obviously annoyed when he sat down and picked up the menu. He glanced at the luncheon specials and put the menu down again.

"Just what exactly do ad people mean by 'sizzle,' Tony?"

"Depends on who's using it. Give me some background."

"Well, like I told you on the phone we're ready to go national with our new product for personal computers. I understand business, but all this advertising stuff is new to me and I'm not comfortable with how my agency wants to approach it. There's this one 'creative' guy, Bart, who keeps looking smug and asking, 'Where's the sizzle in this software?' I think he means, 'What's new and sexy about it?' which I suspect is the wrong question, but I'm not really sure."

"Don't feel bad, Dan. 'Sell the sizzle, not the steak' is the oldest cliché in the advertising book. You can count on someone to ask 'Where's the sizzle?' at least once in each creative conference. It actually pinpoints a profound truth about people and why they buy. The problem is, it has become such a cliché that even some people in the ad business don't really know what it means. Like your friend Bart, they think it means 'Find out what's hot or new or sexy about this product and build your campaign around that.' And by the way, I agree that that's the wrong question for your product."

"So what does it mean, really?"

"To see that, Dan, we need to go back to the original situation that gave rise to the slogan. Imagine you are hungry—*really* hungry. You walk into a restaurant to get something to eat, but you're not sure just what you want."

"That's not too hard to do. I *am* really hungry. What are you having?"

"I think I'll go for the special. But let's suppose your restaurant's owner wants to sell you a steak because she makes more money on steaks. She has given you a menu with tempting pictures of char-broiled steak, and she makes sure the waiter tells you about today's special on top sirloin. But she doesn't stop there. As you are looking at the menu, the chef throws a steak on the grill. From the kitchen you hear this sudden *sizzzzzz*; the aroma fills your nostrils; your mouth waters and you say, 'I think I'll have a steak.'

"But notice carefully what has happened, Dan. When you made the decision to buy, where was *your* steak? Notice that what you really wanted—the satisfaction that comes from eating a cooked, juicy steak—was not there when you decided to buy. The steak was in the kitchen; more importantly, it was in the *future*. And it wasn't that tangible steak you really wanted; it was the delicious but essentially intangible satisfaction that comes from eating a well-cooked steak when you were hungry.

"*So what made you buy?* You were sold on a here-and-now, tangible representation of a future, essentially intangible satisfaction. As marketers say, you were sold the sizzle, not the steak.

"That is really an important understanding, Dan. Whenever someone buys a service from you, what they are getting for their money is a future satisfaction that is essentially intangible. And if that's true about something as concrete as a steak, imagine how true it is of something like software! Our task as marketers is to create a tangible, here-and-now representation that powerfully and accurately conveys that essentially intangible, future satisfaction. We have to create the 'sizzle' in order to sell the 'steak.'"

Dan nodded thoughtfully. "You know Tony, I'm going to have a long talk with my ad agency. You're right: My product needs some real sizzle and I'm not sure these people are the ones to provide it. . . . And you know what else? Here comes our waiter, and I'm going to order the thickest, juiciest steak in the house!"

I didn't have the heart to remind Dan we were in a vegetarian restaurant. He found out soon enough.

Creating the Sizzle

The basic problem in marketing services is getting people to see what they are getting for their money. Their buying decision happens right now; your services and the benefit from them are in the future. The money your customers pay you is very tangible; the benefit they're buying is essentially intangible. Exchanging a tangible, here-and-now thing for an intangible, future thing seems risky, doesn't it? Why would people in their right mind do that?

Often they won't, unless you can cut down their risk. You need to create a tangible, here-and-now representation of your services that is so powerful and so realistic that your customers almost feel as if the services have already happened. That's what presentation is for. In this chapter, we are going to help you create the sizzle to sell your own steak. First we will define exactly what your prospective customers need to see and hear, in order to decide to buy. Then we will decide in what form that presentation is most effectively made to accomplish your marketing tasks.

Before we start in on your specific presentation, though, we need to look at some of the principles involved. How exactly do you go about making the intangible tangible? How do you create the sizzle to sell the steak? The place to start, as usual, is with the benefit to the customer.

Always Give Them Something to Walk Away With

Richard Drake was struggling with a discouraging problem. "Tony, I know I'm doing something wrong, but I can't figure out what. I'm having no success at all getting people to sign up for the second phase of my Career Transition package."

"What do they get in the first phase, Rich?"

"The first phase is really good! We spend a lot of time looking at their work history and finding out exactly what they want in their career. I give them several personality and interest tests, and they fill out these forms that help define their ideal job. Then we sit down and work out a detailed strategy for them to find exactly the right job to match their skills and interests."

"Sounds good. What would you say is the real benefit of all that, Rich?"

"Insight into their own career needs. That, and the job search strategy."

"I'm beginning to see the problem. Tell me, when all this is done, what does your customer walk away with?"

"Like I said, insight and a job search strategy."

"No, Rich. I mean _literally_. What do they have in their hands when they walk away from phase one."

"Well, they usually take notes . . . ."

"So your customer pays you $600 or so for phase one. You call him up and ask him to sign up for phase two. He asks himself, 'What did I get for my money in phase one?' And what does he see? A few pages of notes, in his own handwriting. Does this seem like the buy of the century?"

Rich look flustered. "Well, when you put it like that . . . ."

"I'm not putting it any way, Rich. I'm just describing what your customer sees. I don't doubt for a minute that your services are worth the money. Insight and strategy are scarce and valuable commodities. But they are completely intangible. At the time you are receiving them, you may see their value. But before you get them, and afterward as well, it's hard to see their true worth. Unless you have some concrete thing to walk away with, it is hard to hold onto a sense of really getting something for your money."

Rich's problem was easy to solve. When he sits down now to go over the job search strategy with his customers, he hands them a 10-page report in a high-quality binder. (It's a transcription of his notes for the session; he now dictates them instead of making notes by hand.) He includes copies of the tests and filled-out forms, and all the test results are colorfully charted. All told, this impressive document totals 25 to 30 pages, and it's *all* about this one customer, personally. Rich's customers are now impressed by how much they get for their money in phase one, and he has good success in signing them up for phase two.

But much more important, Rich's sales of phase one have also increased dramatically! Before, all Rich could do was describe how useful phase one would be. Now he can *show* prospects a sample report, and talk them through each piece; by the time he has finished, they are eager to get their own.

Rich has created the sizzle to sell his steak.

―――― **WORKWORK: CARRY-OUT SIZZLE** ――――――――――

Does *your* benefit need some sizzle? You have defined clearly the benefit of your services in previous chapters. Now ask yourself:

What do my customers walk away with when we are done?

What do they have to *show* for their money? What can they point to and say, "There. That's what I paid for."

If you have something that does the trick, great! Be sure that examples of that "something" are always at hand when you are talking to prospective customers.

But if you don't, you have an important gap in your marketing to fill. Filling that one gap may make a tremendous difference in your marketing success.

Don't Just Tell

Rich's example also illustrates the fundamental principle of effective presentation:

Don't just tell them; show them.

This simple principle is easy to put into practice, but you have to discipline yourself to get into the habit:

- Don't just tell them you do a thorough examination. Show them a filled-out examination form and walk them through it step by step.

- Don't just tell them they will get a personalized report and analysis. Show them one, in a very nice binder.

- Don't just tell them how they will look when you finish. Show them before-and-after pictures.

- Don't just tell them that participants in your workshop get their money's worth. Show them actual testimonials.

- Don't just tell them you will save them money. Show them in hard numbers the money you have saved others.

- Don't just tell them that people have fun at your events. Show them pictures or, better yet, videos of an actual event.

Never just tell. *Show* as well.

Involve and Personalize

All this talk about showing and telling can give the impression that the prospective customers should be treated like an audience, sitting quietly and watching the show. Nothing could be further from the truth. At each step your *primary* concern should be with keeping your customers involved with what is being said and shown. Remember, your purpose is to create a customer relationship with this person; telling your story is only a means to that end.

Keep your mind on the person, not the presentation.

Always personalize each point. *Not* "Our first step is to analyze the underlying causes of the problem. We interview every employee individually and . . ." but "The first thing we would do is analyze your situation to find out the underlying causes of your productivity problem. We would talk to all seven of your employees—this is the interview sheet we use—and . . . ."

At each point in your presentation, involve the prospects by personalizing what you are saying. You don't want them to just get a picture of what you do; you want them to get a picture of what it would be like for you to do it for them.

Telling Your Story

Have you ever seen a professional salesperson at work? I don't mean the ones who call you on the phone and try to sell you hot stocks or magazines, or the ones you find at auto dealers or appliance stores. I mean the ones who come into your home to sell you something: vacuum cleaners, aluminum siding, life insurance, or encyclopedias. If you forget about the product they are trying to sell you and concentrate on how they sell, their presentation can be fascinating. You can learn a lot about marketing, both what to do and what not to do by watching these pros at work.

Two things stand out clearly in what these sales professionals do:

1. They have a story to tell, and they tell it the way stories have always been told: from the beginning to the end.

2. They all have props and, most important, a presentation book to support them in telling their story.

"Telling the story" refers to the fact that there are certain things the prospects must see and experience, in a certain order, so they will be prepared to buy. Leave out one of the necessary pieces, or tell them in the wrong order, and the prospects are not mentally or emotionally prepared to become customers. And of course you don't really "tell"; you show and tell and demonstrate.

That's what the presentation book is for. (Real sales pros call it a "pitchbook." Accurate, but some of my clients find it a little undignified.) The presentation book is a set of props and visual aids to support you in telling your story. Usually the book is a three-ring binder, and each sheet is in a plastic sleeve so it doesn't get torn as you flip through the book. As you mention something in telling your story, you flip a page and there it is: an example, or a picture, or at least some "bullet points" that highlight the main statements you're making. The approach is somewhat like using overheads or slides during a speech to a group, only much less formal.

To tell your story, then, you need two things: a presentation book and practice in using it. (Many salespeople write an actual script for what they will say as they use the presentation book. You may find this useful. Most of my clients have found that it suited them better to practice their presentation until they were comfortable with how it came out.)

At this point you may be wondering why all this emphasis on telling your story face-to-face. After all, isn't most presentation done in mailers or brochures or ads?

The face-to-face presentation is the foundation of all other forms of presentation.

All other forms of marketing communication tell some specific part of your story and accomplish some specific marketing task or tasks. When you can tell your story persuasively, start to finish, face-to-face, you have a script for any other marketing communication. Moving to a mailer or ad or brochure becomes a matter of form and not of content. You will know what needs saying and in what order. You need cnly adapt it to the alternate form.

Let's put these principles to work in figuring out how to tell *your* story.

_____ **WORKWORK: A TELLING PRESENTATION** _____

Let's tell your story, start to finish, and design a presentation book for you along the way. Grab a pad of paper, a pencil, copies of all your current marketing letters and other tangible materials, scissors, and tape.

Here's a scenario to orient you to the task. You are talking to Nancy, a satisfied customer. She is enthusiastically recalling how pleased she has been with your services. She picks up the phone, dials a number, and says, "Bob, Nancy here. Listen, there's somebody you've just got to talk to. I've used their services and have been very pleased. I think you would be interested too. What's that? Hold on . . . ."

She puts her hand over the mouthpiece and asks you, "Do you have time to talk to my friend Bob? He's just next door and I think he's a great prospect for you." You nod Yes. She returns to the phone. "Yes. Expect a knock on your door in five minutes."

So you have an interested prospect who knows nothing at all about you or your service, but who is willing to listen. You may be able to sign up a new customer on the spot if you play your cards right. What do you do?

You thank Nancy for the referral, grab your briefcase and your trusty presentation book, and start out to tell Bob your story, start to finish. You know that *how* you tell that story will make a big difference. You have to tell Bob what he needs to hear to move him from where he is now to where you want him to be—your customer.

Fast-forward a bit. You're in the door, introductions have been made, and Bob has graciously pulled up a chair for you. He sits down and asks, "So—what's this great service Nancy is so excited about?"

Sound familiar? It's the "moment of truth" we talked about in Chapter 3. You know what to do. You smile and tell him your mission! And while you are doing that, you reach for your presentation book and open it, on the first page is:

Your Company's Name.

Your Mission.

Both are printed in a readable size and typeface. You may use your letter-head for this or not; in any case, the colors and style of presentation should be completely congruent with the corporate identity projected by your business cards and letterhead.

Bob takes it in. "Interesting. Tell me more." (First hurdle cleared!)

Now that you have Bob's interest, your next task is to turn him into a Qualified Prospect. Show/tell him the pointed questions and scenarios you created in Chapter 8; get him to recognize that you are talking about him! Describe the situations your typical customers find themselves in, or what they are trying to get; illustrate these succinctly but concretely. This task is accomplished when Bob acknowledges: "Yes, it sounds like you are talking about our situation."

(Before we go on, sketch out the pages of your presentation book that will accomplish the qualification. Just jot down bullet points on each page, and boxes for any illustrations. If you already have good qualifying letters, cut out the pointed questions or scenarios and tape them in place; this is just a rough sketch, which you and your helpers can finish later. Remember that it only takes a fraction of a second to flip a page, so don't try to cram too much into a single sheet. Paper is cheap; a prospect's attention is expensive.)

What Bob will want to know next is: "So what do *you* do about it? How can you help?" (That may not be what he says, but it *is* what he will want to know next.) Now you show him your package of services.

First show him the forest, then the trees. Start with a page that just gives the name of the package, and a crisp statement of the Core Benefit. Then an overview page on which the package name is repeated, and each of the pieces is listed in a bullet-point form. (You could even illustrate each piece if you can do so without cluttering the page.)

Then go over each piece in tangible, sizzling detail. Use as many pages as you need; you can flip through them quickly if you need to, but make sure each piece is concretely and tangibly represented. Show, don't tell; illustrate, don't just talk about. By the time you finish with each piece of the package, Bob should have an accurate sense of the benefit the piece will bring him.

A small technical matter: It is very useful to establish some kind of visual key that carries the continuity of the whole while you are showing the parts. For example, you might establish a color and/or graphical convention on the overview page, then repeat it on each subsequent page, to say implicitly: "This is still part of the package." If your package has five pieces, use something like a five-piece shaded bar under the package name as shown on page 158.

MANUFACTURING PROCESS IMPROVEMENT PROGRAM

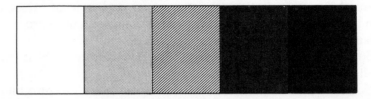

Repeat the bar, perhaps reduced in size, at the top of each page, but with only one box, corresponding to the pieces being described, filled in. The graphic works like one of those "You are HERE" maps in shopping malls. A five-color bar is an alternative, but check on costs for preparation and printing first.

Complete the story by talking about price and payment terms. Be careful not to fall into a defensive posture; just show Bob the price and move on to talk about terms, and any other details, such as scheduling. Don't finish with price and details. Have a final, summary page that repeats the overview of the package and, *most important*, concludes with a restatement of the Core Benefit. As you close your presentation book, the last thing lingering in Bob's mind should be a strong image of the beneficial difference your services will make in his life.

(Grab your pencil and pad and rough out those pages. Make drafts of:

1. Name and Core Benefit of package
2. Overview of package
3. Each piece of package, as many pages as needed
4. Price, terms, and details
5. Summary of package and Core Benefit

If you have examples of reports or tests or whatever you use, stick them in here. Remember, you are trying to give Bob a here and now, concrete experience of that future satisfaction. Make it *real* to him.)

OK. You've told Bob your story. He's seen the sizzle. You've talked it out and he sees the match with his circumstances.

Now show him how to become a customer, and get his "Yes." A Summary Sheet that customizes the package to Bob's circumstances is an excellent tool at this stage. We will design a Summary Sheet for you in Chapter 14.

One last point. Throughout this presentation, you are establishing your own credibility by the professional relationship you are creating with Bob. Along the way you also need to establish your firm's credibility. If you have advertised in *Time* magazine or have been mentioned favorably in a *Wall Street Journal* article (or the good local equivalents of these), by all means include copies of them in your presentation book. Include client lists, testimonials, and any impressive statistics you can lay claim to ("95.7% repeat customers!" "Average increase of 52% in the first year!"). But watch out for overkill; a few great testimonials are better than page after page at this point. Once credibility is established, move on. Bob's really not interested in you, he's interested in what you can do for him.

Where do you put the credibility builders? There's no cut-and-dried rule. Put them where they seem to fit best in the flow of the presentation. Consider scattering them throughout the book; say, one really attention-grabbing item just after the package overview page, and the rest following the relevant pieces of the package presentation. Try it several ways until you find the one that fits most naturally into your presentation.

Now you know how to tell your story, beginning to end. You have a presentation book to support you in doing that. You are ready to talk to a prospective customer face to face.

But you don't do all your marketing through face-to-face presentations, do you? You are going to need some marketing materials that tell your story when you are not there. That's what we will work on next.

Do You Really Need a Brochure?

The most common and costly mistake in marketing is running the printing presses too soon. It's an automatic response for many people: "Time to start serious marketing. Guess I'd better get a brochure." A brochure seems like the first step, when actually it's more like the seventh. Until you have created laser-like alignment with your market, and packaged your services well, you're in no position to create useful marketing communications.

But you've done all that work in the previous chapters, and we have just finished figuring out how to tell your story. Is it time now for the brochure? Almost, but not quite. Before you start designing marketing materials, you first need to decide exactly what materials you need. You may find that you don't even need a brochure!

The principle is simple:

First decide exactly what your marketing materials need to accomplish. Then design materials that accomplish exactly what is needed.

Consider your marketing materials as tools. A surgeon needs a scalpel and forceps; a carpenter needs hammers and saws. Different tools do different jobs. The same is true of marketing materials. Depending on what you are trying to accomplish, you will choose different materials to do it.

The problem with general-purpose marketing materials like brochures is that they usually resemble Swiss-Army knives: you can do lots of different things with them, but you can't do any one thing particularly well. The laser-like alignment you are after is better achieved by getting the right tools for the job. As we shall see, a brochure may be part of your marketing tool kit, but it's only one, specific part.

Before you go charging off to print up a flyer, brochure, or any other marketing piece, ask yourself, "What exactly am I going to use this piece to accomplish?" Will it fulfill one of these worthwhile tasks?

- Introduce your firm and its services.

- Create a Qualified Prospect.

- Get someone to try your services, or convert a tryer into a customer.

- Support an advocate in influencing others to buy or approve your services.

You can accomplish all these tasks with a single, well-designed marketing piece, or you can design specific pieces to accomplish each task. Good quality printing is expensive; before you decide which pieces you need, take some time to analyze your actual needs. Which of these tasks are crucial in your marketing?

Introduce Your Firm and Services

Where do your customers first hear of you and your service? The task of creating a customer has to start somewhere. Word of mouth from satisfied customers is important, but it's risky to try to build a business on *just* word of mouth because you have very little influence over when and how often it occurs. You need reliable methods of insuring that your firm and its services are brought before the eyes and minds of your target market.

Advertising is one means of introducing your firm to its market. Ad media include the obvious—TV, radio, magazines, newspapers—and the not-so-obvious—flyers, circulars, posters, and so on. Another means is public relations: being quoted as an authority in the local business pages, or giving talks to community groups, for example. These all are *impersonal*, in the sense that you are addressing your efforts to a faceless group and relying on them to initiate the first personal contact. Methods and materials for handling these impersonal means of presentation will be covered in the next two chapters.

Right now let's deal with presentations in which you are addressing yourself to a specific, known person. Perhaps all you know about the person is his or her name and address, but that's enough to start.

What materials do you need to introduce yourself and your services? That depends on the economic scale of your business. The most *effective* way to create a customer is face-to-face interaction. If your average customer spends $100 or more for your services, you will almost certainly find that you must talk to each prospect in person before you will be hired.

A very strong combination in these circumstances is an introductory letter that concludes with "I will call you next week to arrange an appointment," followed by a telephone call that leads to a face-to-face presentation. The introductory letter should be on your letterhead and should not read like a form letter; it should begin with a personalized item, such as "John Jones suggested you might be interested . . ." or "As a supplier to Chrysler, you . . ." Remember to get the person's attention with a qualifying question or scenario.

The letter should:

- Succinctly state your mission and the benefit your services provide to people like them;
- Give a sentence or two on your company;
- Say that you are interested in exploring whether your firm's services could be of benefit to them; and
- Conclude with the next step to be taken.

All this must fit on one sheet of paper, leaving room for your signature.

Make sure the envelope is not addressed with a mailing label. Type it. (If it is sent to the prospect's home, consider hand-addressing the envelope; research shows that people are more likely to open a hand-addressed letter.)

Should you enclose a brochure? Probably not, at this point. People are more likely to read a simple one-page letter than a letter-and-brochure combination. Besides, you can do a better job of telling your story in person; if they have seen your brochure, many people will assume they don't need to talk to you.

Create a Qualified Prospect

If your average customer pays you less than $100, or if you need to generate many customers all at once (for example, if your business involves public events like seminars or concerts), you will probably need to find more efficient ways of creating customers than face-to-face interaction.

In this case, the material that introduces you and your services has to generate a response from the prospect. It has to at least qualify the prospect, and perhaps activate some interest in trying your services as well. You might even try to go all the way from introducing yourself to signing up the prospect as a customer in one communication. Remember though, the more you try to accomplish with a single communication, the lower your response rate will be.

If you are simply trying to create a Qualified Prospect, the qualifying letter you designed in Chapter 8 is a good bet. It should be similar to the introductory letter discussed above: brief and to the point, written on your letterhead, and so on. But in addition, it must accomplish the three tasks of a qualifying letter:

1. Get them to recognize, "They are talking to me!"

2. Get them to see the benefit.

3. Make them an offer and show them how to respond.

Again, enclosing a brochure would not be useful at this point. You are trying to stimulate interest and get the prospects to ask for more. A brochure is likely to tell them what they wanted to know and cut down on their need to respond.

Get Someone to Try Your Services, or Convert a Tryer into a Customer

The most useful set of materials for getting people to try your services or to become your customer is your presentation book. Tell them your story in person and make them an offer they just can't turn down.

If you need to get prospects to sign up without talking to them individually, you need a very complete and convincing mailing. It can be either a multipage letter (for years I used a four-page, single-spaced letter on my letterhead to market my workshop; it worked well) or a mailing piece specifically designed as an announcement ("Coming to a city near you!").

Don't try to create a piece like this yourself. It's hard, tricky work best left to the professionals. Take your presentation book with you; that's the story they have to tell in printed form. And definitely take with you all the work you did in Chapter 8. Hand it over to the pros and tell them what you need.

This, by the way, is not a brochure either. It is a direct-marketing piece designed to qualify and activate in one reading. Find someone with experience in direct marketing to do this for you; ordinary writers or advertising people typically do not understand this particular art well enough to do you much good.

Support an Advocate in Influencing Others to Buy or Approve Your Services

You've told your story to Bob. He's impressed and ready to sign up. There's just one little problem . . . . : "I've got to run this by my boss. Just a formality really, but . . . ." *Now* you need that brochure!

Or, something like a brochure the technical term is a "leave-behind." It's what you leave behind when you walk out the door and your customer says; "Now what was that again . . . ."

A "leave-behind" may in fact be your most expensive, impressive, glossy marketing piece because it has to represent you and your story when you're not there. You need a good "leave-behind" for three purposes:

1. To remind the customers of what an excellent choice they have made in selecting you.

2. To help the customers influence others who have to approve your selection.

3. To enable your satisfied customers to tell others about you and your excellent services.

It is possible that you need more than one leave-behind. If your customers spend quite a bit of money for your services, a simple brochure won't do for the first two purposes; you need something glossy, with pockets and inserts, on excellent stock, to keep your advocates from looking foolish. But they don't want to hand such an extravaganza to a friend; a simple but well-crafted brochure that serves as a strong qualifying piece is more appropriate.

___ **WORKWORK: ESSENTIALS ONLY** ___

Take a minute now and draw up the shopping list of marketing materials *you* need. Make notes to yourself on what your business requires.

If your budget is limited (and whose isn't?) look hard at your list and mark the ones you simply cannot do without.

If you have them already and they are working for you, great! If not, your next task is to go get them.

Getting Your Story Told—Tips for Dealing with the Pros

You know what tangible materials you need for your marketing, and what each needs to accomplish. *Now* it's time to bring in the professionals and run the printing presses. *Properly utilized*, professionals can make a terrific, positive difference in your marketing materials. Within their areas of expertise, ask for their guidance and listen. They are the experts.

But always remember one thing in choosing and working with professionals:

You are the expert on your business.

Some designers and writers are accustomed to starting from scratch in designing marketing materials. They assume that their clients know nothing about marketing (this is often an accurate assumption) and act as ad-hoc marketing consultants. Their marketing sense is better than nothing (although not always by much; I've seen a depressing number of useless brochures). Their involvement in this way usually improves the quality of the materials. It always increases the fee.

You don't need or want this. You have worked hard to design a marketing program and materials that are aligned with your market. Supply the professionals with specifications for the materials: This is what needs to be done and said, in this order. They will translate those specs into words and images that do exactly what you want done. If a professional you are considering hiring doesn't like this way of working and insists on starting from scratch, find somebody else for the job.

Whom do you need? Consider these possible resources.

Graphic Designer

You can do letters without a graphic designer, but use the letterhead you paid the designer to develop for you. The layout on the page is important, even on a letter, but most of us have a good enough eye to get that right without too much help.

Anything else—a presentation book, folders or inserts, and certainly any brochures—should be done by a professional if you want it to be taken seriously. Amateur design looks like it was done by an amateur, and that subtly but powerfully says that your services are less than professional quality. You can't afford that message in today's marketplace.

Find a graphic designer you are comfortable with, whose style and visual sense reflect you and your mission well. Start with the Yellow Pages. Talk to a number of candidates. Look at their portfolio; in particular, ask to see anything they have done for businesses similar to yours. The person you select is going to create visual images that represent your mission to your market; do you feel comfortable with what you see in his or her work? Ask about pricing; if an hourly rate is quoted, ask for some examples of how much specific jobs cost.

Be a bit skeptical of "graphic designers" who turn out to be associated with printers or advertising agencies. You may find that they are more interested in selling you printing services or ad space than in simply designing your materials.

Most graphic designers are both willing and able to arrange for printing your materials. This can be a convenience and a good quality-control measure but it may also increase your costs. You may be better off arranging for this yourself. Is that way of working acceptable to your designer?

It's critically important that your marketing materials *all* project the same image. You must not send one message with your cards and letter-head, for example, and another with your brochures. The easy way to make sure this happens is to stick with the graphic designer you pick. Use the same designer for your marketing materials that you used for your letterhead. If this is not possible for some reason, be sure that your new designer is willing and able to stay with the same "look and feel" your old designer created for your materials. (The alternative is to throw out the old materials and replace them, a costly and probably unnecessary move.)

Here are some tips for dealing with graphic designers:

- Be sure that your designer understands exactly what the materials are to be used for, and who will see them.

- Designers are not writers. Most designers want to see the written copy for a piece before they design it. This is the correct order; be somewhat leary of designers who want to lay out the piece and then have copy written to fit. (On the other hand, be delighted with a designer who is willing to make a rough sketch of the layout to give to the writer, who then writes the copy and hands it back for final design.)

- Don't be a back-seat driver. Hand over your material and let the designer work. Your role is to judge the product; the designer's role is to create it.

- Don't pull punches. Once the designer starts showing you sketches and ideas, make clear exactly what you do and don't like about the proposed pieces. Don't accept a design you are not comfortable with; remember, it's *your* business.

By the way, don't be alarmed if your graphic designer does a poor job of marketing his or her own services. There are as many Zorbas in this field as in any other. Lilly Dean is a good example. Lilly bakes nut breads, drinks herbal teas, dresses like a gypsy fortune teller, and raises cats. She also turns out terrific brochures for about half the cost of other local designers. Some of my clients wouldn't use anyone else.

I called her a few months ago. "Lilly, I have some clients who are close to needing a graphic designer. Why don't you send me a half-dozen of your personal brochures?"

There was a short silence on the line. "Uh—Tony, let me get back to you on that, OK?"

The next week the Dean Designs brochures arrived in the mail. Great graphics, subtle use of color—a typical job by Lilly.

A few days later I saw Lilly in a bookstore. I thanked her for the brochures and told her that she should expect calls from three firms soon. "Just one thing, Lilly. Why didn't you send them last week when I asked for them?"

Lilly blushed. "Last week I didn't *have* a brochure for Dean Designs."

Writer

Good writing is the most important part of a marketing piece. It is also the most frequently neglected. Every day I see mailers and brochures that are nicely designed but poorly written. I rarely see well-written pieces that are poorly designed.

Why? It's simple—most of us believe we know how to write, and most of us are wrong. Writing clear, informative copy is fiendishly difficult. Writing copy that is also persuasive is an art that requires a seasoned professional.

Finding a good writer is like finding a good graphic designer, only harder. Use the Yellow Pages strategy we discussed earlier. In addition, pick up every local marketing piece you can get your hands on; when you find one you think is well-written, call the advertiser and ask who wrote it.

Many free-lance writers have some background in advertising copywriting. This is a definite asset, but it can also be a trap if it leads them to insist on starting from scratch to create a marketing strategy for you. You want well-written copy; you don't want another marketing director. Be sure that the writer is willing and able to execute *your* strategy.

Desktop Publisher

This exciting technology is growing every day. You can produce excellent materials for a fraction of the cost of traditional printing in a fraction of the time, using desktop publishing.

Use printers for the marketing materials they do best: highest-quality reproduction (four-color glossy brochures, for example) and large-quantity runs (1000 sheets of letterhead or 5000 flyers are *much* cheaper from a printer). For materials that are one-of-a-kind (a proposal, personalized mailers, your presentation book) or that change frequently (a price list, or résumés of key personnel), desktop publishing may well be the method of choice.

You can do desktop publishing yourself *if* you have the equipment, the time, and the inclination. You may find it preferable to use a free-lance desktop publisher in place of a printer; he or she puts into final form the concepts of the graphic designer, using the words of the writer. Look for someone with *experience* who knows the technology well; you don't want to pay for someone else's education. And be a little leary of desktop publishers who want to design the piece for you. They may in fact be excellent designers, but more often they are people who know the tech-nology but have only a decent amateur's grasp of design.

Perhaps the best combination is a graphic designer who also uses desktop publishing. Savings can be terrific if the design is done on a computer so that the final layout can simply be printed out as the final product.

Printer

Dealing with a printer can be costly and time-consuming. You are often better off to pay your graphic designer to handle overseeing the job for you. Designers usually can negotiate a reduced price on printing; in effect they oversee the job for the same amount you would have paid for the printing alone.

You should select the printer yourself. Ask your graphic designer for recommendations. He or she may have a working relationship with a printer that can save you money. And listen to your designer; not all printers deliver good quality for the quoted price. Shop around before you make a commitment. It's your money.

If you intend to deal with the printer yourself, first look at the "Resources" section of this book. You will find references to books that have some good tips for saving money on printing and for dealing with production professionals.

Not all projects require all these professionals. You know what you need, and you know what you can do yourself—and what you can't. Be honest with yourself and recognize what help you really need, then select the best professionals you can find. Tell them clearly what your business is, who your target market is, and what the materials must accomplish. Work with them, giving them candid feedback until they have produced for you exactly what you are after: marketing materials that will help you create the customers you need.

12

Getting the Word Out

Networking, Seminars, and Other Low-Cost Tactics for Promoting New Business

The sign was posted next to the cash register. It was one of those inexpensive "inspirational messages" you see displayed in racks in souvenir shops, but it had been carefully framed and hung where it couldn't be missed. It stated clearly this immigrant tailor's deeply felt belief about business:

The best advertising is a satisfied customer.

Corny? Sure. Old-fashioned? Unquestionably. It also happens to be true.

This may seem like a shocking admission, coming from a marketer. After all, isn't marketing an *active* process? Aren't you supposed to get out there and *create* customers? What sense does it make to talk about "marketing machines," presentation, and all that, if it ultimately boils down to good word of mouth?

That was Roger's biggest concern when we first started working on his marketing. "I know I need more business, Tony, but I don't see how marketing can help. As I review my client list, they all came to me through word of mouth—somebody I had helped told somebody else about me. It never seems to work when I make the first move. I have to wait for them to call."

"We can do a lot to change that, Roger, but first things first. Word of mouth *is* important in your business. Tell you what: Let's assume for now that you're right and the only way you will ever get business is through word of mouth."

"OK. So?"

"So what are you doing to make sure the word gets out?"

"I'm not sure what I *could* do. Word of mouth just happens. You can't make people talk to each other."

"Of course you can't *make* them, but you can make it a lot more likely to happen. *That's* how marketing can help. Your satisfied customers have good things to say about you and your services. You need some effective ways of making sure this word gets out where it will do you some good."

(Today about half of Roger's business comes from contacts he initiates. The rest comes from word of mouth, which Roger actively works to promote.)

"Getting the word out" is a basic ingredient in marketing success. People have to hear about you before they can become your customers; they have to hear *good* things about you before they *want* to become your customers. Spontaneous word of mouth is priceless but you are already getting as much of it as you are likely to get, and it has not been enough to build the business you want and need. You need to find ways of promoting new business by promoting more and better word of mouth.

In this chapter we will look at "guerrilla" tactics for getting the word out about you and your services. (I borrowed the term "guerrilla" in this context from Jay Levinson's excellent book on advertising and promotion, *Guerrilla Marketing*.) They are "guerrilla" tactics because they don't require a whole army to carry them out, but they can be remarkably effective. All are low-cost; some are free; each is designed to get the word out where it will do you some good.

Networking

Networking is the one essential tactic for getting the word out. Some people are very unhappy with that statement. Networking can call to mind some cloudy images:

- Earnest young professionals dressed for success, systematically passing out business cards at "networking" parties.

- Your daughter's recreation-league soccer coach handing out free samples of industrial-strength laundry detergent and offering to "tell you about my business."

- Friends who are recent graduates of the latest "personal transformation" workshop inviting you to a free introductory program.

Many people have no problem with these images; to them, these activities seem like perfectly reasonable things to do. If that's your reaction you probably won't have much trouble with networking once you see how to do it. Other people find these images of networking distasteful. As Roger put it: "I resent it when somebody uses a social relationship with me to try to sell me something. It puts me on the spot, and I don't like that. It would feel all wrong to me to try to get business through social contacts."

Do you find it somehow unpleasant to think of getting business through networking? Perhaps your reaction isn't as strong as Roger's—few people have opinions as strongly held as Roger's—but you may find yourself doubting whether networking is really for you. Stay tuned. You may find your opinion changing as we dig into this a bit deeper.

Let's begin by clearing up those cloudy images. What is it about networking that turns you off?

- Those earnest young professionals at the networking party seem to be trying too hard for not much return. Networking depends on people having a good opinion of you and then telling someone else. Why would people get a good opinion of you when their only contact with you has been at an event designed for hustling business? Besides, the only reason *they* are there is to hustle some business from *you*. This is *not* the image of networking we will be using.

- The soccer coach may be doing you a real service by handing out the detergent sample. It's not easy to get those grass stains out. But you know it's just a come-on; what he's really after is to sign you up to sell soap. And it's awkward to say "No" when the fellow coaches your daughter. The coach is abusing his position and putting you on the spot. This is *not* the image of networking we will be using.

- Those "personal transformation" friends are well-intentioned but is your state of enlightenment (or the lack thereof) really any of their business? It can be delightful when friends share their enthusiasm with you; it can be a pain in the neck when they insist on *your* becoming enthusiastic as well. Friends who presume on friendship that way run the risk of becoming former friends. Putting friends on the spot is risky and inappropriate. That is *not* the image of networking we will be using.

Here are two images of networking we *will* be using:

- You read about a concert by your favorite musician, scheduled for next month. You pick up the phone and call several friends to let them know about it. You're not sure they will be interested themselves, but you thought they would like to know.

- The disk drive on your computer has started acting up. You're not sure how serious it is. You call a friend and ask if he knows. He doesn't, but he gives you the name of someone who probably does.

She doesn't know either, but she steers you to someone who answers your question.

In both cases you are networking. In the first case you are using your network to get the word out about something of interest; in the other case you are using your network to track down something you need to know.

Notice what you are *not* doing. You are not trying to sell someone something. You are not trying to persuade someone to do something. You are not asking friends to stick their neck out for you, or to go out of their way to do you a favor. You are simply giving and getting information.

Networking is a natural and effective marketing tactic when used properly. The purpose of networking is to *give* and *get* information. If you use networking properly, nobody feels pressured or used or put on the spot. You are not selling, you are telling. You are not asking for favors, you are giving valuable information.

Use networking when:

1. You have information you believe will be of interest to people in your network, or to people they know. For example, if you have worked out an introductory great deal that will be valuable to prospective customers, people in your network will surely want to know about it. They may resent being subtly pressured to try it themselves (don't do that) but they will typically appreciate an "I thought you would like to know . . ." communication.

2. You need information you believe people in your network will have. For example, if your target market includes businesses that have recently gone through budget cuts, it is quite reasonable to ask people in your network if they know of any businesses in this situation. They may or may not be willing to call people in these businesses on your behalf, or to let you use their name to open doors, but they will typically be happy to share with you whatever information they have if you ask.

Let's look at how you can use networking to get the word out about your services.

Activating Your Referral Network

Jill is an unusually enthusiastic person—her normal attitude makes most cheerleaders seem like pessimistic grumps—so I wasn't sure when I answered the phone if she was calling to celebrate a success or to ask for advice. It turned out to be both.

"We finally did it, Tony!"

"Congratulations, Jill! Did what?"

"We finally sent out a mailing to some of our past patients!"

That *was* good news. Jill is office manager for Dr. John the chiro-practor, and I had been nudging them for almost a year to start activating their referral network. "Great! Tell me about it."

"Well, we sent out a letter to 300 of John's most recent patients—it was a really great letter; John wrote it himself—and we included a special coupon they could give to anyone, that was good for a free exam and full diagnosis, including Xrays. We said they could give it to anybody they wanted. But I think we messed up a little."

"How's that?"

"We put an expiration date on the coupon, like you told us. It was good until September 30, but we didn't get it into the mail until the second week of September, so they only had about two weeks to use it."

"That's cutting it pretty close, Jill."

"I know! So we only got 23 people to come in before the end of the month."

"Wait a minute—you sent out 300 coupons, and got 23 responses in two weeks?"

"Yes—and that's why I'm calling. Is that a good response? Should we try it again sometime?"

"That's a *fabulous* response, Jill! Figure it yourself: How many of those people signed up for a treatment program after the free exam?"

"A little over half."

"So you got twelve new patients, who will spend an average of over $400 each—that's about $5000 in new business. Compare that to what sending out 300 letters cost you. Does that seem like a good response?"

Jill laughed. "I guess it is! I think we'll try this again soon."

Word of mouth is the best advertising, when it happens. The trick is to make sure it happens regularly enough to bring you the business you need. How do you make sure it happens?

Give your satisfied customers a good reason to tell others about you and your services, and make it easy for them to do so.

Dr. John's patients already had the best possible reason for telling their friends about him. He had successfully helped them lead lives free of pain and discomfort. That's the kind of benefit you want to spread around to friends who may need it. The letter and coupon provided them with *another* reason to tell others about Dr. John: they were able to hand their friends a valuable, time-limited coupon—and two reasons are stronger than one. Telling people was also very easy: they only had to hand them the coupon which had all the information on it, say "I've had treatments from this guy and they really did me some good," and it was done.

Your satisfied customers will be happy to recommend you to their friends, if they think about it. Give them an occasion to think about it. Send them a letter announcing your next workshop, or a talk, or a time-limited offer. Include a coupon or a brochure that explains the offer, and ask them to pass it on to somebody they know who could use it. You may be amazed at how many responses you get.

It took Dr. John a year to get around to the mailing. "I felt awkward about asking my patients to do me a favor." This is a very common misconception. The "favor" goes both ways here. They *are* doing you a favor by endorsing your services to friends. But it's a favor they are already inclined to do. Satisfied customers are typically grateful for the difference you have made in their lives. You are doing *them* a favor as well, by making it easy for them to give something of value to their friends. You get new customers; they get to do something nice for their friends; the friends get the benefit of your services. Everybody wins.

Some people "sweeten the pot" by offering some kind of reward for making a referral: "Send me a new customer and I will give you . . . ." That may be appropriate for your business, but I recommend you think carefully about it because it may backfire. Offering a reward changes the relationship: instead of being satisfied customers telling their friends, they become like sales agents working on commission. Their stake in getting their friends to use your services changes, and their recommendation becomes perhaps a bit suspect. Rather than risk being seen as hustling their friends, some people will avoid the recommendation altogether.

The Non-Customer Network

So far we have been looking at your network of satisfied customers, for a very good reason:

> **Networking through satisfied customers will give you the best return for your marketing efforts.**

But what if that's not enough? What if you are just starting out, or launching a new service package, or need more response than your customer network can provide? That's where full-blown networking comes in.

Networking is based on two simple ideas and one simple procedure. The ideas behind networking are:

1. *The power of word of mouth*
People are much more likely to do business with you if someone they know tells them about you.

2. The principle of geometric progression

If you know 10 people, and each of them knows 10 people, who in turn also know 10 people each, you have access to 1000 people through a simple two-step network. Let's say the chances of any individual person's having what you want—a piece of information or the burning need for your service—are one in 100. Among your direct contacts, it's very unlikely you will find what you are looking for: one chance in 10, to be exact. But within the two-step network, you should find at least 10 people who have what you want.

The procedure for networking is:

- Make a list of every person who has reason to have a good opinion of you, your services, or your firm. Include *everyone* who has *ever* done business with you; people who know you from community groups, service or social organizations, religious groups, or school; friends—yours and your family's, acquaintances, and even relatives. This is your network.

- Decide exactly what information you want them to have, and/or you need from them. At a bare minimum you want them to know:

  1. Your mission and target market
  2. The Core Benefit of your services
  3. Your upcoming event or offer
  4. What you are asking them to do

- Decide how you are going to communicate with your network and how you will support them in communicating with their networks.

Here are a few tips about the procedure for networking:

- *Don't* include Qualified Prospects in your network. A Qualified Prospect has in effect given you permission to "sell me something"; you can afford to be much more direct in asking Qualified Prospects to try your services themselves.

- *Don't* waste your time and money sending out "I'm in business and here's my phone number" messages to your network. Make sure you are telling them about a time-limited event: a special offer with a discount coupon, a workshop or seminar, a talk or article.

And make sure they understand clearly what you are asking of them: "Pass this on to a friend who might be interested." "Call me if you know anyone who needs this." "If someone you know is in this situation, drop me a note with the name and phone number." "Please come to our Open House and bring your friends."

■ *Do* use personal contact. Networking depends on it, and your contact with your network should be as personal as you can afford to make it. You might consider starting with a telephone call. You will be aiming for getting together in person so that you and your trusty presentation book can make a permanent believer of this person, but be prepared to do what you need to do over the phone. Always follow up with a *personal* letter, which will give you the opportunity to enclose a few brochures or announcements.

The only secret to networking is: Do it. Set goals for how many people you will contact each week, and then keep at it until you achieve them. You may need to talk to 50 people before you get a live prospect. That can be discouraging if you don't keep in mind:

The sooner you get those first 49 out of the way, the sooner you get to the person you were looking for all along.

Increasing Your Network

For decades, marketing in professional service firms consisted of nothing *but* networking. The standard advice the old hands gave a newcomer to a professional firm was: "Join as many clubs and community groups as you can. Get on the board of the local opera or museum. Build up your network. As you become known, people will start referring business to you." That's still pretty good advice.

To make it even better advice, consider these additional tips:

■ *Don't* sit back and wait for people to refer business to you. As long as your communications are appropriate, you can actively communicate with your network.

■ *Don't* merely join the clubs or get onto the board and then expect to get business. You are trying to increase your visibility so that more people will come to have a good opinion of you and your competence. If you only take up space on a board, for example, you may hurt your image rather than improve it. If you do good work for those organizations, people will notice.

- *Don't* join groups solely to make contacts. The efforts of those earnest young professionals at the networking parties are mostly wasted because everybody knows they are there only to hustle business. That image will not generally lead to people's having a good opinion of you. Look for organizations whose efforts you genuinely support and believe in. Enjoy one of life's happy ironies: You have to really believe in what you do in order to get business credit for it.

- *Don't* join only industry or professional groups. Their meetings are often too much like networking parties. Building a network is perhaps the only place where a laser-like focusing of efforts is *not* called for. Of course you should join the appropriate industry or professional groups, but your best contacts are often made when the sharp focus on work is not so prominent.

Make a point of keeping in touch with the people in your network. It's a nice thing to do in its own right, and you can never tell when it may also do your business some good.

Seminars, Demonstrations, Speeches, and Articles

Qualified Prospects are to marketing what high-grade ore is to refining gold: the one essential ingredient. Once you have Qualified Prospects, your marketing machine can turn them into customers. But until you have Qualified Prospects, you have nothing to work with. Anything that will get you Qualified Prospects is worth looking at seriously.

Consider using one or more of these four methods for creating Qualified Prospects: seminars, demonstrations, speeches, and articles. They are low-cost—sometimes even no-cost—methods of getting the word out. Better still, with a little planning on your part, they are methods that enable you to get that all-important first response back. Let's look at each briefly.

Seminars

Free seminars are an excellent medium for telling about your services and creating a pool of Qualified Prospects. They give you that all-important opportunity to establish your professional relationship with an audience while giving them something of value. They attract a strongly qualified group and often lead directly to new customers.

By "seminar" I *don't* mean a several-day extravaganza, or an ongoing group meeting. That is the academic model of the seminar. The business seminar is a brief, to-the-point presentation on a topic of interest to a target audience. It provides them with knowledge they need and want, at no cost except their time; it provides the speaker or moderator with an opportunity to demonstrate professional excellence and create new customers. Both sides win.

You may think you have nothing to offer in a seminar. That may be, but think twice before you draw that conclusion. Your seminar doesn't have to be on some earth-shattering topic; anything that will be of interest to your target market will do the job. Consider these examples:

- A gardener offers a seminar on choosing the best plants for sun and shade.

- A cleaning service offers a seminar on "10 Ways to Save Time in Cleaning Your House."

- "Does Your Workspace Work for You?" is a chiropractor's topic in a seminar on eliminating physical stress and discomfort on the job.

- Forecasting is always popular. Stockbrokers offer an outlook on the economy; computer consultants discuss the trends in new software and hardware; career consultants look at trends in employment.

Can you find a topic like these?

Along with the chance to display your professional competence, a good business seminar should also give you an opportunity to present your package(s) of services in an attractive and natural context. The presentation of your services should flow naturally from the topic, instead of seeming to be tacked on as "a word from our sponsor."

Present the seminar yourself if at all possible. There are few better opportunities to establish that distinguishing professional relationship we talked about in Chapter 5. Why give away that chance to someone else? If you are very uncomfortable with public speaking, don't give a speech. Give a hands-on demonstration, or a show-and-tell; get out among the audience and talk to them informally. *Be yourself* as naturally and comfortably as possible.

Feel free to talk about your services and their benefit but avoid "selling" *during* the seminar. You are being accepted as an authority offering good advice; don't blow that credit by seeming too self-serving. *After* the seminar is a different matter. A good strategy is, during the seminar describe your service package briefly but with enough sizzle to create interest. Tell your audience that you (or sometimes even better, your associate) will be happy to meet after the seminar with anyone who has questions about your package. People who come up to you after the seminar are ready for you to convert them into customers.

Keep in mind a few practical tips:

- Offer your seminar when people in your target market are most likely to attend. If people perceive your services as primarily contributing to their business or career, they will be most likely to attend during time they consider "business time"; seminars on services that contribute to personal satisfaction can be done during "personal time." "Business time" typically means after breakfast but before dinner, Monday through Friday. "Personal time" means weekends and evenings for most people. The lunch hour is considered equally available for either business or personal time; in some parts of the country the same is increasingly true of breakfast.

- Avoid scheduling your seminar during ordinary business hours if at all possible. Well-focused one-hour seminars can be done during the lunch hour. Longer presentations during business time can be done after work but before dinner (make sure you have "wine and cheese" or some equivalent). Longer personal time seminars should be after dinner or on weekends.

- If you schedule a seminar during breakfast or lunch, be sure to let people know whether to expect food. "Brown-bagging" for lunch is perfectly acceptable in many cases; indeed, if you provide lunch, people will tend to see this less as a seminar and more as a sales presentation you are bribing them to attend. (Nothing wrong with that kind of sales presentation, mind you; it's just different in appeal and effect from a seminar and costs a lot more.) Breakfast seminars require "coffee and . . ." or whatever equivalent best suits your audience and circumstances. Be sure to provide at least coffee and water for any seminar.

Don't forget to advertise your seminar! This is an excellent opportunity to activate your referral network with a mailing. Make up attractive flyers announcing the seminar and post them where your target market is likely to see them. Send a press release announcing the seminar to the appropriate section editors of the local newspapers, and be sure to get it on the Events Calendar. Certainly send an announcement to any specialized magazines or journals your target market reads. Make sure that the word *free* appears prominently on all ads and announcements.

Should you pay to advertise your free seminar in the newspaper? My clients' experience with this has been mixed, but the consensus is: Probably not. Your money will be better used for mailings and flyers, or ads that require only a phone call for response. For most people, from reading about a seminar in the newspaper to actually going to it is a pretty long step. The number of those who will take that step is low. Announcements, flyers, and so on cost you very little; they are worthwhile despite the low response rate. Ads cost real money; your cost per Qualified Prospect may be higher than makes sense. If you decide to pay for an ad for your seminar, be sure to keep track of how many people the ad draws. That will let you know certainly whether the ad is worth repeating.

Try a seminar or two. You may find them a great way to create new customers.

Demonstrations

I have fond childhood memories of standing in the local Woolworth's on a Saturday afternoon, watching in amazement as a slick-talking salesman demonstrated the Incredible Vegematic! It sliced and diced and did all sorts of things I never imagined possible to a vegetable, and the first 20 people to buy would get a bonus knife, that . . . well, you know how the pitch goes. I never bought one, but I've been fascinated by a good demonstration ever since. I suspect there are more of us around than you might imagine.

Does your service lend itself to quick, visible demonstration? If so, consider demonstrations as a marketing tool. You don't have to be a slick-talking pitchman like the Vegematic salesman—you probably shouldn't be, in fact—but if you can set up a fun or intriguing way to *show* the benefit of your service, prospects will flock to your booth.

Demonstrations take place at trade shows, health fairs, county fairs, flea markets, malls, and any other place where lots of people can walk by and look. The emphasis is on quick appeal to the senses, especially the eye, to captivate interest, and then a *very* brief informative piece that (you guessed it) qualifies the prospect by getting a response. The demonstrator can proceed to creating customers on the spot, or else get their names and addresses for follow-up.

Use these tips for effective demonstrations:

- Make sure you are actually *demonstrating* your services and, most especially, their benefit. You are wasting your time and money if all you do is announce your availability, or give information about your profession. *Show,* don't tell.

- Personalize the demonstration. Don't just show photos of people whose posture is bad, set up a way for listeners to see objectively how bad their posture is. Don't just talk about "typical cases," give a quick checklist that will tell something about your listeners' cases.

- Offer something free. It's the quickest and most certain way of getting attention. Set up a fishbowl into which people can drop their business cards for a drawing. Make sure what they are trying to win is directly related to your services! Remember, this drawing is a way of getting the names of a number of Qualified Prospects, people who have said, "I would like to win one of those." If "one of those" is a free package of your services, they are Qualified Prospects and will reward your ongoing marketing efforts. If "one of those" is a color TV or some other consumer goody, you have learned nothing useful about their customer potential.

- Before you plunge into demonstrations, go watch a few. Figure out where people in your business might demonstrate their services, and walk around, looking at the booths as a customer would. Notice how other people are doing it. You may pick up some useful tips. You will also notice things you want to avoid.

Demonstrations aren't for everyone—it's hard to see where and how a psychotherapist might demonstrate her services, for example—but for many service providers they can be interesting, useful, and rewarding. Who knows, someday, years from now, some grown-up child may remember a Saturday afternoon when he saw you give this fascinating demonstration. . . .

Speeches

An amazing number of groups meet in your town every month. Professional groups; service groups; social groups; trade, industry, and commerce groups: all meet for lunch or dinner, and almost all are looking for speakers. Their meetings can be a great opportunity to promote new business if you use it properly.

Speeches are like seminars with one crucial difference: You go to your audience instead of their coming to you. People who attend your seminar have qualified themselves strongly; just by walking in the door, they have said, "I have a real interest in your kind of service." You can and should proceed from there to activate their interest.

When you make your speech, you have to start from scratch. You cannot afford to assume that everyone in the audience is a good prospect for your services; indeed, your primary marketing task is to get a response from audience members that will qualify them. And you typically do not have much leeway for "selling." Most groups react negatively to a speaker who uses the podium to hustle business.

Here are some things you *can* do:

- Establish your professional competence by giving a useful, insightful presentation. If everyone in your audience walks away with one new idea that can be put into practice, most will consider the speech a success.

- Write up your own introduction and send it beforehand to the person who will introduce you. Describe yourself and your business clearly and positively. *You* can't say these nice things about yourself, but the MC can say them for you.

- Make sure that everyone hears your "moment of truth" statement of your mission. There will be several places in your speech where it would be quite natural to state your mission briefly. Use one or more of them.

- Create an opportunity to ask for a response from members of the audience. Describe your service package briefly, or mention a paper you have written on this topic, or indicate that a mailing will be sent out soon with a schedule. *Then* ask for a response. For example: "If you are interested in getting a free copy of our next newsletter, please take out your business card, write 'Newsletter' on the back, and pass it to the aisle." You may walk away with the names of several Qualified Prospects to drop into your marketing machine.

Speeches can be a useful way to broadcast your message and create some Qualified Prospects in the process, but be sure a particular speech is really worth your while. Beginning trainers, for example, often try to give a speech to the monthly dinner meeting of the American Society for Training and Development. ASTD is a fine organization; giving a talk to its membership is a professional honor and a contribution to a worthwhile cause. But if you are a trainer, the members of ASTD are your colleagues and/or competitors; they are rarely prospects for your services. You would be doing yourself more good from a marketing viewpoint to talk to almost any other group.

Ask yourself, "Are these people likely to be in my target market?" If so, go for it enthusiastically. If not, you are probably wasting your time.

Articles

Writing an article for a journal or magazine, or a column for a newspaper, can help get you some visibility and credibility. Perhaps surprisingly, it probably won't bring you many prospects directly. It's the usual problem, articles do not make an offer or ask for a response. Typically, you won't get much response.

Don't let that discourage you, though. If you feel you have some-thing worthwhile to say, and know of someone who will publish it, by all means *do* write your article. Why bother? For three reasons:

1. Reprints of an article make terrific credibility builders. Put a copy in your presentation book; send one along with your pro-posals or when you respond to requests for information. You will automatically gain perceived value in the eyes of your prospective customers.

2. Publications provide you with a graceful and natural way of get-ting qualifying responses during a speech. Nobody will bat an eye if you offer to send people a reprint; in fact, even groups that are allergic to "selling from the podium" will be grateful for the offer. And you get their names and addresses!

3. A mailing of reprints gives you an excellent occasion to activate your referral network. "I thought you might be interested in this. Do you know anyone else who might like a copy?"

It doesn't much matter where you publish your article, within rea-son. Sure, *Harvard Business Review* would be nice—your mother would be pleased—but it is likely that very few of your prospects have ever published anything anywhere. A genuine article still carries some weight in most circles, regardless of where it was published.

Just be sure to get plenty of reprints, and use them!

13 | The Media Massage

"Does it really pay to advertise?"

Thirty or 40 years ago some things were simpler than they are today, some truths seemed self-evident. Love meant marriage; horse meant carriage; and marketing meant advertising—specifically, advertising in "the media": TV, radio, magazines, newspapers. You couldn't have one without the other.

Today we have a different view. Love may or may not mean marriage; songs today tend to ask, "What's love got to do with it?" Horses are still with us, but when was the last time you saw a carriage? Perhaps most amazing, we have discovered that it's possible to market services effectively without doing any media advertising at all!

Don't get me wrong. For the large majority, love and marriage still *do* go together. And for many service businesses, advertising is still an important part of their marketing plan. Used properly and judiciously there are few more powerful methods of generating new customers than advertising. But the simple fact is that most advertising campaigns for service firms are costly and ineffective, because the necessary criteria for cost-effective advertising are not met.

The purpose of this chapter is to help you decide whether it makes sense to soften up *your* target market with a media massage. Should you advertise? If so, where? What should you do to make sure you get your money's worth?

Does It Really Pay to Advertise?

Let's ask some real experts, owners of successful service businesses like yours and mine.

183

- "I've never spent a cent on advertising, and I probably never will. I've built my firm without it." That's Marion talking, the owner of the fabulously successful consulting firm whom I introduced in Chapter 1. "I specialize in large systems change. That's not like selling soap. No CEO of a major corporation is going to see an ad in a magazine and say: 'Gee, maybe I should talk to these people about revamping our corporate culture.' If anything, they would assume we weren't heavyweight enough for them if we have to advertise." (On the other hand, one of the largest and most profitable management consulting firms in the world recently ran a series of prominent full-page ads in *Forbes* magazine. The firm obviously assumed that CEOs would react exactly the way Marion assumes they won't. They may have been right. *Forbes* is a heavyweight magazine in the business world; it was worth a try. Naturally enough, the firm refuses to discuss the results of its advertising, so we are left to draw our own conclusions. The fact is, they no longer run those ads.)

- "Depends on what you mean by advertising, Tony." This is Jason, the statistician half of a husband-and-wife team who have made a tidy fortune marketing workshops through the mail. "I can't imagine wasting money on TV or radio or magazine ads. They are just not cost-effective, and there's no way to *really* know what you're getting for your money. But we spend thousands of dollars a month to print and send out our mailers. You could call that advertising if you want, but I think of it just as marketing. It doesn't have much in common with media advertising. For example, I've never met an ad copywriter who could write a really good direct-mail piece."

- "It took me a while to come around, but I advertise now and get good results." Dr. John, the chiropractor, was dead set against advertising when we first started working together. "My Yellow Pages ad makes a terrific difference in my practice. And if I'm careful, I can get good results from advertising my public talks in the local monthly paper. Some of my competitors pay the newspaper to stuff their free-exam certificates in the middle of the paper right along with the inserts from K-Mart and Sears. Maybe it works for them, but it's not for me."

- "How can you be in business and not advertise?" Maria runs a gourmet catering service. "I take every cent I can lay my hands on and plow it into advertising, and it pays! I always monitor the results of each of my ads. Whether it's in the paper, or in magazines or radio, doesn't matter. What counts is how much business it pulls. If an ad doesn't pull, I cancel it and put the money into an ad that does. I'm not big enough for TV yet, but I'm looking at using local cable next. I can't imagine trying to build a business in catering without advertising *all* the time."

So *does* it pay to advertise? Sometimes it does, sometimes it doesn't. The trick is to go full-steam ahead when it does, and either steer clear or get out quickly when it doesn't. Which is which? You can't always know for sure in advance. No ad is guaranteed to pull enough business to be worthwhile. But some are almost guaranteed to be *not* worthwhile. Let's start by getting those out of the way.

It Never Pays to Advertise When . . .

. . .√ *All You Are Doing Is Creating "Awareness"*

Most of us labor under a tremendous handicap when we try to advertise our services:

We have all seen far too many ads.

We have developed a deep, implicit sense of what advertising should be like, and we consciously or unconsciously make our ads like all those others. Unfortunately, more than half of those other ads were unsuccessful, and the rest were for businesses that have little in common with your own. If you go by "what everybody knows" about advertising, you are almost guaranteeing failure.

The clearest and most costly example of this is advertising designed to create "awareness." Ten years ago it seemed that "everybody knew" that the purpose of advertising in service businesses was to create "awareness." We had seen thousands of ads on TV that did nothing but tell the product's name and try to make it look cute or sexy. If it works for General Foods, why shouldn't it work for Maria's Catering? And it makes a certain kind of sense; before they hire you they have to know your name.

So we saw (and still see, alas!) a flood of ads that basically said, "We're really good! Try us next time you need a . . . ." This is the kind of ad that gives advertising a bad name—not with consumers, but with the advertisers themselves. You can burn up a tremendous amount of money for no noticeable gain with "awareness" advertising.

The deadly problem with "awareness" advertising is that it calls for no response on the part of the prospect who sees or hears it. This is a killer for two reasons: (1) you have absolutely no way to assess the ad's actual impact (it could have no impact, or even negative impact, and you have no way of knowing!) and (2) the ad does nothing to move anybody down the funnel toward Customer.

Media advertising for a service business has one specific purpose: to create Qualified Prospects to feed into your marketing machine. Think of your ad as a mass qualifying letter to your market. It must accomplish the three goals of any qualifying communication:

1. Get the prospects to recognize, "They're talking to me!"
2. Get them to see the benefit.
3. Make them an offer and show them how to respond.

Consumer product giants who "own the slot in the consumer's mind" (that's how some ad folks talk these days) can afford to run ads that just create awareness, although that is the subject of hot debate even among ad professionals. *You* can't. *All* of your ads—no exceptions—should be designed to move people through your marketing machine. That means your ads must make some kind of offer that calls for a response, and show the prospect how to respond.

Creating awareness of your firm and its services is an important part of marketing. In the previous chapter, we went over several methods, mostly free or low-cost, for achieving it. Every response ad also serves the purpose of creating awareness, but if your ad is meant to do nothing *but* create awareness, can it. Use your money to buy a lottery ticket instead. At least that will give you a shot at a real return on your money.

. . . *The Only Thing Distinctive About Your Ad Is Word-Play or "Look and Feel"*

Another thing "everybody knows" about advertising is that your ad must be distinctive. It must have a clever slogan or a visual stopper—anything that will grab the prospect's attention.

Fine. You've got my attention. *Now what are you going to do with it?*

For many ads, unfortunately, the answer is: Not much. It's as if the task of grabbing the prospect's attention is so difficult that, having accomplished it, the ad's creator falls exhausted to the ground, leaving the prospect to find his or her own way out. This is bad advertising.

Good advertising uses distinctive verbal and/or visual elements to grab the prospect's attention. It then uses that attention to communicate a distinctive message about your service, and causes the prospect to take action. It communicates what ad professionals have traditionally called your USP (Unique Selling Proposition). (More on this later.) If your ad does not communicate your USP, it won't pay you to advertise.

After all, you're not spending all that money to get people to remember your *ad*; you're spending it to get people to remember your *service*. Make sure your ad makes people notice and remember your USP.

. . . You Have No Way of Measuring the Effectiveness of Your Ad

Decades of hard research have revealed some sobering truths about advertising:

1. Ads do not always increase sales. Many have no impact at all; some actually hurt sales.

2. Small differences in ads, like simply changing a headline, or playing up one benefit rather than another, can increase sales by as much as *ten times* or more.

3. *Nothing* will predict the success of an ad, not expert opinion, not laboratory testing, not focus groups. All of these are useful, but there is no substitute for actually running the ad and seeing what happens.

Adding these up, you can easily see that the worst mistake you can make in advertising is running an ad when you have no way to measure the actual response to it. It is also the most *common* mistake in advertising. Every ad should pull for a specific response. That response should be in some way unique to that ad. When people call or write in response to one of your ads, you should be able to tell without a doubt *which* ad they are responding to. This enables you to improve your ads and weed out the ads and the specific media that don't get response or pull the least. If your newspaper ad gets poor response, you can drop it and put those funds into the media that do produce results. You can't do this unless you can track which ad generated which responses.

When Does It Pay to Advertise?

There is only one honest answer to that question:

It pays to advertise when your ad generates much more revenue than it costs.

In other words, it pays to advertise when it *pays* to advertise. How can you make sure of payback? You can never be *sure*, so you must always keep track of what actually happens. Two obvious approaches will greatly increase your chances with advertising:

1. Pick the right media for your business.

2. Create a great ad and make sure it works.

Let's look first at which media make sense for you.

Where Does It Pay to Advertise?

There are no "perfect" media. Different businesses require different media to reach and influence their target market. Read this section carefully, to decide which make sense for your business.

Choosing media because they are inexpensive, or avoiding them because they cost a lot, is a big mistake. The only "expensive" advertising is advertising that does not generate much more revenue than it costs. A five-dollar ad that gets you no business is expensive; a $1000 ad that draws $20 thousand in sales is a raving bargain.

Yellow Pages

If you have a business phone, you are entitled to a free listing in the Yellow Pages: name, address, phone number. More than that, you pay for annually and in advance, and it's not cheap.

Is it worthwhile? I know of one business that advertises *only* in the Yellow Pages and does very, very well. Many businesses find that a Yellow Pages ad as part of their overall advertising mix is a good investment; other businesses don't bother with the Yellow Pages, for good reason. I have also known some businesses that have hurt themselves badly with expensive Yellow Pages ads that didn't pay off.

Yellow Pages ads are definitely worthwhile if your services meet three criteria:

1. *Customers typically need you urgently.*

They are in pain or discomfort; a disaster has struck; something they have been putting off has finally broken down. They need help *now*; no time to ask around. They reach for the phone book and turn to the Yellow Pages; now whom do they call? This is advertising at the best possible moment: when the prospect is making a buying decision.

2. *Customers typically need you infrequently.*

The less frequently they have need of your services, the less likely they are to already have somebody in mind. They know they need a Caterer, but which one? They look in the Yellow Pages under "Caterers." (If they already have somebody in mind, they will look in the White Pages where you only have to look up the name.)

3. *Customers immediately associate their need with your Yellow Pages category.* Are you listed in the category that automatically pops into mind when customers need your kind of services? If you're not, *don't waste your money on a Yellow Pages ad!* It's like running a great ad in a magazine that nobody in your target market reads—an expensive mistake. Here's

the acid test: Do people ordinarily know that they need your services before they talk to you? Do they usually have an accurate view of when your services are useful and what the benefit is? Or do you usually have to educate your prospect about the need for, and benefit of, your kind of services before they buy? Unless they automatically and accurately associate their need with your category, Yellow Pages ads are not likely to be a good investment.

If you meet all three criteria, invest in a great Yellow Pages ad. It will almost certainly be worthwhile, and may prove to be your best single advertising buy.

If you meet only two criteria—"urgency" and "association," or "infrequency" and "association," a Yellow Pages ad is very likely to be a good investment, but you will certainly need to supplement it with good promotion and perhaps some other advertising.

You only meet the third criterion? Then you need to dig into this a bit deeper before you decide. You may discover that putting your money into promotion or other kinds of advertising is a better use of your resources. Look at the phone book and notice what your competitors are doing. If you see a riot of color and large boxed ads, you can assume that your competitors are getting customers through the Yellow Pages. Do you want some of that action? If you see only some small boxed ads and a sprinkling of color, you can safely assume that your money is best spent elsewhere. (You might consider adding a little red to your listing. That doesn't cost much and is the biggest single boost.)

Specialized Directories

If you provide services for organizations rather than individuals, you might find it worthwhile to advertise in one of the many specialized directories, which are like segmented versions of the Yellow Pages. They list, for example, all firms that provide training or consulting services. Like the Yellow Pages, they typically provide a free listing, which may include a substantial amount of specific information on your services. (If they ask you to pay for a basic listing, you should almost certainly pass them by.) They also provide the opportunity to pay for more elaborate listings.

Should you pay to advertise in specialized directories? That largely depends on your strategy for moving prospects through your marketing machine. It is naive to assume that someone will call you up and hire you on the basis of a listing in a specialized directory; I've never heard of that happening. Instead, you will get requests for brochures and catalogs, and/or requests to submit proposals. In other words, you will get the names and addresses of Qualified Prospects. Are you set up to turn a Qualified Prospect into a Tryer? If so, ask two more questions:

1. How much is each Qualified Prospect worth to you? You determine that by finding out how many Qualified Prospects you need to get one customer and dividing that into the average amount a customer pays for your services. For example, if it takes 20 Qualified Prospects to create one customer, and your average per customer is $250, each Qualified Prospect is worth $12.50.

2. How many Qualified Prospects can you expect from your ad? You find that out by asking the directory's salesperson, who should have solid numbers on past results from ads like yours. Don't settle for the "best-case" results (One company got 500 responses!); insist on knowing the range and average of results.

Multiply the number of Qualified Prospects you can expect by the amount each is worth to you. That's your expected return from your ad. Unless your expected return is *much* greater than the cost of the ad (at least 10 times greater is a good rule of thumb) take the free listing and put your money elsewhere.

General Circulation Magazines

Magazine advertising is great for consumer products with national or at least strong regional distribution. It's a questionable investment for service businesses. You may find some magazines that are a great match for you and are cost-effective. Most service businesses don't.

One simple test: Does the circulation of this magazine coincide with your service area? Unless you are willing to travel wherever your clients are, or you are considering a local or regional magazine, forget advertising in general circulation magazines. Why waste dollars advertising to people who couldn't possibly become your customers?

Magazines have one distinct advantage over other mass media: their readership is more clear-cut and defined. If you are marketing computer consulting, for example, you can find magazines whose readers are all computer users. Your dollars will put your message in front of people who are completely within your target market.

But that can sometimes be a disadvantage as well. The readership profile of a magazine is no secret; every other computer consulting firm is also considering placing an ad in that same magazine. It will take a remarkably good ad to cut through the clutter, and even a great ad may not be enough. The end result of so many ads for similar services in one place can be like hearing 50 musical pieces all played at once: Even great performances get lost in the general noise. (Pick up a copy of *Byte* magazine sometime and just leaf through it. You'll see what I mean.)

Remember that the purpose of advertising your service business is to generate Qualified Prospects. To do that, you must both get your ad in front of people in your target market and get their attention. The easier it is to do the first task, the harder it may be to do the second. Your ad is useless if it fails on either count.

If you decide to try magazine advertising, here are some tips:

- Try to find magazines that are read primarily by people in your target market. (Better to be competing in a tough race than not getting to run at all.) Ask people in your target market where they would expect to see ads for services like yours, and whether they actually read those magazines! Look at *Consumer Magazine and Farm Publication Rates and Data*, put out by SRDS (Standard Rate and Data Service, Inc.), for names of publications that might be a good match for you. Your library probably has a copy. If you see some that interest you, write their marketing departments and ask for data on their readership.

- Start as small as possible. Sign up for *one* ad run in *one* issue. Politely decline the offer of great discounts for long-term contracts. Try the ad once and find out for yourself what your results are.

- Don't necessarily go for the smallest possible ad. Pay for the size that gives you enough space for your message. Better to pay for a full page that generates 1000 prospects than an eighth-page ad that generates 10.

- If you find an ad and a magazine that work for you, stick with them until they stop working. Don't feel you have to change your ad just because you have run it so many times before. Consistency in advertising beats variety every time, and by a wide margin. Keep track of results; when they start to drop off you can change your ad. Until then, be grateful for your success and leave it alone.

On the bottom line, does your ad generate Qualified Prospects for a cost that is comparable to your other methods of qualifying prospects? If it does, keep it. If it doesn't, consider whether those dollars might be better spent for more mailings, or a bigger Yellow Pages listing, or better quality printing for your brochures, or . . . you know the rest.

Trade and Professional Journals

Magazines are like the Yellow Pages; trade and professional publications are like specialized directories. They are well-targeted and may reach exactly the market you want. They are different from magazines in an important respect: Many readers of professional and trade publications are as interested in the ads as they are in the editorial content. They often read these journals specifically to see what products and services are available, so your great ad may have a better chance of getting their attention.

Ask your customers what trade and professional journals they read and which ones they most respect. SRDS has another publication of interest which your library should have: *Business Publication Rates and Data*. You may find some good vehicles for inexpensively qualifying prospects.

Newspapers

Newspapers *may* be your best bet for advertising your services. You're local; they're local. You want to experiment and find out what works; they are flexible and give you lots of chances to try things. They bring people the news; just by appearing there, your ad seems part of what's happening today. On the other hand, there are all those pages and so little time to read. Unless you pick your shots carefully, you run the risk of getting no response.

Consider newspaper advertising if your services are:

1. *Bought by individuals for personal use.*
Products can be effectively advertised to businesses via newspapers; services rarely can.

2. *Used frequently and/or regularly.*
Frequent use greatly increases the chances that the individuals reading your ad will need your service soon. If they don't need it now, chances are they won't remember you when they do need it. If your services tend to be seasonal (lawn care, tax preparation) and this is the season, newspaper ads can be very productive.

3. *Able to be packaged into an enticing free sample.*
Remember, your ad is meant to get a qualifying response. Nothing does that like an offer of a free sample: "Call today to schedule your free . . . ."

If you score a hit on all three criteria, try newspaper ads and see what happens. If you missed on one or more, you're probably better off putting your money into mailings, promotions, or other media like the Yellow Pages.

Radio

Print ads work through the eyes; radio ads work through the ears. This simple fact makes a big difference. When you hear something, you take it in all at once, with no second chance. Because of this, radio more than all other media relies on repetition: repetition within the ad, repetition of the ad. You can run a print ad once and expect some results; running a radio ad once is a sure way to waste money. You must run the same ad many times, and almost certainly on more than one station, before it begins to stick well enough in people's minds to lead to action.

How can you afford so much repetition? Relax. You're confusing radio with television. Radio can be surprisingly inexpensive and very cost-effective when used right.

Should you use radio? To do so effectively, you need the usual ingredients of a qualifying communication, plus:

1. A benefit that can be stated very simply and memorably, like the classic jingle: "It cleans your breath (What a toothpaste!), while it guards your teeth."

2. A business name that is both distinctive and memorable. Remember, you are trying to get listeners to qualify themselves. You are going to ask them to call you, but they won't remember your phone number, so don't bother giving it to them. Instead you must repeat your business name, and it must be one that will stick. "Jones, Smith and Johnson" is not memorable; "Molly Maid" cleaning service or "Mr. Does-All" handyman service is. They will look you up in the White Pages when they know your name. Please, don't tell people to find you in the Yellow Pages. Why spend all that money to invite them to look over your competitors?

Radio can be as plain as a disk jockey reading a prepared text or as fancy as a pretaped "slice-of-life" melodrama, complete with musical sound track and background sound effects. Both cost the same amount to broadcast, but they are quite different in "ear appeal." If you use radio, pack in as much ear appeal as possible. Take those qualifying scenarios you prepared in Chapter 8 and make them into mini dramas. The extra cost of making the tape, spread out over many repetitions, adds little to the cost per repetition. The sizzle can add a lot to the bottom-line results.

TV

We can deal with TV in one sentence: You can't afford it. What's more, you wouldn't want to use TV if you could afford it. TV is a lightbulb medium; you're doing laser-like marketing. Put your money where it will do you some real good.

Want details? Pros say that you must be able to pay for 150 gross ratings points (GRPs) per month before it makes sense to advertise on TV, and you should assume a minimum campaign of three months. How much do 150 GRPs cost? Depends on where you live. In small towns it may cost as little as $1000; in big cities, it can cost as much as $75,000 or more. That's *each month,* remember. Add to that the cost of creating a good TV ad, and you're talking about some real money.

It may be worthwhile, but can you afford the risk of finding out it's not? Consumer products firms usually have no choice; they must advertise on TV or get out of the market. You have a choice. Don't.

. . . But Don't Forget Cable

The upsurge of cable TV has opened up the possibility of TV advertising for even small service businesses. This industry is changing rapidly but in some places you can find "local" slots available on cable for roughly what you would pay for a good radio ad. If you can find a program and time slot that might attract people in your target audience, and if your service can be memorably demonstrated in a short time, consider a cable ad that both shows and tells.

―――― **WORKWORK: YOUR ADVERTISING PLAN** ――――――――――

Now that you've seen the options, let's draw up a quick-and-dirty advertising plan for you. First jot down all the media that make sense for your business. Don't worry yet about whether you can afford them all.

Your advertising budget comes next. Start from the bottom line and work up.

How many customers do you need per year? Write that down and label it "Number of Customers."

How much does each customer pay for your services? That's the "average per customer" you figured out in Chapter 9.

Now imagine I came to you with a business proposition: "I will be your agent. Pay me a fixed sum per customer, and I will provide the customers. You just do the work."

Ask yourself, "How much would I be willing to pay for a customer?"

Think about this *hard.* We are looking for the *most* you would be able to pay and still make your margins. Don't engage in wishful thinking, but don't overpay either. Write down a figure, then try increasing or decreasing it by 10 percent at a time, until you have a figure that looks like the most you could comfortably afford to pay for a customer. Label that figure "Cost per Customer."

Now multiply Number of Customers by Cost per Customer. That's a quick-and-dirty estimate of your overall marketing budget—what it will cost you to generate the new customers you will need.

Try this example. If you need 300 customers per year (Number of Customers = 300) and you would be willing to pay $20 for each customer

(Cost per Customer = $20), then your overall marketing budget will be: $300 \times \$20 = \$6000$.

Don't forget, advertising does only part of the job. It gets you the Qualified Prospects, but you still have to convert them into customers. That costs money. Remember also that advertising is not your only source of Qualified Prospects; mailings and other promotional activities also require some marketing money.

Then how much should you set aside for your advertising budget? Your Marketing Information System will soon give you the guidance you need to fine-tune your own marketing mix, but, for now, pick a percentage that *seems* right to you, and then pay careful attention to what actually happens in your marketing. (If you have no idea, try setting aside 50 percent of your overall marketing budget for the advertising budget at first.)

Where should you advertise? Put your advertising money into the media that give you the lowest "Cost per Qualified Prospect." How much will an ad cost you? How many responses can you expect to get from the ad? Divide the number of responses into the cost, to get the Cost per Qualified Prospect.

For each of the media you have listed as a possibility for your advertising, figure out a Cost per Qualified Prospect. Make a list of these media, in order of Cost per Qualified Prospect, with the lowest Cost per Qualified Prospect first.

Assume you will advertise in the top-ranked medium. Subtract the amount of this ad from your advertising budget. If you have enough left in your advertising budget, advertise in the next medium on your list. Keep going until you have allocated all your advertising budget.

This "best-guess" plan will get you started, but please remember how many pure assumptions are built into it!

Keep track of your expenditures on advertising, and your results, so that your next advertising plan will be laser-like in its focus and effectiveness.

Making Sure Your Ads Work

Now you know *where* you will advertise. All that remains is to create a great ad and make sure it works.

Just one little problem: What's a great ad?

Most of us are sure we can recognize a great ad when we see one. There's some truth to that point of view, but unfortunately not enough to build a business around. Decades of hard research have shown conclusively that not even the most experienced advertising professionals can recognize a great ad when they see it. Some ads you love but they don't work; some ads leave you cold but are tremendously effective. Every advertising pro has a dozen examples of ads that won awards but didn't sell more soap.

Great ads don't get awards, great ads get results. But which results? This is where things can get sticky if you let them:

- People who sell ads will suggest that you should concern yourself mostly with "exposure." This is reasonable from their point of view. Mass media advertising is mostly built around a "per-exposure" pricing structure. You pay so many dollars per thousand readers or viewers, assuming that the more people who see your ad, the more customers you will get. This is a very shaky assumption. You can go broke quickly from judging your advertising on a per-exposure basis.

- People who create ads tend to prefer "recall" figures. They will tell you that what counts is not how many people *see* your ad but how many people *remember* your ad. This is a step in the right direction, but not a big enough step. Too many memorable ads have had no noticeable effect on sales.

- People from a direct-marketing background (and your accountant) will suggest that a great ad is one that increases sales—no ifs ands, or buts. In direct marketing, the only response to an ad is a sale. It's a nice, clean, no-nonsense relation: more sales, good ad; no more sales, bad ad. That's why direct-marketing people are such experts on how to write copy that works. This too is definitely in the right direction but probably goes a bit too far for your business. You almost certainly are using a "two-step" process: first get a qualifying response, then activate that interest and convert it into a sale. The follow-up materials contribute as much (or more) to the ultimate sale as the original ad does. If you take a hard-nosed "sales only" approach to assessing your advertising, you could kill a great ad when the real villain is your packaging or activation offer.

You can avoid all this stickiness by remembering that in a service business, your ad is a qualifying letter sent to a lot of people at once. I suggest you take a hard-nosed stance of assessing your advertising strictly on the bases of how many responses it produces, and how much it costs you to get the responses.

A great ad is an ad that gets you the Qualified Prospects you need at a Cost per Prospect that is a raving bargain.

Five tips follow, on how to make sure your ad is a great one.

1. *Always make sure you know exactly what response your ad has drawn.*

Every ad must make a clear offer and show the prospect how to respond. It should also have some unique element that will enable you to know exactly which of your ads generated the response. For example, if you ask people to respond by mail, give them an address like this:

Tidy Tom's Cleaning Service
Dept. MA6
101 Main St.
Boulder, CO 80302

The "Dept." tells you that they saw your June ("6") ad in the monthly ("M") paper, and it was a version "A" of that ad. You know from the address exactly what ad drew this response. You should also put the code on any response coupon you include in your ad.

When people call for information or to take you up on an advertised offer, *always* ask where they heard about you, and write down their answer. This should go into your Marketing Information System, along with their name and address. At least once a month, sit down with your Marketing Information System and figure out how many responses each ad has drawn, and how much each response has cost you. You will quickly begin to learn what's working and what is not.

2. *Make sure your ad is a good qualifying communication.*

Your purpose in advertising is to get someone to say: "I'm interested; tell me more." In Chapter 8 you worked out in detail what your qualifying communications need to say. Make sure your ads say it. If you can't afford enough space or time to get the qualifying message across, don't advertise in that media.

3. *Be sure your ad presents your Unique Selling Proposition.*

The Unique Selling Proposition (USP) is a traditional advertising phrase for a timeless reality:

Your ad must present to the prospect something about your service that seems both distinctive and valuable.

Notice the emphasis on *seems*. A USP can be an ordinary characteristic that would apply to anyone in your line of work, so long as you are the only one who is making a point of it. Consumer products advertising on television sometimes present extreme cases of USPs; TV copywriters will seize on any feature of a product that can be made to stick in the viewers' minds. (They're looking for "recall," remember.)

If you have worked your way through Chapters 8 and 11, you almost certainly have created a powerful and distinctive statement of the benefit of your services to your customer. That's your USP. Make sure it comes through loud and clear.

✓ 4. Test, test, and test.

Remember the headline that sold all those wildlife books: "Do You Have a BIG Bookcase?" It was an afterthought, the twelfth headline tested and the least promising at first glance; but it was the one that worked.

That's advertising. You can't be sure what will work, so you had better find out.

You don't have to run exactly the same ad every time. Until you are sure you have a winner on your hands, you *shouldn't* run exactly the same ad. Try different headlines; different offers; feature different parts of the package or different ways of talking about the benefit. Keep track of which combinations generate the best response. You will improve your results progressively until you have a sure, tested winner.

Once you have a winner, *don't change it!* Run it exactly the same way, in the same media that drew the best response, until your results begin to drop off. (That will probably be long after *you* are sick of that some old ad.) It takes hard work to fine-tune an ad; please don't throw away all that work by dumping it while it's still working for you.

✓ 5. Find out the tricks of your media.

There are hundreds of useful tricks and "secrets" for using the various media effectively. Experience is the best teacher, granted, but sometimes her tuition can be awfully high. In advertising it's better to learn what you can from other people's mistakes before you begin making your own. Here are just a few examples:

- The Yellow Pages are the great equalizer. Your ad can be as large as that of your largest competitors and, in fact, should be. If you are going to advertise at all in the Yellow Pages, make sure your ad is as large and as colorful as the biggest other ad in the category. "Just a little smaller" in this case means "a whole lot less effective." (You have decided not to advertise in the Yellow Pages? Two tips for making the best of your free listing: If you can, name your company something that will ensure that you get the first listing in the section. That spot will increase your calls substantially. Consider spending just a little money to add some red to your listing.)

- Never let your graphic designer talk you into an artistic ad that prints your copy over a photograph or illustration. Readership drops drastically in those ads.

- Always mention your offer in the ad's headline. If you include a coupon, put it in the middle at the *top* of the ad. Research shows this position gets clipped most.

- Don't let a newspaper write or design your ad. Don't let the Yellow Pages write or design your ad. Don't let the radio people write your ad, and don't let the DJ read it. These are all ways to guarantee that your ad looks and sounds just like all the rest, and will not stand out. Pay your writer and designer to create a great ad for you.

Whole books have been written about how to get the most out of advertising on radio or in magazines or the Yellow Pages. I have listed several books in the "Resources" section that can help you learn the ropes without paying for it in blood. I recommend you start with Jay Levinson's *Guerrilla Marketing*, which many of my clients have found useful for nitty-gritty tips.

A Last Note on the Media Massage

Does it pay to advertise? In the final analysis, you have to try it to find out. Media advertising can be an unbeatable way to generate Qualified Prospects. It can also be a way to spend a lot of money for no real return. It's a *part* of your service firm's marketing mix, but it's *only* a part, and it's not always required. Remember:

You **must** market. You may or may not advertise.

14 Selling Without Fear and Loathing

How to Make Selling a Non-Event and Still Succeed

I recently learned a lot more about waterproofing basements than I ever wanted to know.

We live in a nice old house in a quiet neighborhood. Usually I'm aware of the "nice" part; occasionally I'm reminded of the "old." Like when we had non-stop rains for two days one Spring and the basement flooded. Imagine my surprise and horror when I walked down the stairs to the basement and saw the power supply to my home computer *almost* submerged in water. I walked back upstairs, turned off the electricity to the basement, and started looking in the Yellow Pages under "Basements—Waterproofing." (I also checked my homeowner's insurance; the flood wasn't covered. Rats!)

A few days later a very nice young man was sitting in my living room explaining why it made sense to waterproof by inviting the water in rather than trying to keep it out. I was actually enjoying his pitch quite a bit. He was sincere and well-informed, used a first-rate pitchbook, and had the most fascinating briefcase from which he kept pulling things like lengths of plastic pipe to illustrate his points. He almost had me convinced when suddenly there was a subtle change in the atmosphere. The nice young man seemed suddenly a bit awkward. His voice thickened a little and he leaned forward with a touch too much confidence as he said, "Now tell me, Mr. Putman, if you should decide that this is the way to go, is there any obstacle to your making an appointment tonight so that our crew can get to you as soon as possible?"

The old salesman in me recognized the Asking for Objections and Presumptive Close combination: not badly done, but a bit stiff. But the customer in me was turned off. Suddenly instead of being on my side, he was lining me up for the kill. As kindly as I could I explained that I never sign a contract for something this expensive without sleeping on it. He seemed both disappointed and relieved. (Most sales veterans would have licked their chops at the challenge.) He finished his pitch, made another half-hearted attempt to close the sale, and left me his card. I called him back later to say I had hired someone else. What I didn't tell him was that I might have signed with his firm that night if he hadn't torpedoed the relationship with his premature close attempt. Another sale done in by Adversarial Selling.

Let me be absolutely clear: I have nothing against sales or salespeople. I enjoy selling. I view sales as an honorable and necessary activity without which business would grind to a halt. Some of the finest and most ethical people I know have been in sales. I have earned my living as a salesman and am proud of it. It's hard work, and good salespeople are worth every dollar they are paid.

Unfortunately, that puts me in a small minority among service providers. Almost universally, service providers treat selling like taking nasty-tasting medicine: it may be necessary, but it's distasteful. Even people who *want* to sell often have trouble making themselves do it. As one ambitious young man told me in anguish: "Tony, I just got back from spending $800 on a professional selling skills course, and you know what I did this afternoon? I spent *three hours* just sitting and staring at the Yellow Pages! I couldn't even bring myself to pick up the phone!" And this is a fellow who believes so strongly in his service that he paid for the selling skills course out of his own pocket!

What's going on here? Why do so many people have so much trouble with sales and selling? In my experience people have trouble with selling because they have a fundamental misunderstanding about what it is and how to do it. Change the understanding, and the problems vanish.

That's what this chapter is for. I do not intend to offer you a list of tips and tricks for good selling. (There are hundreds of books that do a good job of that; I have listed a few in the "Resources" section.) Instead I want to help you examine your own view of selling, and remove the anxiety and distaste surrounding it. This chapter is meant to help you free yourself to become the best salesperson you can be.

Fear and Loathing in Selling

Sharon summed it up beautifully. "You know, Tony, I love everything about my job except the selling part. *That* I'm not so crazy about." (That's *strong* coming from Sharon. If she were in traction with two broken legs I'm sure she would say, "You know, I'm not so crazy about this.")

"Why's that?"

"I don't know—I just get so tense and it feels so *different* from everything else I do. I mean, in selling you have to persuade the other person, right? You know what *you* need and you have to get them to agree. But I don't *work* that way. In my work my customer and I are on the same side. So I can't wait to finish the selling part so I can get back to feeling good about what I'm doing."

Sharon dreads selling. She approaches it with fear and distaste. Your reaction may not be as strong as hers, and I imagine you would use different words to describe it, but if you are like most service providers you probably share Sharon's experience to some degree.

The problem is how you are thinking about sales. Most of us have an implicit model of selling that I call Adversarial Selling. The model is this:

> Selling and service are different things. First you have to sell, then you deliver the service. Selling means persuading the prospect to buy what you have to offer. You do that by carefully scoping out what the prospect needs and believes, and then building your case point by point. Once you have established need and benefit, your task is to surface objections and eliminate them, wearing down the prospect's resistance to buying until you see your opportunity and you close the sale. All successful selling ends in that moment of truth, that heady instant of triumph when you ask for the order and get it! From then on, if you're smart, you will continue to stroke the customer (if only to overcome "buyer's remorse"), but your job is essentially done when the signature is on the dotted line. From then on, it's a matter of servicing the account.

In other words, selling is a bullfight in which you are the matador and the prospect is the bull. The sale is the "moment of truth" when the matador–salesperson triumphs over the bull–customer and closes the sale. No wonder things start feeling different when it's "sales time!"

Perhaps the image of a bullfight is a little farfetched for you. That's fine. The important thing is to notice that our typical model of selling is a contest or a struggle; a discrete event, separate from the rest of our service, in which the object is to win over the prospect and make the sale.

If that's how you see selling, things are going to be hard in some very predictable ways:

- Adversarial Selling is hard on the customer. Bullfights aren't such great things for the bull. Prospects who experience you as trying to line them up for the kill are very likely to respond by backing off or going into resistance, like I did with the waterproofing salesman.

- Adversarial Selling is hard on the relationship. In your business you work to align yourself with your customers. If you and your market disagree, usually *you* change to bring about alignment. In Adversarial Selling you line up against your customers until you win them over. This kind of selling distorts the relationship in ways that can be difficult to recover from.

- Adversarial Selling is hard on you. The wear and tear of your Jekyll-and-Hyde switching is enormous. First you are aligned with your market; then you go into sales mode and line up against them; then you jump back into alignment. No surprise, then, that the most common wish I hear from service providers is: "I wish I could find somebody else to do the selling and I would just do the work."

Adversarial Selling is hard on everybody. No wonder that burnout among salespeople is so high! It's not just us amateurs; even the pros experience it. Door-to-door salespeople have an old and very revealing saying: "The hardest door to get through is your own." Adversarial Selling wears you down and, eventually, out.

OK, we know what the problem is. What's the solution?

Relationship Selling

The solution lies in changing your basic model of what selling is all about. Adversarial Selling is a trap and an illusion. Selling that way is hard, unrewarding work. Really effective salespeople don't treat selling as a contest—never have, never will. A secret that successful salespeople have always known will look very familiar to you:

> Selling is the person-to-person process of establishing the relationship of "customer." The sale occurs when both parties acknowledge that the relationship has been established.

In other words, selling is a specific part of marketing, no different in tone or intent from everything else you do in marketing. The "sale" is essentially a non-event, a simple acknowledgment of what has already occurred! Think you might find it easier to sell this way?

I call this model of selling "Relationship Selling." It's not original; people in sales have used the term for years. (Jim Cathcart has written a good book by that title, listed in the "Resources" section.) Let's look at Relationship Selling in detail and see how it works.

Which Relationship?

The magic in Relationship Selling comes from realizing which relationship we are talking about. In the familiar sales situation, the relationship is simple: "I am the prospect and you are the salesperson. Your actions are all congruent with that relationship, and I will see them in that light. You are here to sell me something."

It's such an everyday thing that we sometimes don't notice ourselves doing it. A woman behind a sales counter points out an advantage of this model, and in your mind you respond, "Makes sense—but then, she *would* say that; she's trying to sell me something."

Our guard is up. We are prepared to take everything with a grain of salt and discount half of what we hear because, after all, "They're just saying that because they want to sell us something."

This is the relationship you want to avoid.

The relationship you are trying to create is exactly the relationship we have been talking about throughout this book: the relationship that occurs when you are working with your customers at your professional best. In Adversarial Selling you put the cart before the horse: you sell them, and then you create the relationship they are buying. In Relationship Selling you simply turn the sequence around: first create the relationship they want with you, then sell it to them. In other words:

Never go into sales mode.

There should never be a time when your customers experience you as "here to sell me something." Instead, they should always, consistently experience you as "here to help me get something that's important to me"—that Core Benefit of your services you have examined so thoroughly.

As we saw in Chapter 5, you must begin creating that professional relationship from the first words out of your mouth. Be consistent and congruent, and *never* change to any other relationship. That's the core secret of Relationship Selling. If you have worked your way through this book, that advice should sound like something you will have no trouble doing.

The real trick is to *avoid* doing things that will look like selling! There are two big traps to avoid: persuasion and the "moment of truth." Let's look at those now.

Avoid Persuasion

Joan looked at me in stunned disbelief. "I can't believe I'm hearing this from Tony Putman. For almost a year now you and I have been working on creating an incredible set of marketing materials for me. You've been hammering home that I've got to go out and actively create relationships and sell the sizzle and all that—and now you're telling me that I've got to avoid persuasion when I'm selling! I don't get it. I thought the whole point was to become as persuasive as possible!"

I had to admit she had a good point. "I didn't say avoid *being persuasive*, Joan. I said avoid *persuasion*. It's a subtle difference, but the difference it makes is about as subtle as being hit with a baseball bat.

"I'll give you a good example of what I mean by persuasion. Just last night I got a cold call from a stockbroker who obviously was working from one of those 'get them in the habit of saying Yes' scripts. Every statement he made was immediately followed by a question: 'We estimate the return on this will be 18 percent. Does that sound good to you, Mr. Putman?' After about three rounds of this I was so annoyed I just hung up on him. His persuasion was so lo id I couldn't hear his story.

"Everything you do in marketing, all the relationship building and packaging and presentation and so on, should *be persuasive*. Your marketing is designed to give your customers the best possible chance to decide that they want to hire you. Everything you do and say, and all your materials, must present a single, attractive picture. In that sense, being persuasive is the name of the game.

"*Persuasion*, though, is a different matter. Persuasion is when I'm trying to *make* you see things my way. It's stacking the deck: Instead of respecting your right to decide things your own way, I'm trying to make sure your decision is the one I want. So I crowd you, subtly or not so subtly trying to bully you into agreement with me.

"Problem is, persuasion tends to backfire. Instead of moving you toward agreement, far more often it puts you off; nobody likes being pushed around. And it poisons the relationship that you've worked so hard to create; now you've become just another pushy salesperson, and we all know how to deal with them.

"So stay away from persuasion in selling, Joan. You don't need it. You've worked hard to create persuasive materials; trust them to work for you. Act with confidence, tell your story convincingly, and trust your customers to make up their own minds. You don't have to twist their arms to get them to agree with you. If you've done your homework, you will be so persuasive that you'll never have to persuade."

Make the "Moment of Truth" a Non-Event

Veteran sales trainers know that the hardest part of selling is closing the sale. Almost anybody can call up and make the appointment; it's fairly easy to break the ice and make the pitch. But closing the sale? That's not so easy. That's what separates the real sales professionals from the amateurs.

Salespeople often get cold feet and sweaty palms as the "moment of truth" approaches. Rather than risk rejection or blowing the entire account, they shy away from closing. They become like high-jumpers facing a difficult height: they pace, stretch, fidget, run up, and veer off; they do everything but go for it.

The problem has a simple solution: lower the height of the bar. Closing the sale should not require a great leap on your part or the customers'. Closing should be one more small step in a series of steps already taken, an acknowledgment of something that has already occurred. In your mind and in theirs, they have already become your customers.

Your task then, as it has been throughout the marketing process, is to intentionally create with this person the relationship of "customer." The sale is closed when both of you acknowledge that the relationship has been established.

How do you go about making the "moment of truth" a non-event? Here are three guiding principles:

1. *Assume the relationship.*

Three umpires were discussing the nature of the game of baseball. The first umpire said, "There's balls, and there's strikes, and I call 'em like I see 'em."

The second umpire said, "No, that's wrong. There's balls, and there's strikes, and I call 'em the way they are."

The third umpire said, "You're both wrong. There's balls, and there's strikes, but they ain't nothing 'till I call 'em!"

In creating relationships, think like the third umpire. The relationship is nothing until you create it, so you may as well create it the way you want it from the beginning. The guiding principle is simple:

Assume from the beginning that this person is your customer.

The way you see people strongly influences how you treat them, and how you treat them strongly influences how they see themselves. If you see me as your customer and treat me as your customer, I'm very likely to see it that way myself.

You worked out a detailed relationship description in Chapter 5, and your tactics for creating it. That's really all you need here. All of your interaction and communication with your customers is intended to give them a consistent experience of you at your professional best. You have a service that will make a beneficial difference in their lives, in a package that represents good value to them. As soon as they see that, it's a small step to acknowledge formally what is already a fact: they have become your customers.

To make sure they don't trip in making that last small step, use the next guiding principle.

2. *Cover the details first.*

It's every rookie salesperson's nightmare come true. You've told your story, they seem really interested, you ask for the order, and you hear those dreaded two words: "Yes, but . . . ."

What follows "Yes, but . . ." is called an "objection" by sales trainers. Veteran salespeople actually welcome an objection because it gives them the opportunity to turn the objection into a close. ("Yes, but I can't afford $200 per month." "Tell me what you can afford, and we'll see how we can work it out.") It's a classic sales technique, and there's nothing wrong with it; if you feel comfortable closing on objections, and it works for you, go for it.

Many service professionals are not comfortable with this technique for a good reason: as soon as "Yes, but . . ." begins, it takes enormous concentration and clarity to avoid getting pulled into a contest. Above all, you want to maintain your aligned relationship. "Yes, but . . ." almost automatically puts you on opposite sides, and getting back into alignment can be very hard.

Don't make things unnecessarily hard for yourself:

Deal with the details *before* they become objections.

To help you do this, I suggest you draw up and use a Summary Sheet. The Summary Sheet covers all the details of the relationship and your services. The work you did on packaging will be a good guideline for making up your Summary Sheet. After you have finished the detailed presentation and discussion of the service package, take out the Summary Sheet and fill in the details. "So let's go back over the highlights and custom-tailor this for you. There are 10 sessions, each lasting one hour. The first session could be on Monday, Wednesday, or Saturday. Which works best with your schedule? Saturday? OK, then . . . ."

Figure 5 shows an example of a Summary Sheet for our old friend, the Tahiti Getaway.

Go over each item. Is it clear? Have any choices that are needed been made? As you cover each point, put a check beside it. Whenever customers choose among options, circle their choice; if they don't want something, cross it off. Write in any custom specifications you have discussed. Keep it low-key and matter-of-fact: what you're doing is the equivalent of a tailor measuring the customer for a new suit.

Leave price and terms for last on your Summary Sheet. Your customers will already have seen the price, so this is just repeating something they have already heard. Focus on terms and methods of payment. "We could put this on your MasterCard, or you could pay it off at $75 per month—or of course you could always pay cash in advance! Which do you think you would prefer?"

If they balk at one of the points, stay in your professional relationship and don't try to persuade. Remember that your task is to help them get the service they need. Treat any objections at this point as problems for the two of you to solve. "I can see how that would be a problem for someone in your situation. Let's explore some options to see how we can solve this."

Rehearse using your Summary Sheet until it becomes a very natural part of telling your story. In particular, imagine the places in the Summary Sheet where a customer might have a problem, and run through how you will respond without getting into "persuasion mode." Don't get so involved with the trees that you forget the forest: begin and end the Summary Sheet by reminding your customer of the Core Benefit this package will produce for them.

The Tahiti Getaway

"Two weeks of total relaxation in the tropical paradise."

For: _____

Includes:

- Round trip airfare.
- All taxes, tips, and visas.
- Limos and luggage, door to door.
- Activities: Swimming, sailing, scuba, sunbathing, etc.
- Hotel:

  _____ Blue Lagoon

  _____ Coral Paradise

  _____ Coconut Beach

  _____ Day's Inn

  _____ Marriot

  _____ Other: _____

Food:

  _____ American Plan

  _____ Ad lib.

Optional excursions:

  _____ Bora Bora

  _____ Hawaii (2-day stopover)

  _____ Other: _____

  _____

  _____

Total Package Price $_____

Payment:

  _____ MasterCard _____ Visa _____ AmEx _____ Discover

  _____ Check (5% discount if paid 14 days in advance)

Result: "Two weeks of total relaxation in the tropical paradise!"

Figure 5   Summary Sheet

_____ WORKWORK: DESIGNING YOUR SUMMARY SHEET _____

Let's design a Summary Sheet for you. Get a blank sheet of paper. At the top, write down the name of your service package and its Core Benefit.

Now draw a line on which the customer's name will be written. Label it, if that seems appropriate. Some possibilities would be "Specifications for" or "Designed for" or "For" before the line. So far, using the Tahiti Getaway example, you have something like:

The Tahiti Getaway
"Two weeks of total relaxation in the tropical paradise."

For _____

Now list all the pieces of your service package, one per line, leaving pricing and terms for last. Whenever there are choices to be made, list the options; if there are optional pieces, list them following the others. Leave a few blank lines at the end for any custom details you design for this customer.

Be sure to restate the benefit at the end, immediately below the pricing and payment method.

Now that you have the rough draft of your Summary Sheet, take it to your graphic designer for layout. The look and feel of this sheet should be completely congruent with your mission, your market, and all your other materials. As you use it, the experience of going through it should graphically remind your customer of the presentation you have given, and the experience of you as a service professional. When you finish, the process of becoming your customer should have been completed in your customer's mind.

By the time you finish the Summary Sheet, all the potential objections are handled! If you now "ask for the order" there are no "Yes, buts . . ." remaining.

But don't "ask for the order." That's too much like a moment of truth. Instead, follow the third guideline.

3. _Don't ask, acknowledge._

You've been through the Summary Sheet and gotten agreement on all points. Now the customer is going to turn to you and say, "OK. I'm sold. Sign me up." Right?

Alas, no. That's not how it works. No matter how small the step has become, it's still up to you to make sure it gets taken.

Be careful at this point not to undo all the good work you've done so far. You and the customer are one small step away from acknowledging the customer relationship; don't go all the way back to square zero by saying something like, "So what do you think?" Instead, use one of two strategies:

- Acknowledge the relationship yourself and ask for agreement. "It looks like this is a good match for you and your circumstances. I would like to provide this service for you. Shall we go ahead and schedule the first meeting?"

- Find the smallest possible step that only a customer could take and suggest it. "You said Saturday would be best for you. We could schedule you for this Saturday or the next. Which do you want?" Or, "We need to get your top people together to launch this program. It usually takes a while to get everyone's calendar together. Let's pick some tentative dates for the launch right now, and you can tell us next week which one you have chosen." Or, "You said you wanted to pay with MasterCard. May I have your card number?"

If they get right up to that last step and can't bring themselves to take it, don't push. Continue to treat is as a problem that the two of you can solve together. If they need to consult others before deciding, offer to meet with them or to send some materials that will make their task easier. Be accepting if they insist on time to think about it; nail down a time when you will call them back for their decision. Above all, stay aligned! As soon as you start trying to persuade, you will lose most of the advantage your careful marketing has given you.

Getting Out of Your Own Way

Relationship Selling is low-key but highly effective; powerful without creating power struggles; persuasive without requiring persuasion. It builds up your business without wearing you down. But you have to get out of your own way to use it. You have to be able to tell your story to another person and willing to accept their decision, without getting yourself torn up in the process.

That's hard for many people, but it needn't be. You can free yourself to be the effective salesperson you *can* be. I've seen it happen many, many times. Let's conclude this chapter by helping you look at you.

_____ **WORKWORK: MIRROR, MIRROR . . .** _____

You need to start by being honest with yourself. How do you *really* feel about selling?

Do you enjoy selling your services? Can you hardly wait to get on the phone and line up appointments? Do you feel your spirits lifting as you approach your next sales call? If you honestly answer "Yes" to these questions, skip the rest of this Workwork.

Selling isn't a completely positive experience for you? Don't feel alone. The vast majority of service professionals feel the same way. Let's dig into it a bit.

What's the hardest part of selling for you? Do you feel awkward or clumsy in a sales situation? Do you find that selling is hard work because you're not sure what to do next? Do you find it hard to handle when people keep saying "No"?

If you feel awkward and clumsy, you're probably trying to be something you're not. Don't. Just be yourself, at your professional best, as we discussed in Chapter 5. You don't have to become somebody different in order to sell; in fact, being yourself is your best selling strategy. As you implement a Relationship Selling strategy, the awkwardness will probably go away.

If selling is hard work, you probably need some practice, perhaps even some training. Go back over the chapters in this book on presentation and promotion; they may help you see what you are missing. Then sit down with one of the books listed in the "Resources" section and organize your sales call. You probably have not thought through exactly what you need to do, and what kind of support you need to do it. Consider taking a course in selling skills. There are many good "professional selling skills" workshops around. They cost a lot more than a book, but they force you to practice and that's important.

The biggest reason people have trouble with selling is the last one: how to handle the constant rejection. If you find that hard to handle, the rest of this exercise is for you.

In doing our work, we succeed almost all the time; people like and appreciate our work, and we rarely have to deal with rejection.

In selling, *nobody* wins them all. Some people will turn you down— they won't even talk to you, or if they do, they won't hire you. You can count on hearing a lot of "No's" when you are selling.

Do you find that hard to take? It may help you to understand why. When a prospect turns you down, which of these feelings flashes through your gut?

- "What's wrong? They don't like me!"
- "I've failed! I'm a failure!"
- "Ah, who needs them anyway."
- "They've seen right through my story. I knew nobody would want this service from somebody like me."

Responses like that are irrational and out of proportion—but normal people have them anyway. They are "hangovers" from the past: your childhood or adolescence, when you took *everything* personally and it sometimes seemed as if you would *never* figure out how to get what you wanted.

We have little control over those old unconscious messages. Fortunately, we can replace them with other messages that are more realistic and help make selling a much more pleasant task.

First, recognize a simple fact: When people say "No" to you in selling, one of two things is the case:

1. They in fact are not good prospects for your services, and you just found that out.

2. They in fact are good prospects for your services, and they don't realize it.

In the first case you have succeeded: there was no match, and you both now know it. Perhaps you need five misses before you find a match. One down, five to go. Congratulate yourself and go on.

In the second case, either you have not been clear enough, or your prospects have their own private reasons for not hearing you. You can do nothing about their private reasons, which are not your concern anyway; it's their problem, not yours. Let it be OK with you for them to have their own problems. Move on.

We are left with those occasions when you in fact did not communicate clearly enough. Where exactly did you miss? What should you do differently next time? Fill in any holes in your presentation this review has revealed. Be grateful that it cost so little to fill those holes. Move on.

Where's the need to feel bad?

Finally, let's replace those automatic messages of failure. Many people find that a simple reminder, repeated regularly to themselves, makes a big difference in replacing those old automatic messages. (Some people call these reminders "Affirmations"; whatever you call the technique, it's surprisingly effective.) If you find the "rejection" aspect of selling hard to take, write this down on a piece of paper:

It's OK when they say Yes; it's OK when they say No.
It's not *Me* they are rejecting.

Put the piece of paper next to your phone, or somewhere else where you will see it frequently. Repeat it to yourself a few times daily; *because it's the truth* it won't take long to take root.

15

Staying Alive

What to Do When You Need Business Now

The name-tag said "Roland van Voort" and he was looking at me like starving people look at food.

It had been a satisfying evening so far. I had just finished an after-dinner talk to an overflow crowd at the local chapter of the American Society for Training and Development. The talk had been a big hit. "Marketing Your Services" is always a popular topic with groups like this, and the audience had been pleased with how much time I spent on their specific, burning questions about marketing. I figured I would get around 50 Qualified Prospects out of the evening; quite a few people had come up and immediately signed up for my workshop. A very satisfying evening.

A few of us were standing around afterward, tying up loose ends. Roland stood on the fringe of the group, tall, thin, with a slightly cool and disdainful manner. But his eyes betrayed him; they looked as if they would burn a hole in my tie. He waited until everyone else left before he spoke.

"That laser-like alignment you spoke about. That's exactly what I am missing in my marketing! I will pay you whatever it takes for you to help me get it."

I was intrigued by Roland's directness. "I've scheduled a special session of my two-day workshop for ASTD members in four weeks, and there are still two slots left. You can have one if you want it."

Roland looked anguished. "Four weeks? You don't understand, Dr. Putman; I need that alignment *now*. I'm living on credit cards already. If I don't get a customer soon, I will be out of business."

Staying Alive

Sound familiar? I sincerely hope not. There are few situations more frightening than watching your business sliding to the edge of disaster and having no idea how to stop it. I know this from personal experience: I've been there—twice!—and back, thank goodness. It was to avoid a third trip to the brink that I set out many years ago to create my own high-performance marketing organization, and learned how it was done by doing it.

Let's be clear about something from the beginning:

Marketing takes time.

Marketing is a lot like farming: you can't just make a firm resolution to plant wheat and expect it to grow. You have to actually put time into plowing and sowing and tending the fields before you can harvest the crop. You have to actually put time into researching and packaging and promoting and networking and selling before you can harvest the crop of customers. And just as you can't plant wheat today and harvest the crop tomorrow, you can't expect marketing to work overnight miracles.

Marketing strategies, like cash crops, take time to ripen for harvest.

If you've read the preceding 14 chapters you know what I'm talking about. But if you really need this chapter, chances are you turned to it first, so forgive me for belaboring the obvious just a bit. If your business is headed for the edge, good marketing can help—but not necessarily enough or in time. The time to build your marketing machine is *before* you are desperate for it.

OK, you get the point: It's not good marketing practice to work in "crisis mode." But if you need business now, you need business *now*. Let's see what we can do for you. After all, what good is a book on marketing if it doesn't help you when you really need it?

This chapter is the marketing equivalent of football's two-minute drill: high-energy, high-potential, but also high-risk tactics for generating business in a hurry. Your chances of scoring a touchdown go way up with these tactics; so do your chances of losing the game (and your shirt). Please, don't use these tactics unless you are up against the wall. You can waste great opportunities in the marketplace by charging in with your message before you have done your homework. Take your time and go step by step if you can. But if you can't . . . well, let's see what we can do.

Taking Stock and Filling the Gaps

How could I turn down an appeal like Roland's? I couldn't, so I agreed to work with him on an emergency, one-on-one basis and charge him by the hour. This wasn't a package he was buying, it was a lifeline. I insisted on one condition: When I sent him the bill, it would be stamped: "Due and payable the day Mr. van Voort sells his next consulting program." He was living on credit cards; I wasn't interested in feeling like a vulture.

The first thing I did was sit him down and have him tell me about his business. He showed me his business cards, letterhead, and promotional materials, and told me about his marketing strategy. It was about what I had expected but worse than I had hoped.

What Roland needed to market successfully was *everything*. Nothing he was already using was aligned with his market. If he was to succeed we would have to throw everything out and start from scratch. Roland had only one bright light: the service he provides. Roland is an outstanding provider of a widely needed service. He knows how to squeeze the last drops of performance out of a manufacturing operation without spending much money. People like Roland are in short supply and highly paid— when they can convince customers to hire them. Great professional, pathetic marketer.

My schedule was full, but Roland needed help now, so I agreed to meet him every morning at 7:00 A.M. for a working breakfast. Over omeletts and coffee we revamped his entire business. It took three weeks, and between breakfasts Roland did *nothing* but work on the assignments I gave him, but in the end we had filled the gaps. He had a clear mission and a target market, a new name for his company, new cards and letterhead, a powerful service package, a presentation book, letters, and a brochure. In short, I guided Roland step-by-step through the material in the first 14 chapters of this book.

That's your first step. Go back to Chapter 1 and *work* your way back to here. Don't skip anything, don't take any shortcuts, and don't leave anything half-done. (OK, you can leave the computerization until later if you have to. But come back to it as soon as you can, or you'll be right back in the soup!)

"But I don't have the time and money to do that! I need business now!" Look, the two-minute drill depends on pinpoint execution. When you have the whole game ahead of you, you can afford a few mistakes, a few dropped passes or missed blocks. You can't afford *any* mistakes when the game is on the line. You are going after business in a serious way. You're going to need all your marketing tools to get the job done; when you reach for that intro letter or presentation book or one-sentence "moment of truth" door-opener, you can't afford to come up empty-handed.

Fill those gaps *now*. You don't have the time or money *not* to. Along the way you will almost certainly discover how you got yourself into this crisis in the first place.

The second step is to assess yourself honestly. Are you looking, acting, and sounding like a successful professional these days? Or have you begun to invite failure by acting like one? Look at yourself in the mirror. Do you see someone whose dress and manner would inspire confidence in a prospective customer? Or do you see someone who subtly is saying, "I'm in trouble!"

Do whatever it takes to pull yourself out of fear and desperation. Customers are attracted by a sense that you want their business; they are repelled by the sense that you *need* it. This may in fact be your last shot at success with this business. Either succeed at it or go out with your head held high. *Act* like a success and you may become one; act like a failure and you will guarantee that you will fail.

Clearing the Decks

Roland had one big advantage to start with: he had little to distract him from the task at hand. His children were grown and gainfully employed in another state. His wife had recently divorced him and taken the house in the settlement. He lived in an apartment and saw his friends when he felt like it. There were no demands on his time and energy outside work.

Does it sound cold to you, calling this narrow life an "advantage?" You're not thinking like a survivor. J. Paul Getty put it nicely: "It's not hard to become very rich. All it takes is single-minded devotion to making money to the exclusion of everything else—the same kind of devotion you find in a prima ballerina or a Nobel Prize-winning scientist. Not many people are willing to make that kind of sacrifice."

That's the kind of single-minded devotion you will need to succeed at this marketing blitz. Not for a lifetime—that's for the Gettys of the world and they are welcome to it—but for long enough to get clear of danger. Then, if you choose, you can get your life back into balance.

Don't try this emergency strategy if you are not willing to make the sacrifice. Don't kid yourself. If you are truly against the wall, you won't make it unless you give it *everything* you have.

You have to clear the decks. Start with your family. Your spouse and children and parents are going to get little if any attention for a while. The attentive spouse and dutiful child and, yes, even the adoring parent you have been is going to drop out of sight until further notice. You have to know that and they have to know that, and it must be acceptable to all of you or it's not likely to work. *Single-minded devotion* means just that. If the business collapses, you all will suffer. If people close to you start feeling neglected you will have to make it up to them later; now is the time to be one-pointed and uncompromising.

(Can't do it? Your spouse won't buy it, or your kids are just *too* young for that, or your parents too dependent on you or. . . . It's OK. Don't torture yourself. You have to choose what is more important to

you. If the business truly is less important to you than these other commitments, you need to admit that to yourself and act on it. Don't let it
drag on and drag you down. Skip to the last part of this chapter,
"Thinking About the Unthinkable," and we will talk about what it means
to close your business.)

Simplify your life to the essentials. Forget the hobbies and self-
improvement projects; you'll have to wait to get that basement sorted out.
Look at every social engagement with a clear and selfish eye: "Is this really
contributing to my short-term business goals?" If not, drop it for now, as
gracefully as you can. Take a leave of absence from your civic and political
and charitable duties, unless doing so would hurt your reputation with
your target market. Cancel the vacation and the weekend outings. You
have two minutes to get the ball into the end-zone. Get rid of everything
that might distract you from that task.

Leave your personal habits alone. Perhaps you need to lose 10 pounds
or exercise more or quit smoking or do more of this or less of that. Fine;
you can do these things later, to celebrate your marketing success. For now
just carry on as you have been. You will need *all* your energy and attention
for your business for a while.

Now that you are free of distractions, let's focus on what you need
to do.

Picking Your Plan of Attack

You know how many customers you need. You know when you need
them. You've filled in the gaps in your marketing, and you've cleared the
decks for action. Now it's time to pick a strategy.

I have identified four basic strategies for "crisis-mode" marketing:

1. The Offer They Can't Refuse (and You Can't Really Afford)

2. The All-Out Promotional Blitz

3. Playing All Your Aces

4. The One Big Win

Each has been used successfully by companies who were clients of
mine. None is guaranteed to work, but then most games are *not* won in
the final two minutes. Read the strategies over carefully. See which is the
best match for your situation. Then pick one and put it into action.

The Offer They Can't Refuse (and You Can't Really Afford)

One way of getting customers is to offer them your services at a price
that's too good to turn down. Unfortunately, if it's really such a great deal

you will almost certainly do no better than cover expenses, and you will probably lose money on it.

On the face of it, this may seem like a suicidal strategy. But look beyond the surface. Your task is to get customers *now*. This strategy does that. True, it does not immediately solve your money problems. But it makes sense if it gets you other things you badly need, like time, cash, and a good reputation.

Time

A computer software company asked me for help. They were a collection of talented software developers with an excellent product just entering the market. In six or eight months, they confidently expected sales of their product to make them all mildly wealthy.

Today, however, they were flat broke. They had no money to pay salaries, and no prospect of work.

After a day of brainstorming, we found an intriguing solution. A previous customer of the software firm needed a better, more "user-friendly" interface for their corporate database, but were not willing to spend much money for a "nonessential item." The software firm offered them this deal: "We will build and install your new interface for bare labor cost—no overhead and no profit. In exchange, we will get the marketing rights to the interface software."

The customer jumped at the chance (they were getting great custom software for about 40 percent of its normal cost). The revenue from this interface project (and the forbearance of an unusually patient landlord) kept the company afloat long enough for their product to begin bringing in money. Two years later they were able to sell those marketing rights to the interface software for a very tidy profit.

Cash

A medium-size training firm was facing a cash-flow crunch. They had scheduled a large project for a large manufacturing company. Literally the day before the project was scheduled to start, the manufacturing company was taken private via a leveraged buy-out; needless to say, the training program was cancelled. The training firm had a gaping hole in their schedule. Plenty of work was booked down the road, but nothing much for the next few months. What to do?

They called a financial services company for whom they were expecting to create a performance review system and made them an unusual proposal: start the project next week, instead of four months from now as currently planned, and we will give you a 20 percent reduction. The training firm was candid about the reason for the offer: they would rather work for less money than have so much dead time. After a few internal consultations, the financial services company agreed to the offer. Both firms won. The financial services firm got a planned system for 20 percent less; the training firm got cash instead of dead space and four months' marketing time to replace their lost client.

Reputation

I faced an interesting dilemma when I first began offering my two-day workshop, "Marketing Your Professional Services." I was a well-established and successful consultant to large organizations, and was well-known personally in the local community of professional service providers. But this was my first workshop specifically designed for small-to-medium size business, and nobody knew what I had to offer. What I needed was to create a reputation as a marketing consultant to small businesses.

I gave away the first workshop. It was actually a bit more complicated than that. I hand-picked a diverse group of professionals who knew me personally, and invited them to a free two-day workshop. I set an upper limit on the number of participants, and actually had to turn away some people who were slow in responding. I called it a "Pilot" workshop, was candid about the fact that this was a new format for me, and made it clear that I expected them to give me honest and detailed feedback on what worked and what didn't. I asked them for $30 to help offset the cost of the catered lunches.

I also promised them that the two days would substantially improve their marketing. It did. They gave me some useful feedback that led me to improve the design of the workshop; they also raved about the workshop and its effect on their marketing. My next workshop (full price) was filled with friends and colleagues of the pilot group. Most importantly for *my* marketing, my reputation as a marketing consultant to small service businesses began to spread.

Is the "Offer They Can't Refuse" strategy for you? Notice that its success depends on two factors. First, you must have a plausible reason, one that makes sense to your customers, for offering them such a great deal. "I will go out of business otherwise" will not do the job. Second, you must see a down-the-road payoff. You can afford to make such a (short-term) foolish business deal because you can see explicitly the long-term wisdom of it. It gets you something you need to make your *next* move the one that insures your business success.

All-Out Promotional Blitz

Mark is the model handyman of the '90s: jack of all trades, union card in none. (In our part of the country that still makes a difference.) He survived for years working for "scab" contractors, but then he got married and decided he could do just as well on his own. He did, but he was still barely getting by. When I met him, he was almost ready to go back to work for someone else.

A mutual friend told me about Mark. I needed to have some windows scraped and repainted, so we worked a swap: he did my windows, I helped him with his marketing.

My part turned out to be almost embarrassingly easy. Mark's background as a nonunion worker in a mostly union environment had created in him a habit of keeping a *very* low profile. If you didn't know somebody who knew Mark, you would never know he existed. So we got him going on an all-out promotional blitz.

First he got 1000 business cards and 5000 one-page flyers made up, advertising him as "Handyman Mark, the One-Man Construction Crew" and offering $10 off on any home repair job in this month. (The cards and flyers were nothing fancy, but clean-looking. Lilly Dean knocked the design off in an hour, and Mark fixed her leaky faucets.) He found a printer who needed a new loading dock built and was willing to barter, so he got his cards and flyers plus a little cash in his pocket.

Then he swung into action. He distributed the flyers throughout the "nice but older" neighborhoods in the town. He called up every realtor in the Yellow Pages, introduced himself, and offered to do a minor repair on their own house as a "get-acquainted" special, at half his usual hourly rate. (Realtors are first-rate referral sources, and a surprising number of them took him up on his offer.) He posted a copy of his flyer on every supermarket bulletin board in town.

Within a month, he had more business than he could handle. He kept up the promotions, but scaled down the intensity, to insure a steady stream of new customers. He now makes a very nice living as his own boss.

What's keeping *you* from promoting *your* business? Are you in the habit of keeping a low profile because "somebody" might not approve of your tooting your own horn? ("How unprofessional!") The only important question is: What will your target market think of it? You need customers now. Will *they* be turned off by a promotional blitz? Or will they see it simply as what it is: an appropriately aggressive attempt to get new customers?

Is your own self-consciousness holding you back?

Playing All Your Aces

Are you keeping an ace in the hole that you haven't played yet? It's surprising how many people do that. You say to yourself, "Well, if things ever get *really* bad I can call up good old Charley." And good old Charley would come through for you: *he* would know whom to talk to; *he* would be able to steer you to the right place.

Things *are* really bad, friend, so why haven't you called up good old Charley? Or, to be more exact, why haven't you called up *all* the Charleys you know? You've heard of this strategy before; it's called "networking" these days, and the books have been full of it for years:

> First you sit down and make a list of *everybody* you know, including all those college friends and social acquaintances and old friends of the family, and, yes, even your rich uncle. Make special note of those people who have been impressed by your work, or who owe you a favor, or both. Then call them. Tell them what you are up to: what your mission is, and your target market. Ask them if they know anyone who might benefit from your services. Get the names and phone numbers, and permission to use their name; better yet, see if your friend would be willing to call ahead and introduce you. With each new name, repeat the process until you get a qualifying response: "Sounds like *we* could use that. Let's talk."

That's the "Play All Your Aces" strategy, in a nutshell. It's no big secret; in fact, you already knew it. Why haven't you already done it?

"I hate to ask favors of friends like that. It puts them on the spot." This is the most common reason I hear, and it stems from a fundamental misunderstanding. Get one thing straight: *You are not asking anyone for a favor.* You are simply asking your friends if they know someone who could benefit from your services. If they do, fine; they are in the position of being able to do a favor for their friends and colleagues by introducing them to you! (I can guarantee you that everyone I have told about Handyman Mark is grateful to me. Good handymen are hard to find!) What's more, *you* are trying to do a favor for your prospective customers by letting them know about something they both need and want—your services. Are you still laboring under the delusion that people are doing you a favor by hiring you? Forget it; they are doing themselves a favor by purchasing a service they both need and want. In a clean business transaction like this, there is no room for one-sided favors. *Everybody* benefits, or it doesn't happen. So don't think you are asking for favors. You're not.

"I hate to lose my ace in the hole." When you get right down to it, this is the fear that keeps most people from playing all their aces. It doesn't make sense, but then fear seldom does. If you call up "old Charley" and he *doesn't* come through for you, then you have nothing to fall back on; there's nothing you can comfort yourself with by saying, "Well, if things get *really* bad, I can always . . . ." You're like the man who, confronted with the classic hold-up line "Your money or your life," replies: "Take my life. I'm saving my money for my old age." *What* are you saving those aces for?

The One Big Win

Most of us need a steady stream of customers just to make a living. Each customer pays us $20 or $100 or even several hundred dollars for our services. We put as many resources as we can into our marketing, but we have to spread them around. It doesn't make economic sense to spend $1000 to get one $500 customer.

But some businesses are not like that. A "small" job for Roland brought him $50,000 or so. A typical customer spends hundreds of thousands of dollars over two or three years for his entire program. (Don't worry, they get their money's worth; the savings his programs generate run into the millions.) There is no practical limit on the amount of time and money Roland can justify for marketing to a single client.

There were very practical limits, though, on how much time and money Roland actually had. He decided to play for the One Big Win—concentrating his marketing efforts on two or three prospects with the aim of converting one into a customer.

In choosing this course, Roland was following a strategy laid out by the great Prussian general Karl von Clausewitz (and he knew it; Roland's the kind of guy who read von Clausewitz in the original German as a teenager). Clausewitz advocated as his first principle of warfare the concentration of forces on a single objective. A sure recipe for defeat, said the general, is spreading your forces over too many fronts. In this case, what is true in war is also true in marketing. (It has become very fashionable these days to compare marketing to warfare; the comparisons are mostly misleading but they make entertaining reading. To me, marketing seems to have more in common with making love than with making war; for a few giddy moments one evening I even considered titling this book *The Joy of Marketing*.)

The One Big Win strategy requires you to narrow your focus tremendously. Draw up a short list (four or five at most) of your best targets. Only include prospects with whom you already have a good connection: an internal advocate or a strongly interested decision maker. Be sure there are no obvious "show-stoppers" visible: someone in power who is already opposed to you, or a mandate to cut spending by 30 percent, or policies against your kind of service. (You can get around any of these, of course, but is that a good concentration of forces now?)

Then commit all of your resources to these few targets. Your campaign still may fail, but if it does you should be able to say: "It didn't fail because I held back. I put everything I had into trying to get their business."

OK, time to choose your strategy. Remember, despite the success stories in the illustrations, there are no guarantees. For every one of those success stories, I could tell you about someone who gave it his or her best shot and still went out of business.

But at least they had a fighting chance. If you don't pick a strategy and commit yourself completely to it, you won't even have that.

Hitting the Bricks

Finally—and quickly, I hope, for your sake—the time comes when there is nothing left but the doing. "Hit the bricks," as salespeople say; get out there and send your letters and make your calls and talk to people. Start moving people through that marketing funnel; crank that marketing machine with all your might until you've got what you need from it.

Yes, I know: easier said than done. But here are some reminders to help you keep going. I call them reminders because you've probably heard them all before, but don't let that get in your way. These help, and right now you need all the help you can get.

Set Goals

Few worthwhile things can be accomplished all at once. When you move steadily forward a step at a time, it's much easier to see and take your next step than to see the final destination.

Set goals for yourself. Not just the final goal of so many customers or so much revenue, but short-term goals. Weekly goals. *Daily* goals. You can't create five new customers today, but you *can* send out 20 introductory letters. You *can* make 10 follow-up phone calls. You *can* make four presentations. Set those as your goals for the day.

Write your goals down. Make them clear and explicit and measurable. Don't set a goal to "try" or to do "better"; set a goal to *do* a particular number of things successfully. Make sure there can be no doubt in your mind whether you did it.

Make sure your goals are both stretching and attainable. It's self-defeating to set goals that require no special effort to attain; it's equally self-defeating to set goals you won't accomplish. Get in the habit of achieving your daily goals *every* day; your larger goals will fall in place automatically.

Chart Your Progress

After you have set your overall goals—so many letters sent, so many Qualified Prospects, so many sales calls made—make up wall charts for each. Make them big and colorful. Draw a red line on the chart to show your goal for this month, and then every day, without fail, chart your progress. It can get very discouraging, going out every day and feeling like you are getting nowhere. A visible chart will keep you reminded: "There's the goal, and there's where I am. I *am* accomplishing something!"

Set Up a Buddy System

Competition bodybuilders rarely lift weights alone. They know that a time comes in every lifting session when the mind and body want to give up.

But if you stop there, you have wasted the session; real gains come only when you push past that point, to achieve the goals you set for the session. Bodybuilders work on a "buddy system." Two work out together; when one starts to quit, the other yells and exhorts and demands that the lifter finish the set. That external push is enough to keep going.

An all-out marketing push can be discouraging, hard work. You may feel at times like giving up, chucking it all in, or at least taking a day or two off. At times like that, it can be useful to have a "buddy"—someone who shares your commitment to success, who can help you stay on track, and who won't let you back down because the buddy is counting on you to keep him or her moving ahead in turn. Meet with your buddy regularly and faithfully to applaud each other's successes and urge each other on when the going is tough.

Can you think of anybody who might be willing to be your "marketing buddy?"

Thinking About the Unthinkable

You've seen what it takes. You know what you need to do, and how to do it. You've got a fighting chance, at least. All that remains is to go out and give it your best shot. Are you going to go for it?

If so, then I sincerely wish you the best of luck, and I *want you to stop reading this chapter right now!* You need to keep clearly in your mind an image of success. What we are going to talk about from here on is what to do when you have done everything you can, and it still isn't enough. Go hit the bricks, and I hope you *never* read the rest of this chapter!

If you're still reading you're either just curious or you're wondering if the best thing to do is close up shop *now*. Either way let's get right to the heart of it.

Time for a hard-nosed, honest appraisal. Look at your business. Look at your situation. Most important, look at yourself. Do you see signs that it's time to call it quits for now?

- Is your income a lot less than your expenses, with no turnaround in sight?

- Have you run through your reserves? Does the thought of piling on more debt make you feel cold and sick inside?

- Do you have a family situation that makes it impossible to give your full attention to your business?

- Have you run out of people to call?

- Do you find yourself feeling increasingly paralyzed—going through the motions of business but spending less and less time productively?

- Most important of all: Have you lost your confidence in this business? In your heart, do you believe the party's over?

You know what your answers to these questions are, and you know what they mean. Either it makes sense to you to keep going or it doesn't. There's no point in going down with a sinking ship. Scuttle it and get into the lifeboat. Sometimes it's best just to make a fresh start.

I know what you're feeling. A little over 25 years ago I was in your shoes: I gave everything I had to a business, and still, finally, had to close it down. Making the decision to close down was one of the hardest things I had done, because it wasn't only the business that was dying: it was my hopes and dreams and my image of myself as a success, or so it seemed at the time. My partners and I got together and packed up the business records. We laughed as we remembered the good and funny and absurd things we had gone through together; we told each other sad tales of what might have been, if . . . . Then we divided up the debts, locked the doors for the last time, went home and got mildly, sorrowfully drunk. I was a much younger man then; it seemed like one of the blackest days of my life.

But a funny thing happened. Next day, contrary to expectation, the sun actually rose in the sky. It was a glorious day with warm, clear, sunny skies. The universe didn't even do me the courtesy of putting on a display of gloom. And I noticed an amazing thing: I hadn't changed at all! I was still the same Tony; same dreams and hopes and only a small bruise on my sense of being a winner. In fact, mostly what I felt was *relief*. It was over and I knew it. It felt good to finish it and begin to move on.

That is what happens, you know. Your life continues, and you do move on. If you have decided to close the doors for now, do it as quickly and cleanly as possible. Tie up the loose ends with your head held high. Work with the landlord to arrange a sublease. Pack up the equipment and inventory; keep what you need, sell what you can, and store or give away the rest. If there are debts to pay, acknowledge them and work out a schedule for paying them. If people have helped you along the way, call them and thank them for their help; explain what you are doing and why, and let them know you will be back when the market and your capital are ready for it.

That *is* most likely what will happen. Cold statistics say that eight out of 10 small businesses in this country will close their doors within two years. (My personal mission is to help reverse those numbers to eight out of 10 solidly successful after two years. Unfortunately, that will still leave two out of ten who didn't make it this time.) What those cold statistics don't show is that the large majority of those "failures" come back and open another business, and sometimes a third, or even a fourth, until they get it right. This is a country of second and third chances.

But what about those feelings of failure? You didn't succeed this time; maybe you're not cut out to own your own business. Shouldn't you just accept that about yourself?

I respectfully suggest that you don't. Of the successful independent business owners I know, *every one of them* has had at least one business failure in the past. It almost seems like tuition or dues that have to be paid; you have to be incredibly lucky not to have failed at least once. If you have tried and failed three times, ask yourself those hard questions. Until then, don't worry about yourself. Chances are very good that you were right about yourself to begin with.

Go ahead and regroup. Get a paying job and build up your capital; on evenings and weekends get your marketing materials ready for your next business. When the time comes, you will be ready to try again and to succeed.

What about Roland? Did he make it or not? I wish I could end this chapter with yet another rousing success story, but that's not how this one turned out. As this book goes to press, Roland is still struggling to keep his business alive. For a while it looked like his One Big Win strategy was going to do the trick. His best contact was close to signing a contract when one of life's little ironies clobbered it: Roland's internal advocate was given a nice promotion and sent to head up South American operations. His replacement didn't know Roland at all, and there's not much time left on the meter.

Roland is an honorable man. A former client unexpectedly paid him for work he did last year (the company had been having problems with sales and Roland had written his fee off as an uncollectible debt). I received a check for the full amount of my bill for marketing services. He wrote a note that explained: "Your marketing consultation was superb. After all, it wasn't your fault I started too late. I know exactly what to do, and even if I don't make it this time, I intend to try again, using these same materials, as soon as I have enough capital."

I was touched, but I sent the check back with a note reminding him that payment was not yet due. Roland hasn't experienced the *benefit* of my services yet.

I'm not worried. Roland van Voort will build a good business for himself. If he has to close his doors, he'll be back. And the next time there will be no stopping him.

16 | Success and Beyond

Keeping Marketing Alive in a Large or Growing Firm

Congratulations! You have done such a splendid job of marketing that you are now a large and growing firm! All the parts of your marketing machine are in place and working well:

- Your mission is perfectly aligned with your market.
- Your marketing efforts create exactly the relationship your customers most want and need.
- Your services are well-packaged, presented with terrific sizzle, and priced so that your company can grow and thrive.
- You know exactly where and how to advertise and promote your services.
- Your marketing machine routinely and predictably creates the new customers your business requires.
- Everything you do and say to your market sends a single, clear message of positive benefit.

Your biggest problem is finding enough good people to do the work and keep track of the money!

Now what?

Now, unless you are very careful and a little lucky, you may learn the profound wisdom of an old saying:

Be very careful what you pray for. Your prayers may be answered.

Perhaps prayer did not figure heavily in your business success, but hard work, persistence, and unswerving commitment certainly did. You have worked hard to get exactly where you are now. This is where you have wanted to be, but unless you are careful you will look back years from now and realize that this was the *high point!*

Somehow from here on your business success may get harder and harder. The company you worked so hard to build will lose its edge and its focus; the excitement and satisfaction of the early years will give way to a long, slow drift and decline. If you are lucky you will sell before the decay becomes obvious. If not, your firm may continue on for years among what venture capitalists call "the living dead"—companies that never do quite poorly enough to kill off completely, but never fulfill that early, bright promise.

Before you lie two paths. The first, which you may already have begun following, is the path of least resistance. If you follow it, you will find that less and less energy goes into marketing. You will notice more and more people busily employed in your firm doing things that have no obvious connection to "creating and maintaining the relationship of customer." You may see this as inevitable. It leads to progressive growth and stagnation.

The second path is a little harder to find and to follow. It requires you to resist the "inevitable" and to make certain you do *not* fall into the "obvious" management structures. It takes as its first priority a single overriding task: keeping the marketing perspective alive in your firm. This path leads to that rarest of outcomes: a large and growing organization that markets with laser-like power and effectiveness.

"Rust never sleeps." Unless you make it your *first* priority to keep marketing alive in your company, the marketing perspective will be overwhelmed. That laser-like focus and alignment will blur and become distorted; in the crush of "more urgent" agendas, marketing will first become ritualized and then, finally, will cease to be an all-encompassing perspective. It will become "Marketing," one of many functions reporting to the CEO, ranking in actual importance somewhere between Finance and Human Resources.

The purpose of this final chapter is to help you take that second path. We will look at what you need to do to continue your marketing success.

If you have an MBA from a typical business school (and you believed everything they taught you about management), you are probably going to hate this chapter. If you have learned to see a company as simply a pile of assets to be deployed strategically for greatest financial return, I *promise* you will hate this chapter (or else dismiss it as hopelessly naive). That's OK. I consider it an honor to be seen as naive by the fine folks who gave us the philosophical underpinnings for corporate raiders, defensive restructuring, and junk finance.

If you want to *continue* to succeed without having to change your definition of success; if you want to keep the marketing perspective alive and vigorous in your large or growing firm, read on. I think you will like what you see.

Some Unhappy Truths About Organizations and One Happy Solution

To travel that second path, you need to understand why organizations work the way they do. (Don't worry; this won't take us too far off into theory.) When you are with a smaller firm, you can afford to ignore these organizational realities. As you grow larger, you ignore them at the risk of being overwhelmed by them.

I have been a consultant to organizations for over 20 years. I have worked closely with hundreds of organizations, and have observed and influenced thousands, ranging from some of the world's largest organizations to one-person firms. In the course of that work and observation I have come to appreciate the importance of one fundamental fact of organizations:

All organizations have *two* missions: the external mission and the internal mission.

The external mission is what we have identified as your mission throughout this book. It is the organization's original and continuing reason for existence: to make a beneficial difference in the lives of some group of customers.

Energy put into the external mission results in creating, maintaining, and/or satisfying the organization's customers.

The internal mission consists of all those activities which maintain the organization and advance the personal goals of its members. The fundamental internal mission of any organization is to survive: to maintain itself, its structures, and its valued practices in the face of threats to its survival. Each member of the organization has his or her own needs and wants, which each acts to accomplish. Together these "maintenance" and self-oriented activities make up the internal mission.

Energy put into the internal mission results in maintaining the organization and advancing the personal goals of the organization's members.

When your business is small, the internal mission is almost invisible. You take care of business and let the business take care of itself. You don't need elaborate performance reviews, for example, when you are the only employee. As the business grows, the organization begins to have a life of its own: meetings and memos and quarterly reports; pro formas and SEC filings and the company picnic. As one successful entrepreneur told me:

"There came a time when I was leaving the office after a full, hard day of work and it hit me: I hadn't done one thing all day long that had anything to do with a customer! That's when I started to worry that we had gotten too damn big for our own good."

The problem, which this unhappy entrepreneur was experiencing, stems from another fundamental fact about organizations:

> **The larger the organization, the more energy is needed for the internal mission.**

That's a fact, and there is not much one can do about it. When you're cooking for two, you can pretty much wing it and everything comes out fine. When you're cooking for 200, you need a lot of planning and advance buying and preparation; plenty of energy goes into making it possible to cook. That's just common sense.

But there is one more important fact about organizations that is perhaps not so obvious. I first observed it over 25 years ago in working with community mental health organizations. Its implications for any growing business are sobering.

> **Left to follow the path of least resistance, an organization will devote increasing amounts of energy to its internal mission. In the absence of a strong and clearly defined external mission, an organization will devote virtually *all* its energy to the internal mission.**

It may be possible to have an organization so divorced from its external mission that it accomplishes nothing at all outside of maintaining itself and serving as a vehicle for the gratification of its members. In my practice I have seen some that come chillingly close, and they are not all in the federal government. These organizations are like black holes: From the outside, you would have no way of knowing they were there except for the immense amount of money that disappears into them.

Realistically, your organization will not disappear into a black hole. A service business has to accomplish *something* for its customers, or it will have no resources to maintain itself with. But unless you take firm action to prevent it, there is grave risk that so much effort will go into your internal mission that it will sap the vital force of your business.

It's a real dilemma: You can't get big without increasing the internal mission, but you can't thrive when so much energy goes into maintaining the organization. Your organization has only so many resources, remember; if they are being used to accomplish the internal mission, they are not available to accomplish the external mission. One CEO of a growing company put it bluntly: "You know, you really can't win. You succeed, so you get big and bulky and before you know it some hungry little start-up company is eating your lunch."

Those are the unhappy truths about organizations. Fortunately, there is a happy solution to the problems they create. The solution is very simple, and by now it should seem very familiar. It's actually a prescription for organizational success:

> **The high-performance organization creates laser-like alignment between its external mission and its internal activities.**

The solution is to *not allow* your organization to take the obvious path of least resistance.

- The organization must be maintained, but make sure those maintenance activities also contribute directly and obviously to accomplishing the external mission.
- People have their own wants and needs and will act to satisfy them. Just make sure that they do so by contributing directly to the accomplishment of the organization's external mission.

As a small and growing firm you established a firm ethic: *All* activities must contribute to the laser-like alignment between our mission and our market. As a large and growing firm you must maintain that same ethic in the face of growing internal pressures to abandon it.

That is the challenge that faces you: keep marketing alive in your organization by creating laser-like alignment between your mission and all internal activities. For the rest of this chapter we will examine the five key tasks required for meeting the challenge.

The Five Key Tasks

Keeping marketing alive in your large or growing firm is not easy but it can be done. To succeed, you must:

1. Keep the mission alive and vital.
2. Create and maintain internal alignment with your external mission.
3. Live with your market.
4. Create new for old:
   - New customers for old packages;
   - New services for old customers;
   - New packages for old services.
5. Become the Model Marketer for your people to follow.

Keeping the Mission Alive and Vital

Does your organization suffer from Framed Mission Syndrome? FMS is a deadly disease of large organizations. I've seen hundreds of cases. You walk into a manager's office and there, on the wall behind the desk, is a handsomely framed document. Ask about the organization's mission, and the manager smiles, points proudly to the framed document, and reads it to you. Unfortunately, as you watch what goes on in that organization, you quickly see that the mission on the wall has very little relation to what people actually do. The organization is suffering from FMS, a deadly disease characterized by steady and progressive loss of customers.

Don't get me wrong; there's nothing wrong with framing your mission statement and hanging it on the wall. You could also print it on your letterhead and business cards, and certainly *should* feature it prominently in all advertising and marketing communications. Your mission statement is essentially a promise made by you to your market, and you should be justifiably proud of it.

But promises aren't for framing. Promises are for keeping, and that's where organizations suffering from FMS fall short. At best their mission has become an ideal, to be aimed for but never really accomplished; at worst it has become an irrelevant leftover from earlier times, or the brainchild of staff planners who never have to worry about implementing it.

How can you avoid FMS? How can you keep your organization's mission alive and vital? A full answer would require a book at least as long as this one (the "Resources" section has some examples), but you can get a long way with this short answer:

> **Never forget where the mission comes from and never let anyone in your organization forget it.**

Your mission comes from the alignment of the best you have to offer and the needs of your market. Your mission is to make a positive, beneficial difference in the lives of your customers. Exactly *what* that difference is, and *how* you go about making it, and even *who* your customers are can and probably will change over time. But what does *not* change is the need to make a difference in your customers' lives and to put everything you have into that effort. At all times, your mission should be as perfectly aligned with your market as it is humanly possible to make it.

If you start allowing your competitors, or your technology, or the capital markets to dictate how your people spend their time and energy, your mission will move progressively out of alignment with your market. It's only a few easy steps from there to FMS.

Keep the customer in the foreground *always*. Get in the habit of asking, "What difference does this make in the lives of our customers?" If it makes no difference, or makes the wrong kind of difference, ask, "Then exactly why are we putting resources into it?" Use the mission constantly and visibly to make decisions about what your firm does and does not do.

Keep your mission alive and vital by keeping it constantly in front of you, not behind you in a frame on the wall.

Creating Internal Alignment with Your External Mission

A mission is alive and vital only if people act on it. Everyone in your firm should be able to look at your mission statement and feel, "Yes. That describes our firm, and it describes my job. What I do on the job contributes directly to accomplishing that mission."

The mission should serve as a guiding light for your people. When they are faced with resource decisions—What should we do next? How much should we spend? Should we give priority to this or that?—they should refer to the mission as the final point of reference. If this is not the case in your organization, you have some work to do.

Start with the jobs themselves. Whether you have a formal system of job descriptions or not, everyone in your organization has some more or less fixed idea of what "my job" really is. Every job should be defined fundamentally in terms of its contribution to accomplishing the mission, that is, in terms of its contribution to making a beneficial difference in customers' lives. *Every* job.

Even the "support" or "staff" people need to see clearly that success in their jobs depends essentially on their making it possible in some way for the firm to serve its customers. Can you really afford to keep employing someone who makes no real difference in accomplishing your firm's mission?

Once every job has a clear and strong connection to the mission, organize to make the connection a reality. When goals or objectives are set, be sure that they are directly anchored in the mission. When rewards are given, be sure the connection between contribution to the mission and the reward is clear. When people strive for advancement and promotion, make it clear that the path to advancement is through contribution to the mission.

All of this alignment is based on enthusiastic acceptance and endorsement of the mission by the people in your firm. As we shall discuss later, the most essential ingredient in creating such enthusiasm is your own willingness to be the Model Marketer for your people to follow. From the beginning, let everyone see your commitment to making that specific beneficial difference in the lives of your customers. Let everyone see clearly that the mission is your first priority and that you invite and expect their enthusiastic commitment. Then align your rewards with your expectations.

Suppose your company has a history of confusion or indifference to overcome. How can you create a sense of "our mission" and "our customers" among people who have not had it? Again, that is the topic of a long book but you can get a long way with one principle:

Enthusiastic commitment results from involvement and ownership.

You can't just hand down a mission and expect people to cheer. You must involve your people in hammering out the best mission possible. Everyone has some piece of the puzzle, so get everyone together and get them talking to each other. Don't go in with a fixed agenda, to "sell the troops" on your ideas. Ask for their involvement in creating a mission that will energize the firm and delight the market, and then step back and listen. Be unyielding on only one point: The mission ultimately will be defined in terms of the benefit to the customer.

If ego clashes and power struggles erupt, resolve them by insisting that all issues be viewed from the market's perspective, that you want only the best your people have to offer, and that there will be *one* clear mission with which the firm will align all its efforts. If someone refuses to support the mission wholeheartedly, find someone who will support it to take his or her place.

That is the involvement part. What about ownership? In one sense, ownership is already taken care of. People have a *feeling* of ownership in anything they have been meaningfully involved with. When we are involved in working out the mission, it becomes "our mission." When we have actual responsibility for creating and maintaining the customer relationship, the customers become "our customers." This is the psychological meaning of ownership.

I suggest you consider a more concrete, economic meaning of ownership as well. As part of the process of creating internal alignment and congruence, ask yourself:

How can I say, "It's *our* mission, *our* customers" on the one hand, and, "But it's *my* company" on the other?

What happens when you give people responsibility for the customer relationship but no ownership stake in the company? One of three things:

1. They take no real responsibility for the customer relationship. They probably won't be rude or indifferent—people usually aren't—but neither will they work enthusiastically to stay aligned with the market. This is the most common response.

2. They will take matters in their own hands and make those customers their own. This is good news and bad news. While they are with you, they will help grow the business, but they have every reason to go out on their own and probably will eventually.

3. They act like owners even though they are not. They are everyone's ideal employees. There are people like that. You know how
   often you find them.

I have a radical suggestion for you:

Make your employees owners. ?

You built the company and it's yours by rights. Granted. If you want to
build it even further, and you recognize that you can't do it all on your
own, the *most effective method* is to recognize that *future* growth will be a
function of two things: the hard work of the past and the hard work of
the future. As the company grows through future hard work, acknowledge the contribution of those who have done that hard work by giving
them their share of the company. A company of owners will outperform a
company of employees any time, and you won't have to worry so much
about your best people going into competition with you.

Please be clear: This is not a pitch for "workplace democracy." It's
one more attempt to create the alignment and congruence on which your
continued success depends. If you follow this suggestion, you may find
yourself having to adjust from 100 percent ownership of a $1 million busi-
ness to 65 percent ownership of a $50 million business.

As someone said when asked how she would adjust to the pressures
of winning the lottery: "Give me that kind of problem!"

Living with Your Market

Success contains the seeds of its own destruction. They need not sprout,
but they will unless you carefully weed them out.

The seeds of marketing destruction are sown in the field of neglect
and distance. You did not build your firm by sitting in an office chairing
executive group meetings. You did not build your firm by spending your
time courting the financial markets, or huddling with consultants, or
creating a strategic plan for sustainable competitive advantage. You built
your firm by living with your market, so that you *knew* exactly what they
needed, in what form. If you expect marketing to stay alive and vital in
your firm, you must continue to live with your market. You. Not just
your field reps or "marketing people." You and all your executives.

The most dangerous move you can make is to create a corps of executives or staff who are insulated from interaction with your customers. They
will create policies and procedures that lead you steadily *out* of alignment
with your market, every time.

"Management" as taught in MBA programs is essentially a set of
tools for accomplishing the internal mission of the organization. As such,
it can be critical in making the transition to a larger firm since, as we saw

before, the larger the organization, the larger the scope of the internal mission. But never forget that *the external mission is primary.* You are not in business to manage assets; you are in business to make a beneficial difference in the lives of your customers, and you can't do that unless you are precisely aligned with your market.

Get out of your office and into the field. Talk with your people and talk with your customers. *Live* with your market.

Creating New for Old

Alignment is a never ending process. Your current service package was perfect for what you knew when it was designed. It is probably a very good match for your market right now. It will almost certainly be out of tune with your market in the future.

Keeping marketing alive and vital is fundamentally a matter of keeping that laser-like alignment. To do that, you have to create new for old.

New Customers for Old Packages

New customers are the lifeblood of any business. You may believe you have grown so large that you can succeed by serving only existing customers. This is an illusion. As soon as you stop the flow of new customers, your business begins to stagnate and die.

New customers are everywhere! Look for them especially:

- Within your current target market. Your marketing communications have reached only a fraction of your target market. Go for the rest, step by step, and keep track of responses.

- Within subsegments of your target market. Your Cost per Customer may be quite different in different media and in different subsegments. Turn your MBAs loose on working out exactly where you are getting the most bang for your marketing buck, and emphasize those subsegments more.

- Within new target markets. Perhaps you have covered your target market well, and still have marketing resources available. Or perhaps your target market requires new service packages, leaving you with a perfectly good service package that is no longer aligned with that segment. In either case, you have a service package that is a proven winner. Go through the market segmentation exercises again. Find another segment for whom your service package is an excellent match.

New Services for Old Customers

New customers are lifeblood. Old customers are a gold mine. The single best source of continued business growth is marketing new services to old customers. The reason is simple: Your hit-rate for marketing to customers is far higher than your hit-rate marketing to anybody else. Your customers have bought from you before; they know you provide satisfaction. If they need this new thing you are offering, they are very likely to buy.

To make sure they *do* need this new thing, you must do some research and development (R&D) work.

Research and development is a critical component of continued marketing success.

This statement surprises and upsets some owners of service businesses. After all, they don't have an R&D lab. How can they compete?

A service business engages in R&D at the front line. Your R&D worker is the person who lives with the customers, watching their response to your current packages, listening to their complaints and compliments and suggestions. The ongoing design of your service packages must respond to the shifting and emerging needs of your target market, as represented primarily by your current customers. The best ideas for your next packages come from listening carefully to current customers.

Make R&D an accepted, explicit part of every service providers' job. They *must* watch for opportunities to improve alignment. They *must* report what they see and hear. And they *must* be heard.

The folklore of American business includes hundreds of success stories that begin with a front-line service provider who lives with the market and sees the need for a new service. Loyal worker tells powers-that-be; powers-that-be fail to respond; loyal worker forms own company and becomes a raving success. Don't be one of the "powers-that-be." Empower your front-line R&D troops, and *listen* to them. They will guide you to the new services you need for your old customers.

New Packages for Old Services

Remember "Handyman Jeff," the one-man media phenomenon? He created one excellent package for his services—a book—and followed it up with a lecture tour, a newspaper column, a cable spot, and a workout video. New bottles for the old wine; new packages for old services.

Perhaps it's time to consider the repackaging strategy for *your* services. Finding a new package for your services is mostly common sense, mixed with a willingness to listen to your customers. Look at how your services are currently delivered, then ask yourself (and your customers), "How could we do this differently?"

Consider these suggestions:

- If you deliver a standardized package of services, offer a custom package. Or vice versa. (Vice versa applies to each example; I will assume you will apply it without my writing it each time.)

- If you do workshops or instruction, write a book.

- If your materials are in books, put them into Computer-Based Coaches, or interactive video, or film, or a correspondence course.

- If you do public workshops, consider customized in-house versions.

- If your services typically take place in a single block, spread them out over time.

- If they are done in one location, conduct them in several locations.

- If your documentation is in binders or manuals, put it on-line.

- If your customers come to you, try going to them.

Again, most good ideas for profitable new packaging in service firms come from front-line R&D folk. They listen to the complaints and suggestions of customers and to the objections of the prospects who never became customers. Ask them for ideas, and listen.

Becoming the Model Marketer

In the final analysis, one factor will determine whether marketing remains alive and vital in your business: *You.*

It seems appropriate to end this book the way we began it, by noticing that success at marketing depends essentially on seeing your business through "marketers' lenses." You have worked hard through these 16 chapters to master the marketing perspective. You have examined every aspect of your business from the marketing perspective, and seen how to align your business to create laser-like power and focus. Keep doing that, and make sure your people see you doing it.

With success comes the temptation to change, to become more of a "CEO." It's easy to get caught up in the long-range plans, or the next stock offering, or that new headquarters building you've always dreamed of.

Don't. Stay with what got you here—alignment between your mission and your market. Now more than ever, it is important to keep your own view of that alignment clear and sharp.

Remember the lesson of marketing communications: you must send one, clear message to your market. If you send conflicting messages, or multiple messages, you confuse your market. That caveat is equally true for your communications with the people who work for you. If you want them to see the enterprise through marketers' lenses, show them how. Show them what you value by sending one, clear message:

> **We are in business to make a specific, beneficial difference in the lives of our customers. We do that by providing the best service we have to offer, to people who need and value it. Everything we do must reflect that alignment with our market.**

That's the strategy. As the owl told the grasshopper, "The details are up to you."

The good news is: you don't have to become a cricket to do it! You don't have to become something you are not. All it takes is the best *you* have to offer. That best, with a little luck, will be enough.

Good luck, grasshopper.

This book was written for one purpose only: to help you, the reader, to become an effective marketer. I attempted to include in the book *everything* and *only things* required for that purpose. That meant making some tough choices: Should I go into this in more depth? Would more detail here help? How much of that do readers *really* need?

Inevitably, some compromises were made between thoroughness and readability. Some readers will be left wanting to know more about a particular topic, or wishing to explore a technique at greater length than seemed reasonable in this book. To assist those readers, I have put together this partial listing of Resources for further growth as a marketer.

Doing the Workwork. Every chapter of *Marketing Your Services* was written with the specific intent of enabling you to apply the ideas easily and effectively to your own business. To that end, I provided the Workwork exercises, and constantly invited you to think along with the book on each topic. Feedback from early readers (and years of workshops) indicates that the strategy works well for most people.

If, however, you find it difficult to simultaneously read a book and work through exercises, here are two suggestions:

1. *The Marketing Coach.* Here's the ideal situation; first you read the book, then the author would sit down with you and talk you through your own situation step by step. Take this author and put him in your PC: you've got a Computer-based Coach, or in this case, *The Marketing Coach.* It's the next best thing to having Tony Putman as your private marketing consultant. Try *The Marketing Coach* if:

    - You want someone to talk you through the tasks of building a high-performance marketing organization, step by step and in personalized detail.
    - You have a PC (IBM PC, XT, AT, or PS-2 or any 100% compatible) with the MS-DOS (or PC-DOS) operating system with at least 512K memory.

    Cost: $49.95. Available from: The Putman Marketing Group, Software Division—Dept. B, 1019 Baldwin Avenue, Ann Arbor, MI 48104.

2. *Form a Study Group.* There is nothing like group support in thinking through marketing issues. Brainstorming and reality-checks are vastly improved with group input. A good old-fashioned study group may be just what you need to really do the work. Get together a group of three to six people, each of whom makes a commitment to the group. Start at the beginning and work your way through *Marketing Your Services:* read a chapter, discuss it, and support each other in working through it. Many groups have found that meeting for two to three hours at a time, about once every two weeks, is ideal.

Finding Your Work. If you don't love what you are doing, you're probably in the wrong business. Work can be the source of tremendous satisfaction if you are doing the right work for you. Here are two resources for helping you to find your work:

What Color Is Your Parachute? by Richard Nelson Boles; Ten Speed Press, 1989. (New edition annually.) This is a classic, best known as a job-finding resource, but it contains some very useful exercises and guidance for figuring out what job to find.

Do What You Love, The Money Will Follow by Marsha Sinetar; Del', 1987. A good book for extended contemplation on finding your "true" work. A bit "new-agey" for some, but if the philosophical slant doesn't put you off, you may find it useful.

Learning More About Marketing.   Many books about marketing are available. Most are useless (or worse!) for the small service business: they are either too academic, too anchored in product marketing, too oriented toward advertising or sales, or written for CEOs of multinational corporations. I originally decided to write this book because I couldn't find a book I could recommend to my clients. But there are nonetheless some excellent books on marketing. Two in particular may give you some ideas for your own use:

The Marketing Imagination by Theodore Levitt; The Free Press, 1983. Anything by Ted Levitt is worth reading, but you may have to think long and hard before you can figure out how to apply it. Levitt is the marketer's marketer.

Maximarketing by Stan Rapp and Tom Collins; McGraw-Hill, 1988. Makes a lot of sense, especially on what the authors have learned from direct marketing.

Getting the Most Out of Advertising, Media, and Presentation.   *Guerrilla Marketing* by Jay Conrad Levinson; Houghton Mifflin, 1984. Levinson's book is full of helpful tips for nitty-gritty matters of advertising, promotion, and dealing with presentation professionals.

Getting It Printed by Mark Beach, Steve Shepro, and Ken Russon, 1989. Just what the title implies: how to deal with printers, in detail. Available from: Coast-to-Coast Books, Inc., 1115 S.E. Stephens Street, Portland, OR 97214.

Confessions of an Advertising Man by David Ogilvy; Macmillan, 1980. Terrific, no-nonsense account of what works and what doesn't in writing advertising copy. Tells you about the USP (Unique Selling Proposition) and how to use it.

Selling.   If you like selling and sales talk, you will love these books. If sales talk turns you off, read them anyway and translate them into language you can live with.

Zig Ziglar's Secrets of Closing the Sale by Zig Ziglar; Berkeley, 1984. Ziglar is a legend among sales professionals; this book shows why.

Relationship Selling by Jim Cathcart; 1988. I like the title and the basic concept; the book is a good step in the right direction. Available from: HDL Publishing Co., 1315 Antigua Way, Newport Beach, CA 92660.

Integrity Selling by Ron Willingham; Doubleday, 1987. No, he does not mean you have to sell your integrity; he means selling *with* integrity, and does a good job of explaining some basic points.

Creating a Vital Mission and Organization.   For those who are facing Framed Mission Syndrome, some ways out:

Management: Tasks, Responsibilities, Practices by Peter F. Drucker; Harper and Row, 1973. Still the best (and most complete!) book ever written on management. Don't be put off by the size; Drucker writes very well and clearly. If you haven't thoroughly studied Drucker, you have no business calling yourself a professional manager.

A Passion for Excellence by Tom Peters and Nancy Austin; Warner, 1985. Peters himself is passionate, a good writer, and a bit of a scold. Lots of great cases.

Thriving on Chaos by Tom Peters; Knopf, 1987. Like *A Passion for Excellence*, only more so. Offers detailed prescriptions.

Service Wisdom by Ron Zemke and Chip Bell; 1989. An excellent collection of articles; contains some very useful ideas for keeping your mission alive and vital. Available from: Lakewood Books, 50 S. Ninth Street, Minneapolis, MN 55402.

Index